A History of the RAF Servicing Commandos

Badge of the RAF Servicing Commando Association

RAF Servicing Commando Units

3201 SC
3202 SC
3203 SC
3204 SC
3205 SC
3206 SC
3207 SC
3208 SC
3209 SC
3210 SC
3225 SC
3226 SC
3230 SC
3231 SC
3232 SC

A History of the RAF Servicing Commandos

J Davies and J P Kellett

Airlife
England

THE FOUNDER

Among the various military papers held by the Public Record Office at Kew, was found a copy of a letter written by the late Lord Louis Mountbatten, then the Commodore Combined Operations, sent to the Air Ministry and other Commands, dated 22 January 1942. (PUBLIC RECORD OFFICE REF AIR 37/161.)

Resulting from his recommendations, 15 RAF SCUs were formed to take part in various Combined Operations, 12 units were created in the United Kingdom, together with three other units in the Middle East Area, thus becoming our Founder. This book is dedicated to the men who gave their lives while serving in these units, either lost at sea or buried in various parts of the world, so that their names shall not be forgotten.

Also to the memory of our Founder, who years after the formation and disbandment of the 15 RAF Servicing Commando Units, also lost his life through unforeseen circumstances. He was a military man who died a military death.

J Davies

British Library Cataloguing in Publication Data

Kellett, J.P.
A history of the R.A.F. Servicing Commandos.
1. Great Britain. Royal Air Force. Servicing Commandos
I. Title II. Davies J.
358.4'00941
ISBN 1-85310-051-X

First published in the UK
1989 by Airlife Publishing Ltd.

Airlife Publishing Ltd.

101 Longden Road, Shrewsbury, England.

Contents

Acknowledgements

This history is the result of a team effort by ex-Servicing Commandos and others who have supplied much of the information which has enabled us to present a comprehensive record of the 15 Servicing Commando Units.

First, our heartfelt thanks to Gordon Graham who set us on the path and to Reg Stride who wrote or telephoned with vital data.

Next, our thanks must go to Mrs Betty Goodman for typing the original manuscript. As the wife of an RAF ex-serviceman her knowledge and understanding of the subject were invaluable in deciphering the several hundred scrawled pages which we handed to her.

To all the members of the SCUs who have written, telephoned or sent photographs, newspaper cuttings and other memorabilia, we give our grateful thanks and list the names of those who helped and encouraged us in our researches.

Gwyneth and Eddie Pritchard; Doug Gladwell; Ken Wilson; Eric Sterling; George Nuttal; Harry Schofield; J H Shearwood; J F Craig; C F Dunkason; Sqn Ldr A G Haggar; Ray Honeybone; Alan Magualin; Ken Hurst; Ron Sawyer; Sqn Ldr C F Smith; Emrys Morgan; Harold Worthington; Johnny Bagley; Bill Davies; Ray Merrett; Robert Breeze; Davey Blair; Peter Wareham; Jack Elsdon; Ken Tweedie; Jack Emms; S King; Pete Siddle; 'Timber' Woods; Jack Russel; Reg Reddaway; P C Bevans; Ches Morris; Fred Wright; Hal Baker; Joe Grainger; D D'Eath; J H Hind; George White; Jim P Hogan; Les Flanders; Sqn Ldr W J Fenton; Les Sulkeld; the late Bill Langridge; Sqn Ldr C Berry Savory.

Our special thanks to Sqn Ldr F L Brown for his information on the three Servicing Parties that were formed in India and for his account of his experiences during *Operation Thursday*.

We would like to thank all the officials at the Public Record Office, the Ministry of Defence, Air Historical Branch, the Imperial War Museum, the RAF Museum, Hendon, and the Commonwealth War Graves Commission, who were particularly helpful in dealing with our queries, and the staff of Cwmbran Library for obtaining books and information.

We would also like to thank all those who have read this history. Our intention was to bring the history of the RAF Servicing Commandos to the attention of the general public, and you have helped us to accomplish that which we set out to do.

Finally, our thanks to Peter Dobson for editing the manuscript and reducing it in length down to a publishable size.

J P Kellett J Davies

Introduction

There has been very little mention in the annals of Royal Air Force history of the activities of the RAF Servicing Commando Units that were formed and used in various Combined Operations during World War II.

For many years their history has remained dormant and it was not until 1983 that an attempt was made by us, in conjunction with the newly-formed RAF Servicing Commando Association, to find out as much as possible about these units from the records held by the RAF, the Public Record Office and other sources.

Very little information was available, but after some two and a half years' research and the gathering of recollections of the units from many ex-commandos, a one thousand page history was compiled covering the 15 units that were formed; 12 in the United Kingdom and three in the Middle East.

During the course of this research we learned of three small units that had been formed in India in 1943. These units had been trained along commando lines, but were known as Servicing Parties. No records of these units were held by the RAF, or the Public Record Office and consequently we decided to include a special Chapter recounting their involvement with the Chindit forces in Burma and in the early part of 1944.

Our self-appointed task is now completed. In this adaptation we have tried to give an overall picture of events and to comment, criticise or praise according to our findings. We are both proud to have been members of the Royal Air Force and, as ex-servicemen and ex-Servicing Commandos, we now present this previously untold part of the history of World War II.

J P Kellett — ex-3205 SCU

J Davies — ex-3232 SCU

CHAPTER 1
Formation and Training

In the early years of World War II, after France and the Low Countries had been so quickly overrun by the German military machine, senior officers of the British Army, the Royal Navy and the RAF began to analyse the enemy's success, and to identify and look closely at the reasons for our defeat.

Numerically at least, the opposing armies were of equal fighting weight, but the German army was equipped with modern weapons, its troops were better trained than any of their Allied counterparts and many German units had gained valuable experience in the Spanish Civil War and in Poland. The Luftwaffe had also benefited by taking part in these campaigns and was a ruthless, modern fighting force with almost twice as many combat aircraft as the combined Allied air forces, whose aircraft were, with the notable exceptions of the Hurricane and Spitfire, mostly obsolete.

The German forces were also much better led, with the exception of Hitler and to some extent Reichsmarschall Goering. There was little co-operation between the three arms of the British forces and many Allied generals still thought in terms of trench warfare. Nowhere was this failure to grasp the modern principle of mobile war more clearly demonstrated than in the Allies' dependence on the Maginot Line for the defence of France, an almost medieval concept which was soon proved to be irrelevant by the Blitzkrieg tactics of the Germany army.

The word *Blitzkrieg* means 'lightning war', an apt description of a technique that depended upon close co-operation between powerful groups of heavy armour and dive bombers. This was a devastating combination that could first smash through or isolate the opposition, promptly followed by fast-moving infantry and well-organised supplies.

The key to the success of Blitzkrieg lay in the Luftwaffe's capacity to keep its aircraft in the air over the battle areas for long periods of time while in constant contact with armoured units on the ground. It was this twofold domination that overwhelmed the Allied armies and led to the traumatic evacuation of Dunkerque.

During World War I the Allies had contemplated the co-ordinated use of tanks and aircraft but had not implemented the idea. Many serving officers in both the army and the RAF had recognised the need for such co-operation long before the outbreak of World War II, but unfortunately their opinions had no impact on strategic planning. Once the Germans had so convincingly demonstrated the error of our ways it was obvious that any recipe for Allied victory must include close co-operation between our forces in the air, at sea and on the ground. Then things began to change.

One important change was the acceptance by the planners that it was desirable to have a mobile force of combat aircraft capable of flying from airfields near the battle zones. The advantages of such proximity were obvious enough but so were the drawbacks. Any airfield close to the front line would be vulnerable to attacks by enemy tanks and infantry and to constant strafing from the air, but the military structure of the RAF was not designed to cope with defending its own airfields. Furthermore, every front-line pilot needs a back-up team of several tradesmen to keep his aircraft operational. Transporting men to vulnerable airfields and keeping them supplied with large quantities of fuel, oil, coolant, spares, bombs and ammunition, not to mention food and water, would present a major problem.

Nevertheless, on 31 January 1942, the Director of Organisation at the Air Ministry gave instructions for the formation of three Servicing Commando Units (SCUs), although the idea was greeted with some scepticism by both the army and the RAF. It was not to be the duty of the Servicing Commandos to fight for airfields, rather, 'The object of these units will be the occupation of advanced landing grounds as soon as they are captured by the army'.

Duties and operation of SCUs

This occupation was to operate as follows: the Commando units would be put ashore from landing craft, complete with transport and equipment and make their own way to the airfield. Once the airfield had been captured, the front-line Squadrons would fly in and, while the Servicing Commandos attended to the aircraft, convoys of trucks would bring up their supplies. As Fighter Command would be responsible for the deployment of the SCUs, each unit would be trained to service fighter aircraft and to keep those aircraft operational to support the front-line troops until the battle had moved on and Squadron personnel could be brought in. The SCUs would then pack up and move to another forward airfield as soon as it was safe to use. (At the time 'fighter aircraft' meant Hurricanes and Spitfires, but as the war went on the SCUs were called upon to service almost anything that flew, with or without special training.) While not primarily intended as a fighting force, all Servicing Commando personnel would undergo intensive combat training and would be expected to defend their airfields without reliance on the army, who might have neither the time nor the men available to 'wet nurse a bunch of Brylcreem boys'. This mirrored the German system: all Luftwaffe ground crews were combat trained and organised as army units; consequently they were able to defend their airfields without seeking help from front-line units of the Wehrmacht.

Staffing and equipment

The Air Ministry instructions specified that each RAF Servicing Commando Unit would comprise two officers and 148 other ranks. The Commanding Officer was to be a Technical Officer holding the rank of Squadron Leader or Flight Lieutenant, while his second-in-command would be an Admin Officer with the rank of Flying Officer or Pilot Officer. There was to be a Warrant Officer, responsible for discipline, and the units were to be divided into Flights, three technical and one headquarters Flight, with a Flight Sergeant in charge of each. There would be a Sergeant responsible for every trade and the Flights would be split up into four sections, with a Corporal responsible for every section.

Each unit would have fifteen three-ton trucks, a jeep for the CO and one motorcycle. Only the minimum of servicing equipment would be carried in the trucks which was to be evenly distributed between them to minimise the effect of the loss of, or damage to, a truck. They would also carry pickets, ground markers, windsocks, entrenching tools and two-man bivouac tents, plus additional tenting for the air crew. Each unit would include a cook or cooks and carry facilities for the provision of hot meals to both the unit and the air crew.

Early in January 1942 orders were sent to Training Command to form three volunteer

SCUs, and notices appeared on Station Standing Orders asking for officers and men of selected trades to volunteer for a dangerous task, which was not specified. On 6 April the Army Co-operation Command requested the formation of two further SCUs to service army aircraft, but permission was refused until the AOC-in-C made the point that reconnaissance aircraft were just as vital to the army in battle as the fighter aircraft.

By May there were sufficient volunteers to form the first three units, known as 3201, 3202 and 3203 SCUs and two more, so Training Command were given the go-ahead to form 3225 and 3226 SCUs, each comprising two officers and 74 other ranks.

During 1943, following the valuable contributions made by the first three SCUs to the success of *Operation Torch* (see Chapter 2), Fighter Command formed five more SCUs, Army Cooperation formed two more and Fighter Command Middle East asked for volunteers for the three units required for *Operation Bigot Husky* (see Chapter 3). Only 400 officers and men were selected from the volunteers, so these last three units were slightly under strength until their numbers were made up with tradesmen transferred from 3225 SCU when it arrived at Hadera in May 1943. The three Middle Eastern SCUs were disbanded by January 1944.

A block of unit members, 3201 to 3232, were allocated to the SCUs, but in the event only fifteen units were formed, as follows:

Unit number	Command centre	Date of formation	Training location
3201 3202 3203	UK Fighter Command	March 1942	United Kingdom
3225 3226	UK Army Cooperation Command	August 1942	United Kingdom
3204	UK Fighter Command	February 1943	United Kingdom
3205* 3206*	UK Army Cooperation Command	April 1943	United Kingdom
3207 3208 3209 3210	UK Fighter Command	April 1943	United Kingdom
3230 3231 3232	Middle East Fighter Command	April 1943	Palestine

* Later transferred to UK Fighter Command.

Training

The training syllabus was similar for all the SCUs, whether they were trained in the United Kingdom or the Middle East, so that any unit could be sent to any theatre of war.

Upon arrival at the training centre the Resident Senior RAF Combined Operations Staff Officer gave an introductory briefing, after which all personnel exchanged their RAF blue uniforms for the standard Infantry khaki battledress. RAF blue badges of rank were retained and new blue berets were issued with RAF cap badges. In the Middle East, tropical uniforms were issued and all personnel were given greatcoats as the winter months approached. Berets were not issued in the Middle East, where both officers and men retained their blue Glengarry caps and badges. Combined Operations flashes were not worn until the landings in North Africa had taken place, after which a special AMO authorised their use by personnel who had taken part in an invasion landing.

Rigorous training for all ranks began with drills, forced marches, bayonet practice, battle courses, weapons training, self-defence and unarmed combat classes, swimming, PT and compass and map-reading exercises. All these activities were presided over by instructors on loan from the Commandos and anyone who did not measure up to the high standard set was posted elsewhere without delay.

Every member of the SCU had to learn to drive and take a course on motor transport maintenance, together with instruction for waterproofing vehicles which were to take part in invasion landings onto beaches, in case they were dropped in reasonably deep water.

In the United Kingdom the survivors of the first stage of training were sent to Inveraray (Loch Fyne) where they were embarked on the Royal Navy Landing Ship Infantry (LSI) HMT *Etterick.* The Inveraray Combined Training Centre was staffed by members of all three services. At the time of SCU training, the resident RAF Commander was Squadron Leader C B Savory. His staff devised and carried out the training programme and were responsible for the co-ordination of the other two services.

At Inveraray, Naval units were trained in the handling of all types of landing craft, including Landing Craft Tank (LCT). The SCUs used these for the transportation and handling of their mobile equipment. SCU exercises concentrated on embarking, loading equipment, lowering the fully-loaded craft into the water, unloading equipment both in daylight and under night-time conditions and the use of scrambling nets which were dropped over the ship's side for boarding purposes. The landing of heavy transport on a beach could be a hazardous operation, especially if the vehicles were driven down the ramp into several feet of water and practices, in full operational kit, often resulted in casualties, although the Navy anticipated the occasional sinking and had small rescue craft and rafts standing by. Final practice landings usually took place using live ammunition and simulated air cover and/or smoke screens which were provided by pilots from the Combined Operations Squadron No 516 from RAF Bogside, Dundonald, commanded by Squadron Leader J Drinkwater.

After fourteen days of day and night training, the SCUs went to sea in an LCT, whatever the weather conditions, later disembarking and undertaking final practice landings on the beaches at Troon, Ayrshire.

A secret film was made at this time entitled *The RAF in Combined Operations,* with a foreword by Lord Mountbatten. It shows the SCUs in this training and later operational scenes of *Operation Torch,* North Africa. This film was used extensively for the training of other units, prior to D-Day in Normandy.

Whilst on the subject of beach landings, the diagram on page 0 and the following notes issued for the guidance of units taking part in *Operation Bigot Husky* gave a clear picture of the composition, and the function, of an invasion landing beach.

Beach Bricks

The composition of a Brick is illustrated in the accompanying diagram. It will be seen that whilst the Brick is primarily an army organisation, there is in each an RAF element. This element is divided into

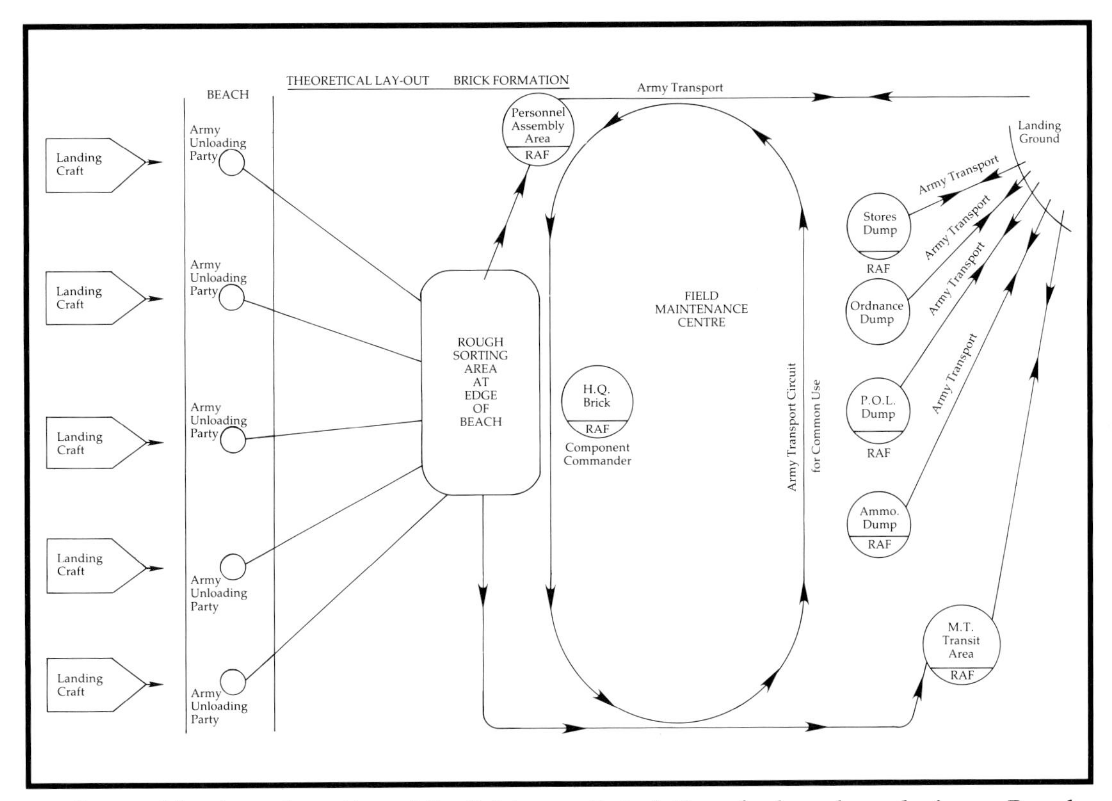

parties working in each section of the Brick through which all personnel, MT or stores will pass.

1 Personnel All personnel landing on a beach will pass through the Army Provost section where a small RAF staff will be located. It is essential that personnel proceed to this assembly area immediately on landing, leaving the beach clear. Unit personnel must not remain in the beach off-loading area.

2 Motor Transport All vehicles will be accompanied in ships by their drivers, who will then proceed as directed to the MT transit area, remaining there until further instructions are received from the unit or Beach Brick Commander. In no circumstances are units to remove from the MT assembly area any vehicle of any other unit. If for any reason a unit is deficient of a vehicle, that unit will remain deficient until such time as the Force HQ (or, until their arrival, the senior RAF officer) re-allocates.

3 Aviation fuel and explosives Rough sorting of aviation fuel, and explosives will be carried out on the beach and then transported to the Field Maintenance Centre, where detailed sorting will be effected (by an RAF Dump Section). Issues will only be made from the FMC. Army are responsible for transportation from beach to FMC, and from FMC to landing ground, upon call. This will apply until such time as the RAF can relieve the army of this responsibility. Initial stocking of landing grounds is the responsibility of the COs of the Servicing Commandos who are to place demands upon the RAF Dump Section. The responsibility for ensuring that stocks are delivered to landing grounds when required rests with the CO RAF Beach Brick component.

4 Oxygen Oxygen will be supplied over beaches in transit cylinders or in crated bottles and cleared to the RAF Dump Section. Used cylinders or bottles are to be returned to Army Section who will be

responsible for ensuring that they are despatched by the quickest available means to a Wing Base for refilling. If, of course, air transport direct from the landing ground to base is available, it will be used in preference to the above.
5 Long Range Tanks Long range tanks will also be received over beaches and are to be cleared to stores dumps. Issues will be made in a manner similar to that instituted for explosives, POL and oxygen until such time as the tanks are required.
6 General Stores It is not expected that in the early stages any large quantities of unaccompanied stores will pass over the beaches. Instructions have been issued that units are, as far as possible, to pack their equipment into unit vehicles. It is possible, however, that through shipping limitations stores will be shipped separately from unit personnel. In these circumstances the OC Unit will contact OC RAF Beach Brick component immediately on arrival to ascertain the whereabouts of such stores.
After the beach landings the unit would move off again for training in the servicing of a variety of aircraft currently in service with the RAF and USAAF, as an SCU would be expected to be capable of looking after three squadrons of fighter aircraft, or two squadrons of light bombers and one squadron of medium bombers, and to keep them operational from a forward airstrip during daylight hours. The more skilled tradesmen were trained to become experts on one type of aircraft so that they could instruct other members of an SCU who were not familiar with the type.

The training course was rounded off by instruction in anti-aircraft weapons and techniques and aircraft recognition lectures.

After the first SCUs had completed their training programme at Inveraray, the structure of the Army Co-operation SCUs was changed from the RAF Flight system to the army pattern of four Technical Sections and one Headquarters Section, subdivided into four platoons. A Technical Platoon would include two Bren gun teams, other personnel being armed with Sten guns or rifles. Each platoon would have a three-ton truck. There were to be two Corporals to each truck, one would be in charge (I/C) of the platoon, and the second would be his second-in-command (2 I/C). A Sergeant would be I/C of two platoons and a Flight Sergeant I/C of every section. A Warrant Officer would be I/C of the four Technical Sections, and the Headquarters Section would include a Warrant Officer I/C discipline. The HQ Section would comprise approximately twenty men including a Flight Sergeant/Signals, an Aircraftsman/Signals, an Admin Clerk, cooks and MT drivers. This made a total of 150 men, not counting officers, per SCU, but in actual practice the number varied from 130 to 160 men, with two to four officers per unit.

The Director of Military Operations had originally instructed that the two Army Co-operation Units, 3225 and 3226 SCUs, were to be trained only to service army reconnaissance aircraft, but it was soon realised that all sorts of aircraft were likely to drop in, quite literally, at any forward airstrip and the Army Co-operation SCUs were brought up to the same strength as the RAF SCUs and given the same training. In May 1943 a further twenty-eight men were added to both Army SCUs to form Beaufighter Flights. It is doubtful if these men were volunteers as they were hastily drafted from a sheltered life on Squadrons and put through a crash Commando training course.

Later in the war, 3225, 3226, 3205 and 3206 Army Co-operation SCUs were transferred to RAF Fighter Command as their activities with army reconnaissance aircraft were very limited in comparison with the overall requirements of the RAF.

In addition to the fifteen SCUs formed in the United Kingdom and the Middle East, three small units, each consisting of one junior officer and thirty other ranks of various specific trades, were formed in India during the summer of 1943. Although these units were trained along Commando lines, they were not designated as Servicing Commandos but were known simply as Servicing Party No 1, 2 and 3. Unit personnel retained their RAF blue uniforms, but were issued with bush hats, ammunition boots, and six-inch gaiters, and displayed an Assault Wing badge comprising a sword and trident across a background of wings.

No 2 Servicing Party was never operational and was used mainly as a personnel reserve in the event of postings. But Nos 1 and 3 were deployed in Burma on *Operation Thursday* where they played a role similar to that of an SCU; keeping RAF and USAAF aircraft flying from remote airfields and landing strips. They were disbanded as soon as *Operation Thursday* ended.

CHAPTER 2
Operation Torch – The Invasion of North Africa

In 1942 vast areas of North Africa were French colonial possessions under the control of Vichy France. Under the terms of the Franco-German armistice of 1940 there were no German troops in French North Africa, but, although the Allies assumed that the French forces loyal to Vichy France were anti-German, they also knew that the French were pledged to resist invasion and had to be considered as potential enemies.

Operation Torch was mounted to gain control of Morocco and Algeria, and to provide a springboard from which the British 1st Army could rapidly seize Tunisia, thus forestalling an occupation by the Axis and trapping Rommel's desert army between the 1st Army, pushing eastwards from Tunis, and Montgomery's 8th Army pushing north-west from El Alamein. This was intended to prevent the Italo-German forces under Rommel from escaping into Sicily and Italy and to discourage Franco's Spain from entering the war on the side of the Axis powers.

The Allies had no wish to replace French forces in North Africa by deploying their own, believing that French co-operation would be very useful in controlling a potentially troublesome Arab population

North Africa – part of the convoy carrying the invasion troops and their equipment.

and would leave the British and American armies free to concentrate on smashing Rommel. They had to hope that the French would not resist, but there was a problem. While *Torch* was a combined Anglo-American offensive it had to appear to be purely American in concept and execution in order, at the very least, to miminise resistance to the Allied landings because many Frenchmen were fiercely anti-British due in part to the destruction of the French fleet ordered by Winston Churchill after the fall of France and in part to the savagery of the attack made by the Royal Navy upon French warships anchored at Mers el Kebir.

To allay French fears of an Allied take-over in North Africa, leaflets were dropped both into the target area and into mainland France, carrying a tactful message from General Eisenhower, the Commander-in-Chief of *Operation Torch*. The message ran:

FRENCHMEN OF NORTH AFRICA

Faithful to the traditional and ancient friendship of the government and people of the United States for France and for French protected North Africa, against the menace of an Italian-German invasion, our principal aim is the same as in 1917, namely, the annihilation of the enemy and the complete liberation of invaded France. The day when the Italian-German menace ceases to weigh upon French territories, we shall leave your soil.

The sovereignty of France over French territories remains complete. We know we can count on your co-operation to clear the way which leads to victory and to peace.

All together, we shall get them!

Dwight D Eisenhower
Lieutenant-General

To begin with the leaflet raids and clandestine meetings between Allied sympathisers in Algeria and Major-General Mark W Clark, Eisenhower's Deputy Commander, had little immediate effect and in most places the French put up strong resistance until the landings were complete. Then a deal was made with Admiral Darlan, Marshal Pétain's second-in-command, thus avoiding a pointless, tragic and time-wasting struggle with the French armed forces.

The first phase of the biggest amphibious operation ever mounted by an army got under way with the sailing of three Task Forces. Early in October 1942 the Western Task Force, entirely made up of American troops under the command of Major-General Patton, sailed from ports along the eastern seaboard of America and headed straight for their objective — Casablanca. On 1 November the Centre and Eastern Task Forces sailed in convoys from Glasgow and Liverpool. The Centre Task Force was bound for Oran and consisted of American troops under the command of Major-General Lloyd R Fredenhall. The Eastern Task Force was to make the initial landing in the Algiers area. It was predominantly British, made of up Lieutenant-General Anderson's 1st Army and a comparatively small number of combat troops from the American 34th Division under Major-General Charles W Ryder.

A change in strategy by the Allied air forces played an important part in the invasion of North Africa, for it was planned that fighter aircraft were to operate in close liaison with front-line forces on the ground. Two RAF Servicing Commando Units sailed with the Eastern Task Force in the convoy out of Liverpool. Their role in the landings was to take over and defend key airfields as soon as they were captured by the army and to be ready to service the aircraft of the front-line Squadrons as soon as they flew in. The two officers and 130 other ranks of 3201 SCU were aboard the USS *Leedstown*, while the similar number of officers and men that made up 3202 SCU were divided equally between ships H 10 and P 27.

During the voyage the SCUs occupied their time by taking part in ship's drills and general exercises, by making petrol filler funnels from old petrol tins and re-arranging the cargo to facilitate unloading. Many of the men were seasick, but morale was high and a concert was held on board H 10 one evening.

The convoys carrying the Centre and Eastern Task Forces passed through the Straits of Gibraltar on the night of 5-6 November, heavily escorted by Royal Naval warships. Early the next day the convoys were attacked by aircraft carrying torpedos but no casualties or damage were sustained.

7 November

At 10.00 hours Flt Lt E H Webster, commanding 3201 SCU, and Flt Lt B E Wheadon, commanding 3202 SCU, were called to a conference aboard the *Leedstown* with the Officer Commanding 323 Wing, whose aircraft the two units would be servicing once the initial stages of the operation were completed and the aerodrome at Maison Blanche, eleven miles east of Algiers, had been secured. Meanwhile orders had been given that the next day was to be D-Day and all personnel were busy with their preparations. Vehicles were checked, refuelled, and ammunition issued and the landing craft (LCMs) were slung out on derricks ready to be launched. The airmen's living quarters were evacuated in order to gain access to the holds, and as darkness fell all lights were doused and all noise was prohibited. The men of the SCUs made some attempt at sleep, sprawled in the corridors, and in the mess rooms, keenly aware that the serious business of *Operation Torch* was shortly to begin.

The assault began at 04.00 hours. There was no preliminary bombardment and artillery and small arms fire was heard as the French forces resisted the invasion. It had originally been intended to land the Servicing Commando Units at Algiers but as the area was strongly held they were put ashore on beaches a few miles to the east.

8 November

At 10.15 hours parties A1 and A2 of 3201 SCU, who had been cruising in the vicinity of the *Leedstown* in their LCMs since 04.00, set off in rough seas for Charlie Red Beach at Surcouf to supervise the landing and unloading of the unit's LCMs. Shortly afterwards parties B1, B2, C1 and C2, who had also been cruising around in some discomfort, set off for the shore. As they approached the beach a mist came up and while B1 and C2 parties landed slightly to the west of Ain Taya, due to an error by the coxswain of their LCM, B2 and C1 landed slightly to the east of Surcouf.

3202 SCU also had its problems. At 04.00 hours H 10 had moved to a position three miles off Surcouf beach, but due to H 10's derricks proving to be unsuitable for unloading motor transport into LCMs in heavy seas, the party from H 10 did not land on Charlie Red Beach until 08.30 hours. They were two hours late and had lost many items of equipment when an LCM capsized before it reached the beach.

The party under PO Hatton disembarked from P 27 into an LCM at 04.00 hours intending to go ashore at Charlie Blue Beach but half the party landed by mistake on Charlie Red Beach. As it turned out this was a lucky accident as the organisation on the beach was ineffective and PO Hatton and his party took on the job of unloading petrol and equipment from the LCMs. The beach was in fact unsuitable for landing motor transport but PO Hatton and his party worked on, aided by other RAF personnel, until 12.30 when Grp Capt Appleton gave the order for the beach to be abandoned and for the unit to assemble on the aerodrome at Maison Blanche at 14.00 hours.

The other half of the party that had disembarked from P 27 under the command of WO Reffell had gone ashore at Charlie

Blue Beach at 05.30 hours as planned and marched the eleven miles to Maison Blanche, meeting a little token resistance from a unit of French tanks and enduring a few half-hearted air attacks that caused no casualties before the airfield was secured and aircraft from Malta started to fly in.

B1 and C2 parties from 3201 SCU, under Flt Lt Webster, were machine-gunned as they left the beach and strafed by two enemy aircraft during their three-hour march to Maison Blanche but they arrived, intact, at 09.30 to find that squadrons of fighter aircraft had arrived before them. The two parties proceeded immediately to 43 Squadron dispersal and refuelled the aircraft. They then removed the long-range petrol tanks that had been fitted to the Hurricanes, working only with the tools they carried with them, until one of the unit's three-ton Bedford trucks arrived with technical equipment.

PO Hatton's party assembled on the aerodrome at 14.00 hours as ordered and, though badly handicapped by lack of their equipment which was still at sea, they immediately began to service the Spitfires of 93, 111 and 242 Squadrons. At 14.30 B2 and C1 parties who had landed to the east of Surcouf turned up to lend a hand and at 16.00 hours A1 and A2 parties were collected from the beach where they had been unloading LCMs. 3201 and 3202 SCUs were at full strength again. Flying ceased at dusk but servicing and inspecting aircraft went on until 22.30, by which time everyone involved had begun to feel that they had had a busy day but had acquitted themselves well.

Major-General Mark Clark's visit to Algeria had achieved a measure of success. The landings of the Eastern Task Force met with little opposition although there was some fighting in Algiers, which was the

North Africa – RAF weapons and equipment being landed on the beach prior to an assault on an aerodrome.

seat of government for the whole of French North Africa and the most important objective of the operation as it was the closest to the town of Tunis. The Centre Task Force had landed all its troops without much trouble, but the next day the French forces launched a strong attack and fierce fighting continued until Allied armour entered Oran when the French authorities surrendered. The Western Task Force met with the most resistance and, while the landings were accomplished, heavy fighting went on until 11 November when news came through that a ceasefire had been arranged in Algiers.

In planning *Torch*, the High Command had not thought it would be necessary to deploy the RAF Servicing Commandos in the Western and Centre sectors as they were too far away from German airfields to need more than the degree of fighter cover that could be provided by the Fleet Air Arm from aircraft carriers. In fact, the Western Task Force made their landings with no air cover whatsoever and the Centre Task Force were able to use ordinary RAF servicing personnel on the airfields in the Oran area, where squadrons of Mitchells and Bostons had been flown in from America to support the US forces.

A local ceasefire was agreed in Algiers on the afternoon of the first day. The next afternoon the remainder of 3201's transport, eleven Bedford trucks and two motorcycles, arrived at Maison Blanche having finally been off-loaded at Algiers docks. By this time petrol stocks were running low and a party of forty men in six of the Bedford trucks made nine round trips down to the docks and transported 50,000 gallons of aviation fuel back to the airfield. Transporting petrol and supplies was really the RAOC's responsibility, but they already had their hands full with the army and were quite unable to provide a back-up service for the RAF.

While half of 3201 were at the docks, the other half were refitting the long-range tanks to the Hurricanes of 43 Squadron and servicing the Hurricanes of 253 Squadron between sorties against the enemy and sheltering from air attacks. At the same time 3202 SCU were hard at it keeping three squadrons of Spitfires operational, although many of the aircraft were overdue for major overhauls and the men were hampered in their work by the lack of their equipment which was still stowed in trucks somewhere in Algiers.

In the meantime, 3203 SCU under Flt Lt Roberts had disembarked at Bône on 10 November from the SS *Volendam* after an uneventful voyage from Liverpool.

11-17 November

3202's transport did not arrive at Maison Blanche until 11 November, by which time half the unit, under Flt Lt Wheadon, was aboard the SS *Awatea* bound for the aerodrome at Djidjelli, on the coast halfway to Bône, to support Lieutenant-General Anderson's 1st Army in their advance to Tunis. The departure of Red and Blue Flights of 3202 for pastures new left one and a half SCUs to cope with two squadrons of Hurricanes, three squadrons of Spitfires, six Spitfires of Eagle Squadron, six Hurricanes of a Photographic Reconnaissance Unit and four tubby Grumman Martlett belonging to the Fleet Air Arm.

The first half of November was both hazardous and exhausting for the two SCUs at Maison Blanche. The Luftwaffe bombed and strafed the airfield every day, dropping antipersonnel devices and delayed action bombs and as there was no bomb disposal unit in the area the armourers had the unpleasant task of dealing with these things, but in spite of these diversions work went on. Servicing began at dawn each day and continued until all refuelling, re-arming and repairs were finished, although flying ceased at dusk.

At 10.00 hours on 11 November all personnel were fully armed, pending the

French acceptance, or possibly non-acceptance, of an armistice between the Allies and French forces throughout North Africa. During the night a number of French tanks had arrived at Maison Blanche and parked on the aerodrome perimeter with their guns trained on the dispersal areas. Work went on, in a tense atmosphere, with all ranks hoping that Admiral Darlan would sign the document. In the afternoon the French tanks went away.

On 12 November the men of 3201 SCU were constantly refuelling and re-arming the fighter aircraft belonging to 43, 93, 111, 242 and 253 Squadrons. They were also called upon to see to the refuelling and general servicing of an assortment of odd aircraft that dropped in at Maison Blanche throughout the day. In the afternoon 43 Squadron's ground crew arrived and the following morning the work of servicing their Hurricanes was handed over to that squadron's own personnel.

At 10.30 a.m. on 13 November PO Hatton received orders to proceed immediately to Algiers docks with the remaining half of 3202 and to embark aboard the *Princess Beatrix,* a Combined Operations LST due to sail for Bône at 18.00 hours.

In the afternoon 253 Squadron's own ground crew turned up at Maison Blanche and immediately took on the job of servicing their aircraft. 3201 were then reorganised to cope with twenty aircraft from a Photographic Reconnaissance Unit and the Fleet Air Arm in addition to the three remaining fighter squadrons.

On 14 November personnel from 81 Squadron took over the servicing of aircraft belonging to 111 Squadron and later in the day more men were drafted in to take over the servicing of 242. In the afternoon the Spitfires of 152 and 225 Squadrons arrived and 3201's Flights were reshuffled once again to cope with them.

On the morning of the next day personnel of 225 Squadron took over their own aircraft and at 16.00 3201 was withdrawn

North Africa: Maison Blanche aerodrome – aircraft are serviced while kitbags and equipment are dumped at the edge of the airfield.

from servicing and the unit pitched camp just off the airfield boundary. On 16 November the unit received orders to move and on the morning of 17 November 3201 SCU left Maison Blanche in their own transport to rendezvous with Blade Force, an American contingent attached to the 1st Army, to make their way to the aerodrome at Souk el Arba, in Tunisia, to the east of Bône, to service the aircraft of 72 and 93 Squadrons attached to 324 Wing who were providing air support for the advance on Tunis and Bizerta.

It is almost 400 miles from Algiers to Tunis. The 1st Army element of the Eastern Task Force had begun its march on 9 November and had made good progress over dreadful roads and rough, inhospitable terrain, but while they were advancing great numbers of Italian and German combat troops poured into ports and airfields around Tunis and Bizerta. They were unopposed by the French forces who were awaiting orders from Algiers to resolve the question of whose side they should be on, and it was not until the middle of November that the French formed a defensive line to keep the Axis forces occupied until the 1st Army could arrive to help.

In order to clarify the further history of the three units' contribution to *Operation Torch* we will follow the fortunes of each unit separately, beginning with 3201.

3201 SCU

3201 left Maison Blanche on 17 November at 07.10 and drove north-eastwards to rendezvous with Blade Force at Bouria at 13.30. They bivouacked at Mzita at 18.00 and moved off early the next day, bivouacked at Le Khrouba at 18.30 and on 19 November arrived at Souk el Arba at 15.00 after a tiring but uneventful journey. 72 Squadron flew in at the same time, and while B Flight re-armed and refuelled the aircraft A Flight organised petrol and ammunition dumps at a dispersal in readiness for the arrival of another squadron.

The following morning all personnel reported to dispersal for 'Dawn Readiness'. 93 Squadron flew in early in the day and both Flights were kept busy with refuelling and re-arming. At 10.00 hours two ME 109s flew round the aerodrome, dropped long-range tanks and flew away. No attack was made, so it was assumed that they were on reconnaissance, and as that probably meant trouble, slit trenches were dug for the men to shelter in when trouble came and the aircraft were dispersed as widely as was possible.

Trouble arrived in plenty on 22 November. In the morning a reconnaissance JU 88 flew across the airfield. In the afternoon a dozen ME 109s and FW 190s flew in from the east and blitzed B Flight's dispersal with bombs and cannon fire, setting fire to petrol, oil and ammunition dumps, destroying one aircraft and damaging six others. One Bedford truck went up in flames and AC1 Clarke and LAC Gallagher were killed. AC2 Edgar and Cpl Frazer were badly wounded, while LACs Harlow, Jones and Baxter and AC Wilson received slight wounds.

An hour later a formation of ten Stukas turned up from the east and dive-bombed and machine-gunned both dispersal areas, destroying a Spitfire. Nobody was injured.

At 16.45 another formation of Stuka dive-bombers, this time with a fighter escort, flew in from the south. They bombed and machine-gunned the airfield indiscriminately — and ineffectually. No damage was done and no casualties were sustained. However, because of the frequency of these attacks it was not possible for the unit to bury the dead airmen. This was finally attended to by the 67th General Hospital who were receiving all the local casualties.

Servicing of aircraft went on between the raids, and was finished by 19.00. Both Flights then salvaged what they could and made new fuel and ammunition dumps. While this was going on enemy aircraft attacked the aerodrome again, but caused no casualties or damage and work went on until the early hours.

On 23 November all personnel were at dispersals at 06.30 hours, as usual, for 'Dawn Readiness'. A Flight serviced all the remaining Spitfires of both squadrons while B Flight prepared a new dispersal area on the east side of the aerodrome. Work ceased at 20.00, but fifteen minutes later the airfield was attacked by unidentified but obviously hostile aircraft that dropped HE bombs and antipersonnel devices. The only casualty was a civilian camel, pressed into service as a makeshift tractor to haul heavy loads out to dispersal. In the darkness it trod on an AP device, and was killed instantly.

The next day there were no raids on Souk el Arba. Spitfires of 152 Squadron arrived and flew several sorties, keeping B Flight busy, and flying went on till dusk.

At dawn on 25 November, when work had just begun, a lone JU 88 appeared, machine-gunned the aerodrome, and bombed the town. Later in the morning several Spitfires were flown in to replace those lost by 72 Squadron during the air raids on the aerodrome. Once again, flying went on all day, although three Spitfires crashed on landing when they returned to Souk el Arba after dark. The remaining Spitfires were refuelled and re-armed by 10.00 and all personnel, excepting those on guard and other duties, retired to bed, only to be woken, first by an air raid that caused no casualties and then by heavy rain.

There were no air raids on 26 November, but a great many AP bombs had been dropped the night before. While the two Flights worked on the aircraft, FO Pilcher-Clayton, using gun cotton and a safety fuse, courageously exploded 25 AP devices in torrential rain. Worked stopped at 19.30 and rain continued throughout the night.

By 27 November both the aerodrome and the surrounding countryside had become a quagmire. Flying continued, but several Spitfires crashed on take-off, 'nosing' into the soft ground. This badly damaged the propellers, and caused the fitters a great deal of extra work. Enemy aircraft again dropped AP bombs on the airfield after dark, but nobody was hurt and there was no damage to the aeroplanes.

From 28 November to 1 December the pattern of early rising for all personnel and hard work for fourteen hours or more a day continued, as sorties against the enemy were flown as frequently as possible, despite the rain. There was some excitement when a warning was received to prepare for a possible attack by German paratroops, but no attack occurred. There were several more air raids that left the airfield littered with AP devices, but these were soon dispatched by FO Pilcher-Clayton, who had perfected his technique.

On 1 December six Bisleys belonging to 18 Squadron landed at the airfield for refuelling and 111 Squadron's ground crews arrived, although their Spitfires were still flying from Maison Blanche. The unit was ordered to send a party to Medjez el Bab, some sixty miles along the road to Tunis, where the Southern Brigade of the 1st Army was in contact with units of the German army. They were held up by Allied troop movements along the road, and drove much of the way in total darkness, to arrive at 21.00 hours that night to find the situation precarious. They were sniped at, slept in the open air in heavy rain and were strafed by ME 109s at dawn. At 10.30 they were located by a dispatch rider with orders that they should return to Souk el Arba straight away. They arrived, worn out and wet through, at 16.00 hours and started work immediately. While they were away two Beaufighters had arrived, complete with their own ground crews.

For the next six days things were quiet at Souk el Arba, with very little flying and no attacks upon the airfield due to the bad weather. On 3 December the Spitfires of 111 Squadron were flown in from Bône aerodrome and on 4 December advance parties of the three squadrons' own ground crews arrived. The rain stopped, briefly, on 8 December and late in the afternoon a gaggle of ME 109s and FW 190s attacked the airfield, destroying two Spitfires at dispersal and killing the pilot of one of them before he could take cover. LAC D Williams bravely fired a Bren gun at the attacking aircraft, but with no discernable result. The heavy rain began again that night, and went on for some days, although a JU 88 did manage to drop bombs on the town of Souk el Arba on 10 December. On 11 December more squadron personnel arrived to bring the ground crews up to strength. But 12 December saw the arrival of the first mail that the unit had received since they left Liverpool.

On 13 December 3201 SCU handed over their equipment to the squadron personnel who were now servicing the aircraft and the unit was withdrawn from the dispersals. At 15.00 hours they moved out in their remaining trucks and drove westwards, in convoy with their two motorcycles, to Ghardimaou a few miles inland from Bône and further from the fighting around the Axis bridgehead. Here they made camp, and rested for two days.

On 16 December Flt Lt Webster and WO Brownrigg visited 135 Advance Servicing Post at Medjez-Sfa to obtain replacements for the clothing that had been lost when the USS *Leedstown* had been sunk, off Algiers, by German aircraft on 9 November. Clothing was in short supply and several visits were made to the ASP before the unit could be re-equipped.

On 17 December the unit resumed route marches and general training until on 22 December, the equipment they had loaned to the squadrons at Souk el Arba was returned to them, in poor condition. All personnel worked hard to overhaul it, which kept them occupied till Christmas Eve. So ended 3201 SCU's active participation in the fighting in North Africa.

Christmas Eve also marked the end of *Operation Torch.* General Anderson's 1st Army had been reinforced by Blade Force and other units of the US Army, as well as by the French, but the Germans and the Italians were far too strong and well prepared. By late November there were 47,000 German and 18,000 Italian troops in Tunisia. To make matters worse the Luftwaffe had regained local air superiority and supplying the Allied combat troops had become a difficult and costly business. On 24 December 1942 General Eisenhower decided that the Axis forces defending Tunis and Bizerta could not be quickly overcome and that the assault upon them would have to be abandoned, at least for the time being.

3202 SCU

Let us return to 10 November when Red and Blue Sections of 3202 SCU left the aerodrome at Maison Blanche for Algiers docks, to embark at midday aboard the SS *Awatea,* with forty tons of petrol, oil and ammunition.

Once aboard the men enjoyed the first cooked meal that they had had for days, followed by several hours' sleep which was just as welcome as the meal. The ship sailed that evening to take part in the assault on Djidjelli.

They arrived early the next day only to find that, once again, the beaches were not suitable for landing transport, so the ship went back to Bougie, forty miles or so west of their designated landing area, thus causing more delays and problems. The SS *Awatea* lay off Bougie harbour while 3202 personnel unloaded fuel and ammunition from the holds into waiting LCMs. They were under constant air attack, but all equipment, stores and personnel were on the quayside at Bougie by midday.

They had hoped that they would be setting off immediately for Djidjelli but no transport was available and the afternoon was spent in an exposed position on the quayside under almost non-stop attack by German aircraft. As darkness fell a small party was left on the quay to look after the stores and equipment while the main body of the unit marched through the town and climbed a hill where they camped with a good view of Allied shipping burning in Bougie harbour. Dawn saw the resumption of German air attacks, proving the wisdom of camping on the hillside.

During the morning, a Sergeant and ten men were sent to Djidjelli with an army convoy, arriving at the airfield as the Spitfires of 154 Squadron came in to refuel. Although the party were severely hampered by lack of tools and fuel, the Spitfires were kept flying somehow until night fell, by which time their number had been reduced to three.

The remainder of Flt Lt Wheadon's unit spent the morning of 12 November unloading ships and clearing the dock area until six LCMs arrived to take them to Djidjelli. As the harbour was still under heavy air attack each LCM sailed for a rendezvous outside the harbour area as soon as it was loaded, the airmen aboard firing back at the attacking aircraft with Bren guns, Sten guns and rifles.

The voyage to Djidjelli took seven hours, and was no pleasure cruise. The sea was rough, heavy rain storms were encountered and the convoy was attacked several times by enemy aircraft. Fortunately none of the landing craft laden with the unit's stocks of petrol were hit. Two enemy aircraft were shot down by Spitfires during these attacks and an Italian Savoia bomber crashed into the sea close to the leading LCM. Three Italian aircrew were

North Africa – RAF Servicing Commandos set out on a route march as part of training to keep them fit and ready for action.

taken prisoner when they baled out of a damaged aircraft and everyone agreed that the trip had been most uncomfortable, but quite exciting. As dusk fell the convoy became separated and in the poor light and heavy seas one LCM was beached ten miles from Djidjelli, and was stranded there for days.

The five remaining landing craft reached Djidjelli safely after Flt Lt Wheadon and Cpl Webberley had waded ashore to inspect the beach adjacent to the airfield and come to the conclusion that it would be both easier and quicker to unload on the quayside at the harbour, although it was further from the airfield.

By this time it was dark, but the unit's equipment, fuel, stores and ammunition were once again unloaded and transported to the aerodrome, three miles away, with the welcome help of a company of Buffs and their Bren Gun Carriers. Once the unloading, and transportation of all items was complete, the unit began the task of servicing the Spitfires. They worked into the night refuelling and re-arming and several defective cannons and machine guns had to be replaced before anyone lay down to sleep in the open air. All personnel were very hungry as they had had no food since disembarking from the SS *Awatea*.

On 13 November the Spitfires flew many sorties from Djidjelli but the big event was the arrival of the compo rations. A cook and cookhouse were quickly organised and a small hangar was cleared out to provide a mess that doubled as the sleeping quarters for a number of the unit's personnel. Others made impromptu shelters from all sorts of odd materials and while these habitations were inadequate and primitive they were a great improvement on sleeping in the open air as the temperature fell sharply when the sun went down.

Bône

Meanwhile the men of Green and White Sections of 3202 SCU were on their way from Maison Blanche to Bône, taking only a small proportion of their equipment with them for there was very little space on board the *Princess Beatrix*. The remaining equipment was loaded onto trucks to be driven to the aerodrome.

The men were tired and hungry when they went on board the ship, but ate and slept well during the short voyage and arrived at Bône refreshed at 07.00 hours on 14 November. Their landing was covered by Spitfires of 81 Squadron that had arrived the previous day. PO Hatton and his men were immediately transported to the aerodrome where Cpl Millar and Aircraftsman Lee were already hard at work, having been flown in from Maison Blanche on the previous evening with tools, fuel and ammunition. They had re-armed and refuelled 81 Squadron's aircraft during the night with the assistance of the pilots so that the Spitfires were prepared for dawn patrol.

Work began at 08.30 and went on all day and half the night, interrupted by frequent strafing from low flying ME 109s and JU 88s, the constant need to take cover, very quickly, or to man the few machine-gun posts — set up by 3202 personnel — which were the airfield's only form of air defence.

The Spitfires of 111 Squadron flew in from Maison Blanche at dusk and were serviced in the dark. This was made difficult by small-arms fire from snipers in the surrounding hills and by the wide dispersal of the aircraft, an inconvenient but very necessary precaution against the frequent air attacks. At this stage of *Operation Torch* the only Allied troops to the east of Bône were small patrols. A handful of Airborne troops made up the perimeter defence and they were supplemented after dark by 3202 personnel.

On 15 November the Spitfires of 242 Squadron flew in to Bône and 3202 SCU ran short of petrol. The situation was eased, but not eradicated, by fuel flown in from Maison Blanche in DC 3s escorted by

Hurricanes of 233 Squadron. In spite of this, many of the Spitfires were obliged to take off with partially-filled tanks until a large convoy of trucks with petrol arrived the following afternoon. In addition, due to the modest dimensions of the airfield, a number of Dakotas crashed on landing and some very unorthodox methods were adopted to keep the runway clear. Air attacks continued on both days: on 15 November the airfield was attacked by HE 111s and JU 88s and work parties were sniped at from the hills; on the following day the attacks included several by the Italians, during which one of the Italian machines was hit and crashed nearby. The aircrew was taken prisoner by 3202.

The workload increased on 16 November with the arrival of seven Army Co-operation Hurricanes, but on 19 November 81 Squadron's own ground crew turned up and 3202 left the aerodrome to take up residence at a transit camp set up at a disused tobacco factory to the west of Bône before moving on to Phillippeville, where they arrived on 21 November.

Djidjelli

During this period the other half of 3202 SCU had their share of work and hardships even though they were further from the fighting and suffered fewer air raids. Like their comrades at Bône they suffered from fuel shortages and had problems caused by short runways. On 15 November there were several crashes as the Spitfires of 242 Squadron came in from Maison Blanche, and on 16 November major salvage problems developed when six long-range Hurricanes arrived, fully laden, to land at an airfield which was too small, followed by a Bisley which had been damaged in an air raid on Bizerta which made a forced landing and had to be manhandled off the runway in the first rain of the season.

On 17 November the unit's transport arrived and Green and White Sections' vehicles were sent on to Bône. Servicing of Hurricanes and Spitfires went on throughout the day, on which the most notable event was the crash of a German HE 111, with loss of all crew.

Rain proved to be the major concern for the next two days. It curtailed flying and played havoc with the surface of the airfield. Take-offs and landings became extremely dangerous, and even taxying an aeroplane was fraught with the risk of bending a propeller by nosing over into the mud, but despite the foul conditions efforts were made to carry out inspections, as some of the aircraft had flown over 80 hours with no real maintenance. All were found to be in good condition.

The weather cleared up enough on 20 November for some sorties to be flown, but that night there was an air raid that cut off the supply of water to the airfield when a bomb fell on the town.

During the morning of 20 November the unit was alerted that a move was imminent, as the squadron's own ground crews were expected. They arrived the following day and the Red and Blue Sections of 3202 were ordered to proceed to the aerodrome at Phillippeville. They left at midday on 22 November, arriving at Phillippeville at 14.00 the next day, where they found Green and White Sections at work servicing the Hurricanes of 253 Squadron.

3202 SCU was reunited, although the two teams were billeted in separate farmhouses, but they had only one squadron to service. Green and White Sections continued working on the Hurricanes while Red Section dug slit trenches in case of trouble and Blue Section took time off for domestic duties. It was apparent that the first hectic phase of *Operation Torch* was over for the SCUs.

Desultory flying and servicing went on at Phillippeville until early in December throughout appalling weather. Continuous torrential rain turned the airfield into a quagmire and there were many crashes.

On the credit side, there were no air raids, NAAFI supplies became available for the first time and they received their first pay-cheque since leaving Liverpool.

4 December brought a signal which read '3202 Commando will return to Maison Blanche to rest and refit'. The unit moved out early the next day. It was the first time that they had been on the road together as a complete unit since the move from Ipswich to West Kirby. They travelled on the coast road via Djidjelli, Gorges de Taza, where they camped for the night, and Bougie, arriving at Maison Blanche on 7 December after an uneventful journey.

Two days later they moved out again to billets at Farm St Philippe at L'Abra. They stayed here for the next month, making Combined Operations badges, which had not been issued, manufacturing new transit cases and working on the aerodrome at Maison Blanche, mostly in the pouring rain.

On 13 December 1942 the unit was mentioned in Command Routine Orders.

> DEVOTION TO DUTY. The Air Officer Commanding Eastern Air Command is pleased to draw the attention of all ranks to the splendid work carried out by 3201 and 3202 Servicing Commando Units at Maison Blanche, Djidjelli, Phillippeville and Bône, where they maintained a large number of aircraft under the most difficult conditions and repeated attacks by enemy aircraft. The highest credit is due to the Officers, NCOs and airmen of these units.'

By this time *Operation Torch* was in the doldrums with the assault on Tunis and Bizerta bogged down by strong opposition, heavy rain and lack of reinforcements. General Eisenhower was holding the four divisions of the American 5th Army on

North Africa: Maison Blanche aerodrome – preparing a quick meal.

the western borders of Morocco, because of the possibility of a German counter offensive against the Allied forces in that country, launched from mainland Spain and so there were only three divisions deployed against the Axis bridgehead.

Although *Torch* ended in December, the fighting in North Africa went on. On 5 January 1943 Flt Lt Wheadon and the men of Red and Blue Flights were sent off to Djidjelli to dismantle Spitfires belonging to 154 Squadron. When they arrived they found that there was little left to do and returned to St Philippe the following day.

On 8 January, 3202 SCU was ordered to proceed to Bône to assist 102 Repair and Servicing Unit (R&SU). They left on 9 January and spent the day looking for the unit, which had moved to a transit camp at Djidjelli.

On 11 January, 3202 was split up once more, this time into three separate parties. One party went to Phillippeville, one to Bône and the third joined 102 R&SU, which was now at Qued Frarah. All three units were employed on repairs and salvage work during the remaining weeks of January, through February and into March as the Allies steadily rebuilt and greatly strengthened the air force in North Africa.

February 1943 saw an improvement in the weather. On 12 February the party at Qued Frarah moved to Bône, under the command of a Flight Sergeant from 3201 SCU, to help remove numerous crashed aircraft from the aerodrome. On 19 February Air Vice Marshal Tedder ordered the air forces under his control to mount a massive six-day operation against airfields, troop concentrations and ports and harbours in the Tunis area and on shipping bringing in supplies from Sicily.

On 16 March a party was dispatched from Bône to the airfield at Le Kroub to service aircraft. The next day this party was ordered to proceed to the USAAF airfield at Canrobert to service the B25s of the 12th Bombardment Group. On 19 March the remainder of 3202 SCU joined the party already at Canrobert and the unit was united once again.

During the early stages of the assault on Tunis the 1st Army had been hampered by a lack of air cover. Allied aircraft were operating from bases a hundred miles and more away from the front line and targets in the Axis bridgehead, but Italian and German aircraft were flying sorties from airfields that were only thirty miles, at most, from the front line. During the winter the Allies remedied this situation by building airstrips in the forward areas. These airstrips were named after famous railway termini. On 15 April, Red, White and Green Sections moved to 'Kings Cross', the scheme being for the Mitchell bombers to operate from there throughout the day and return to Canrobert at night where Blue Section would service them.

By April the Italian and German armies in the Turnis bridgehead were in trouble. Heavy shipping losses had forced them to rely on air transport for supplies although the Luftwaffe had lost control of the skies over Algeria and Tunisia. On 10 April the Germans lost forty transport aircraft and thirteen fighters and bombers, and the next day a further thirty-one transports, mostly three-engined JU 52s, were shot down over the sea. On 18 April one hundred JU 52s were intercepted off Cape Bon, and half of them destroyed, together with twenty-three escorting fighters. On this last occasion the Allies lost nine aircraft.

In the closing stages of the battle for Tunisia, the Luftwaffe used ME 323s. These huge, six-engined transports could carry twenty-two ton loads or a company of infantry and were nicknamed 'packing cases' by the RAF. On 22 April thirty-one of them were downed, with eleven fighter escorts. The Allies lost four aircraft.

On 19 April the order was given for the elimination of the Axis bridgehead around Tunis and Bizerta. 3202 SCU at 'Kings

Cross' and at Canrobert were very much involved in this operation, keeping the USAAF Mitchell bombers in the air for frequent sorties against the enemy. Several of their B25s were shot down or crashed and many suffered heavy damage.

On 25 April Blue Section left Canrobert and joined the other sections at 'Kings Cross' where all servicing and maintenance was carried out until the German forces in the area surrendered to the Allies. On 13 May 1943 General Alexander reported to Churchill that the campaign in North Africa was over.

3203 SCU

When 3203 SCU disembarked from the SS *Volendam* at Bône on 10 December 1942, the main impetus of *Operation Torch* was spent. The Allies had gained control of Morocco and Algeria but failed in their attempt to take Tunis in one swift assault.

3203 moved into the tobacco factory at Hippone that had been taken over as a transit camp. That night they were welcomed to North Africa by heavy air attacks on Bône. The next few days saw the unit at Bône docks, unloading their transport and equipment that had been brought from Liverpool on board the *Kiamatra*. In view of the night air raids the unit bivouacked outside the town, although they returned to the transit camp for meals, cooked in four-gallon petrol tins over wood fires, until their own kitchen equipment could be unloaded.

On 14 December, 3203 received the order to proceed by road to Blida, near Algiers, almost 400 miles away. Much of the unit's transport and equipment was still on board *Kiamatra*, but the convoy of twelve Bedford three-ton trucks, one DR and 148 officers and men set out for Blida two days later.

3203 SCU had been trained in the United Kingdom for work on Spitfires, Hurricanes, Blenheims and Bostons. They arrived at Blida aerodrome on 19 December to find that they had been brought in to service Wellingtons and that most of the equipment that they carried with them would be of little use!

There were twenty-four Wellingtons belonging to 142 and 150 Squadrons of 323 Wing. The SCU was split into two Flights for servicing and the work pattern for the next two weeks was bombing-up and then de-bombing Wellingtons when flying was cancelled due to rain. The day on which 3203 had landed in North Africa had been very like an English summer day, but now the weather had turned wet and cold. Blida aerodrome was meant only for light aircraft and was not suitable for bombers trying to take off with heavy, lethal loads. When bombed-up the Wellingtons could hardly taxi on the airfield without getting bogged down in the mud.

On 24 December the aircraft were flown out, lightly laden, to the aerodrome at Maison Blanche a few miles away. Every day a work party went to Maison Blanche to bomb-up and frequently de-bomb the Wellingtons, as the mud at Maison Blanche was very like the mud at Blida. On 29 December Flt Sgt Flanders and a party of armourers were attached to 323 Wing and stayed at Maison Blanche. By now the weather was extremely cold, with snow on the mountains to the south of Blida. In late December, and early January, a few operations were flown against the enemy, and two of the Wellingtons that mounted these attacks were equipped to carry 4,000lb HE bombs.

3203 personnel who were not employed on servicing the aircraft, or on fatigues and other duties, were kept busy with maintenance work on the unit's transport, as there was a possibility that the SCU would be instructed to proceed immediately to a front-line airfield, which would mean a journey of 600 miles. Once these preparations were completed there was little work to do at Blida. Flt Lt Roberts, the CO of the unit, ordered the setting out of an assault course, and a tough programme of battle training, including a rope crossing of the cold and swollen Chippa River, as the seventeen-day voyage from Liverpool had adversely affected the physical condition of all members of 3203 SCU.

These battle courses, together with route marches, training in map reading, and the digging of slit trenches, went on throughout the month of January. By the end of the first week the airfield at Blida had dried out sufficiently to allow a loaded Wellington to take-off safely and the aircraft and all 3203 personnel returned from Maison Blanche.

On 8 January four airframe fitters and four engine fitters were detailed for inspection work on the Hudsons of 608 Squadron. The next day more men were detailed for this task, and a Corporal and two Aircraftsmen armourers were given a quick course on the safe handling of depth charges. In the afternoon 3201 SCU arrived at Blida from Ghardimaou, for a rest and refit.

Although the Wellingtons were back at Blida, 3202 SCU were not fully employed, and Flt Lt Roberts went into Algiers on a motorcycle to ask Grp Capt Simpson of 323 Wing to find more work for 3203 to do. This visit resulted in all sorts of odd jobs. Eight fitters and riggers were loaned to 500 Squadron to help with servicing their Hudsons, the CO of RAF Blida asked 3203 to support the Duty Flight in dealing with the servicing and refuelling of all stray aircraft that arrived and on 19 January the Engineering Officer of 608 Squadron asked if 3203 could provide a salvage party to bring back as many undamaged parts as possible from a Hudson that had crashed ten miles to the west of Djidjelli.

On 22 January more work was found for fitters with 107 R&SU, also at Blida. During the day a hot wind, the Sirocco, blew up from the south and dust and sand were everywhere. The remaining personnel spent the rest of January servicing transitory aircraft, and vacating their quarters in the barrack block. By 29 January all members of the unit were sleeping under canvas.

In early February the weather was unsettled, varying from warm to cold and wet. On Sunday 7 February, 3203 received orders to proceed by road to Ghardimaou with all equipment and tents where they were to be temporarily attached for duty under the direction of the Officer Commanding 110 R&SU.

The convoy moved off from Blida at 10.00 hours on 9 February and arrived at Ghardimaou at midday on 12 February having covered 444 miles, over 300 of them through heavy rain and snow. The last night of their journey was spent at Souk Ahras, only forty-seven miles from their destination, but the way ahead was blocked by blizzards. The unit put up their tents, in an icy wind, on the parade ground of the local gaol, as the transit area was under water. By the next morning the road to Ghardimaou was considered passable and 3203 set out on the final leg.

The unit stayed at Ghardimaou with 110 R&SU until 23 February salvaging crashed aircraft that included a Bisley, a Martin Marauder and a Lockheed Lightning. Sgt Hailstone and his salvage party were attacked by an Arab while searching for a crashed Bisley, and were obliged in their own defence to kill the man with two bursts from a Sten gun. Personnel not working at the crash sites were engaged on repairs and modifications to Hurricanes and Spitfires to make as many aircraft as possible serviceable for return to front-line squadrons which needed them urgently. All trades were required to carry out this task.

During the latter half of February the Axis forces in the Tunis bridgehead launched a strong and entirely unexpected counter offensive that met with some considerable success, and 22 February was a tense time at Ghardimaou. Flt Lt Roberts was called to a conference at Soul el Khemis to discuss a possible retreat as the 10th Panzer Division, backed up by a detachment of Rommel's elite Africa Korps, had broken through the Kasserine Pass after inflicting a serious defeat upon the Allied forces led by Major-General Fredenhall, and were threatening the right flank of the 1st Army. Flt Lt Roberts was informed that in the event of a retreat being ordered the Servicing Commando would stay at Ghardimaou servicing the combat aircraft until all squadron personnel had been withdrawn to other airfields to carry on that task. Due to a miscalculation by the German High Command, and stiff resistance by the British 6th Armoured Division and the American 9th Division the counter attack failed and no retreat was ordered.

'Paddington', Thibar and Souk el Arba

On the following day Flt Lt Roberts returned to 324 Wing HQ and was instructed to send a party to 'Paddington' at Souk el Khemis, to service the Mk VB Spitfires of 242 Squadron that were scheduled to arrive at noon. 1 and 2 Flights moved immediately to 'Paddington' and the remaining two Flights followed the next day, 26 February.

3203 was then split into A and B Flights and Echelon, in the manner of a home-based squadron, and by evening fifteen of 242 Squadron's eighteen Spitfires were serviceable. Although less imposing than its namesake, 'Paddington' had been laid out beside a railway and as soon as work on the aircraft had been completed at 10.30 hours all personnel were set to work unloading 20,000 gallons of petrol from a train that had conveniently stopped within 300 yards of the main runway. The airstrip was ankle deep in mud and the job was not completed until the early hours.

For 3203 SCU there began a period of sporadic and confusingly varied activity at a number of locations. On 27 February 324 Wing HQ ordered a party to be sent to Souk el Arba to service a squadron of USAAF Mitchells that were expected in the afternoon. The party discovered that there was no oil or petrol stored at Souk el Arba and only a limited amount of ammunition, but this made little difference to the war effort as the Mitchells did not arrive.

From 1 March until 16 March the unit was split between 'Paddington' and Souk el Arba. Flt Sgt Flanders and fifty NCOs and men were stationed at the latter airfield, living in the village school and servicing the Spitfires of 242 Squadron. Between their arrival at 'Paddington', and their departure for Tingley on 13 March, 242 flew many sorties, escorting bombers raiding German transport in the Tunis bridgehead and other well defended targets, but only lost one aircraft in three very active weeks.

After the Spitfires had departed, the unit took on the servicing of aircraft of 242 Group Communications Flight and the Air Freight Service, dealing with a steady flow of aircraft that included Bisleys and Douglas C 47 transports that flew a daily service with supplies for the front line. They were also employed unloading fuel and ammunition and creating storage dumps, with the help of Arab labour.

On 16 March the main body of the unit left 'Paddington', by road in heavy rain, and moved to Thibar, near Souk el Arba, where they were once again attached to 110 R&SU. For the next three weeks they were engaged on salvaging crashed aircraft and general repairs but, due to a lack of aircraft spares, there was insufficient work to keep all personnel fully occupied.

On 7 April the men detached to 110 R&SU at Thibar were sent to join the men at Souk el Arba, and the unit was once more split up into four Flights.

During the days that followed there was considerable activity in the sky over the airfield as Allied bombers rendezvoused with fighter escorts. During the morning twelve Bostons were seen, and in the afternoon eighteen Flying Fortresses and eighteen Mitchells collected escorts overhead, two fighters to each bomber. At 16.00 hours 3 Flight was ordered back to 'Paddington', and there they stayed until the Hurricanes pulled out again on 26 April. Two squadrons of Spitfires landed at Souk el Arba at 17.30, and were airborne again at 06.15 hours the next morning.

On 12 April twelve Bostons came in at 08.00, followed one hour later by another twelve. They arrived bombed-up, but were topped-up with fuel and oil. The first squadron took off for its target at 12.30, returned intact within the hour, refuelled, and took off again for home. The second squadron took off at 15.00 and returned direct to base.

On 13 April twelve USAAF Bostons flew into Souk el Arba with their own ground crews. Two dozen more arrived, complete with ground crews, two days later. As soon as they had landed they were attacked by eight or more FW 190s, but they inflicted little damage. Throughout the next few days the Luftwaffe carried out slight and sporadic air attacks on Souk el Arba, but the skies were full of Allied bombers and their fighter escorts.

The weather, which had been changeable, started to warm up. In view of a full moon night air raids were expected and Beaufighters began patrolling this section of the Medjera Valley.

Number 3 Flight returned from 'Paddington' on 26 April. The next day 3203 were ordered to proceed to an unfinished frontline airstrip outside Medjez el Bab, which they reached early in the day on 28 April. While they were unloading their equipment a number of USAAF P40s came in low and bombed the airstrip by mistake destroying some transport.

Here the unit was only thirty miles from Tunis. British artillery was in action day and night close by the airstrip and German long-range guns were shelling the road through Medjez el Bab. Some shells fell near the airstrip and air attacks, mostly by FW 190s, were frequent.

29 April was spent unloading oil and petrol from a convoy, and on 30 April number 3 and number 4 Flights, under WO Miles and Flt Sgt Flanders, were put on stand-by for a move to an airstrip at a map reference near Djebel Abiod. They left Medjez el Bab at dawn on 2 May, and found the airstrip by 08.00. Spitfires of 93 and 111 Squadrons flew in next day and were serviced and refuelled. The pilots bedded down in a marquee supplied by 242 Group and took off on patrol at dawn next day. The detachment hung about for orders, and finally returned to base on 7 May.

Meanwhile back at Medjez el Bab the Aerodrome Construction Company had returned and finished off the runway, and no sooner had they gone than squadron after squadron of American P40s came in to refuel, each carrying one 500lb bomb destined for the docks at Tunis. Shells from the German guns were still falling on the town and late in the evening on 5 May Allied artillery all around the airstrip began a barrage that went on till dawn, when the distant battle appeared as a vast dust cloud, hundreds of feet high, in the sky to the north east.

At 06.30 three Spitfires landed at the airstrip, piloted by Air Commodore Cross, the Air Officer Commanding 242 Group, his PA and Grp Cpt Hallingspott, who had flown up to observe the final stages of the battle. A few minutes later twelve Spitfires of 4 Squadron USAAC came in to refuel, and at 07.00 a Taylorcraft piloted by Air Vice Marshal Coningham, the Air Officer Commanding Group, with Capt Balfour as his passenger, landed at the airstrip. They were driven off by car to view the battle from the top of Grenadier. At 08.40 the six Spitfires of the AVMs Duty Escort Flight came in, as squadron after squadron of Mitchells and Bostons passed overhead.

At 10.00 the AOCG and his escorting Spitfires took off again and the three Spitfires of the AOC's party followed shortly after. In the afternoon a damaged Spitfire was seen to crash on the north side of the town, and WO Wright went out with a party to see if they could help the pilot. He was found to be concussed and was taken to the nearest hospital. While this was going on squadrons of Blenheims, Bostons and Mitchells flew over on their way to bomb the bridgehead, until by the end of the day over 400 sorties had been observed.

7 May was another busy day at Medjez el Bab. The artillery around the airfield had moved forward and could not be heard above the roar of Merlins as squadron after squadron of Spitfires flew in and out again as soon as possible, although operations were held up when PO Keith of 72 Squadron came in, his Spitfire trailing Glycol smoke, and crash-landed on the runway.

8 May was even busier, as six squadrons of Spitfires were instructed to make use of Medjez el Bab which was nearer to the fighting than their own base at Souk el Khemis. In addition to these Spitfires, the unit serviced 242 Group's aircraft, several squadrons of Spitfires belonging to the USAAC, the Spitfires of the Free French 217 Squadron and two squadrons of American P40s. They also looked after several aircraft that had been damaged in the fighting. Early in the day Air Vice Marshal Coningham and Air Commodore Cross arrived by air and set off by road to be present at the fall of Tunis, and in the afternoon 3203 were ordered to stand-by to occupy a captured airfield in the Tunis-Bizerta area. Normal servicing of aircraft went on next morning, but no re-arming was necessary as there was no resistance from the enemy. The Servicing Commando's active contribution to the Allied victory in North Africa was at an end.

CHAPTER 3
Operation Bigot Husky — Sicily

The Casablanca Conference of 1943 was originally intended to be a tripartite meeting between the political and military leaders of the three great Allied powers, but as Stalin had understandably declined the invitation, on the grounds of pressing business with the German army trapped at Stalingrad, the conference was strictly an Anglo-American affair between Roosevelt and Churchill and their respective Chiefs-of-Staff, although Generals Giraud and de Gaulle were invited to express their views on the government of French North Africa and the direction of the Free French war effort.

The conference began on 14 January 1943, some months before the Allied victory in Tunisia. Its purpose was to formulate a grand strategic plan for the future conduct of the war, not only in the European theatre but world-wide and how best to bring about the unconditional surrender of the Axis powers. In simplistic terms, the major considerations were the timing of a direct assault across the English Channel, code-named *Operation Round-up,* and what proportion of the American war effort should be diverted to the fight against the Japanese, for although Churchill and Roosevelt had agreed on a 'Germany first' policy in 1941, the Americans were anxious not to let the Japanese become too powerfully entrenched, as they suspected that the British might leave them to carry on alone in the Pacific, once the war against Germany was won.

The Americans, who at this stage of the war were inclined to over-confidence, were as keen to mount *Operation Round-up* in the summer of 1943 as they had been in 1942, but the British Chiefs-of-Staff had long since realised that, although *Round-up* had been postponed until the satisfactory outcome of *Operation Torch,* it was still unlikely to succeed against massive German opposition, although they had some trouble in persuading Churchill to curb his naturally aggressive instincts and see their point of view.

The British scheme, presented by Sir Alan Brooke, was to put off *Round-up* once again until the summer of 1944 and to maintain the pressure on the Axis forces by an invasion either of Sardinia or Sicily, thus bringing some relief to hard-pressed Russia while at the same time exploiting the possibility of an Italian collapse. It was thought that such an invasion might also persuade Turkey to come into the war on the Allied side and it would certainly divert the Luftwaffe from the defence of German oil resources and other equally important targets. Churchill reluctantly agreed to this proposal, with the proviso that *Round-up* would go ahead if Germany should show signs of imminent collapse brought on by losses on the Russian front.

With the support of Air Chief Marshal Portal, Brooke then turned his attention to the US Chiefs-of-Staff, leaving Churchill to convince Roosevelt that the Allies were not ready to take on 44 divisions of the Germany army in a direct attack on France. The large number of British and American combat troops and substantial air force already in North Africa were a powerful argument in favour of the British view and after much discussion the conference agreed that the invasion of Sicily, not Europe, was the best course open.

The codename for the new offensive was *Operation Bigot Husky* and planning for the landings was already well advanced when Tunis fell in May. General Alexander would command the 15th Army Group, made up of Lieutenant-General Patton's 7th Army and Montgomery's British 8th. Eisenhower was, once again, Supreme Commander, but much of the credit for the success of *Bigot Husky* must go to Montgomery. The original planning for the operation was based on the assumption that after the catastrophic losses inflicted on the Italian and German forces during the Tunisian campaign resistance would be slight, but Montgomery insisted that the Allies should anticipate fierce resistance — and was proved to be right.

It was estimated that there were some 300,000 Axis troops in Sicily, comprised of twelve divisions, ten of them Italian. The two German divisions were the 15th *Panzergrenadier* and the 'Herman Göring' Panzer Division. The two German divisions were later reinforced by two paratroop regiments and the 29th *Panzergrenadier* and between them they held the north western tip of Sicily for much longer than anticipated.

By May 1943 the Allied Strategic Air Force had 4,000 aircaft in North Africa, and they were put to work in June to 'soften-up' the enemy. Flying Fortresses, Wellingtons, Bostons, Baltimores, Mitchells, Marauders, Mosquitos and Mustangs pounded Axis airfields and centres of communications in Sardinia, Southern Italy and Sicily, paying special attention to Messina, and to other ports through which the defenders could be supplied and reinforced. By the end of June the defences lay in ruins and the roads and railways were damaged so

Sicily landings – photograph taken from one of the ships, showing invading troops going ashore with their stores and equipment.

extensively that food distribution was seriously disrupted and there were shortages in many areas.

The offshore island fortresses of Lampedusa and Pantelleria were also bombed. The 12,000 already demoralised Italians on the latter island were the unhappy recipients of 6,000 tons of high explosives in six days of aerial bombardment before Admiral Pavesi surrendered the garrison to the Allied forces on 12 June. Pantelleria, together with Gozo and Malta, provided useful front-line airfields for fighter aircraft covering the landings that took place on 10 July 1943.

The landings were no surprise to the defenders. On the evening of 9 July the crew of a German aircraft had seen six convoys leaving Malta, where General Eisenhower and General Alexander had set up their headquarters. In all, 2,500 ships of all shapes and sizes, under the command of Admiral Cunningham, sailed from several ports to take part in *Operation Bigot Husky* and successfully landed 180,000 Allied troops in the first phase of the invasion.

Eight SCUs were involved in *Bigot Husky,* as their records show in this operation, which says as much for the fortitude and efficiency shown by the first three units, and the useful part they played in *Operation Torch* as it does for the correctness of the concept and structure of the Servicing Commandos. In the opinion of the AOC-in-C of Administration at HQ, Eastern Air Command, 'The success achieved by the fighter squadrons during this period was undoubtedly due very largely to the loyal and extremely hard work of the Servicing Commandos who have most certainly proved their value in a campaign of this nature'.

Only 3201 and 3230 went in behind the combat troops on the first day of *Operation Bigot Husky.* 3202 and 3203, the other veterans of *Operation Torch,* were next and 3232, 3226, 3204 and 3231 joined in the invasion at intervals over the following two weeks, with 3225 held in reserve in Palestine.

3201 SCU

3201 had been resting, refitting and undergoing routine training in Algeria since the end of *Operation Torch.* In June they were informed that Cpl Frazer and Sgt Bannon were each to receive the British Empire Medal and that Sgt Tee, Cpl Dawn, LAC Garlick and LAC Williams had all been Mentioned in Dispatches.

By the end of June the unit was at sea, the CO, Flt Lt Webster and A Flight aboard LST 331 and B Flight in cramped quarters split among three LCIs, all bound for Tunis. They arrived at midday on 1 July.

B Flight went ashore at La Goulette, where they camped uncomfortably without blankets in a field of rubble. They were pleased to re-embark aboard LCI 237 on 5 July to sail in convoy to La Sousse, where they arrived next day. They landed, briefly, for an eight-mile route march on the evening of 8 July before re-embarking at midnight to set sail for Sicily.

During this time, the men aboard LSI 331 had remained at Tunis, but they set out for Sicily at the same time. Conditions on board were appalling: there were far too many men aboard for comfort and there was nowhere to lie down to rest. By the afternoon of 9 July, twenty men of A Flight were suffering from heat exhaustion. Then, during the night, a wind sprang up. By dawn it had increased to gale force and the convoy was tossing in waves 35-40 feet high.

The convoy was escorted by a powerful fleet of warships which included six battleships, fifteen cruisers and 120 or more destroyers, monitors, aircraft carriers and submarines.

At 07.00 hours 3201, in their respective craft, were anchored off the south-west coast of Sicily, with a heaving grandstand

Sicily – men of the Army Airfield Construction Unit preparing a landing ground.

view of the invasion for those who weren't too ill to care. The monitors were shelling shore defences as wave after wave of landing craft went in, but there were no enemy aircraft to be seen, for which all ranks were truly grateful.

The 3201's objective was the aerodrome at Cosimo, twelve miles or so inland. By 10.00 hours infantry and armour of the US 7th Army had established a beach-head, against strong opposition, and B Flight went ashore at 'Cent' beach, near Scoglitti. Their LCI hit the beach too hard, but everyone landed safely and dispersed behind the beach to take cover in an almond grove a mile inland. They found out later that to reach the almond grove they had walked right through an uncleared mine-field!

Heavy fighting was going on not far ahead, so in the almond grove they stayed, being sniped at and occasionally strafed by JU 88s and FW 190s, though nobody was hurt. Twin-boom Lightning fighters of the USAAF and RAF Spitfires constantly patrolled the skies above the beaches, but could not prevent two FW 190s from shooting down a Kingfisher 'spotter' seaplane. The afternoon was taken up with digging-in and B Flight went to earth at 21.00 hours, but sleep was impossible as salvoes of shells were screaming overhead all night.

Due to the heavy seas the unloading of A Flight was delayed by thirty hours. They disembarked at midday on 11 July and discovered that there was no transport or US personnel, as had been arranged, to unload RAF supplies. The unloading was carried out by the whole unit, with twelve Bedford trucks. It took thirty-six hours and was quite exciting when enemy aircraft bombed the beaches. There were two heavy raids late in the evening and ships and anti-aircraft batteries put up a terrific barrage, succeeding in shooting down several American DC3s that were flying in reinforcements. One of them came down in flames near B Flight's trenches in the almond grove. The MO and others rushed to help, but nothing could be done.

The unloading of LST 331 was completed by midday on 12 July. Thinking dark thoughts about the organisation of the US Army Transportation Corps, A Flight left the beach, and drove to Cosimo aerodrome which had been captured by troops of the 45th Division of General Bradley's army the afternoon before. The unit's transport was unloaded and went straight back to the beach to pick up petrol, oil and ammunition. The aerodrome was bombed at 14.45 and strafed a little later, FW 190s taking part in both attacks.

Cosimo had already been severely blitzed by Allied aircraft. The administration building, sleeping quarters and three hangars were very badly damaged and the control tower was a ruin. There were abandoned aircraft everywhere, some forty-five ME 109s, both Fs and Gs, several Macchi 202s, a JU 52, two JU 87s, two JU 88s and a Feisler Storch. Some of them were serviceable, while others could obviously be written off.

Early the next morning two Luftwaffe pilots absent-mindedly landed their Stuka divebombers at Cosimo, realised their mistake and tried to take off — quickly. They may have been misled by the presence of the Messerschmitts and the lack of Allied aircraft but 13 July was not their lucky day and they were both shot down. Three of the four occupants were killed in the ensuing crashes, but one pilot survived to be taken prisoner.

B Flight arrived at 08.30 and the unit's transport went on ferrying fuel and ammunition from the beach. This misemployed one hundred craftsmen, but there was still no sign of the US personnel and transport whose task this should have been. The advance party of 3203 SCU turned up at 13.30 and ninety men of 72 and 111 Squadrons arrived, without rations, later in the afternoon expecting to be fed, although they should have brought their own food with them. This left 3201 very short of food as the ration distribution system had somehow broken down. Shortly after they arrived the Spitfires came in to land, followed by three more squadrons of Spitfires: 93 Squadron at 17.00, 243 Squadron at 18.00 and 43 Squadron at 19.00.

Routine patrols and servicing went on for several days. There were no air raids, but on 17 July one of 111 Squadron's Spitfires collided with an American roller that had stopped on the main runway. The unit's MO rushed to give first aid but the Spitfire pilot died of a broken neck and severe facial injuries. The accident appeared to be the driver's fault and an enquiry was set up by the HQ of 324 Wing.

The remainder of 3203 arrived at Cosimo on the morning of 18 July, and the Spitfires of 72 and 111 Squadrons were handed over to them in the afternoon. Personnel belonging to the other squadrons arrived next day.

On 20 July most of 3201's equipment was transferred to a new camp beyond the perimeter track in the north-east corner of the airfield. The enemy's R&SU had been situated there and a great deal of the technical equipment found there was in good condition. Several ME 190Fs were parked amongst the trees, and with them were two brand new engines, only recently unpacked. The work of servicing the Spitfires was handed over to the squadron personnel at 18.00 hours that evening.

For the next few days 3201 SCU became an R&SU, repairing three out of five badly damaged Mk VC Spitfires and returning them for squadron use. On 25 July they were instructed to pack up and move on to service the Beaufighters of a night-fighter squadron who were to operate from the airfield at Cassibile, which was forty or more miles away by road on the south-east coast ten miles south of Syracuse. Leaving a rearguard to clear up the site, the main body of 3201 left Cosimo shortly after midday and arrived at Cassibile at 19.10 to find themselves unwanted, as the Beaufighters of 600 Squadron were already at the airfield, complete with squadron personnel.

The unit camped down in an almond grove. During the night there was a heavy air raid, and a terrific Ack-Ack barrage was sent up, so that the main danger seemed to be from falling shrapnel and unexploded shells. The next day trucks were dispatched back to Cosimo to collect the rearguard and the residue of the equipment and the unit were reunited by 18.00 hours.

3201 awaited further orders at Cassibile for the next few days. They helped with servicing the Beaufighters and slept or tried to sleep in stone-roofed slit trenches, listening to the rain of red hot metal from the anti-aircraft barrage that went up every night against German bombers attacking shipping just offshore.

Meanwhile, *Operation Bigot Husky* had been progressing well. The burden of responsibility for the defence of Sicily fell on the shoulders of General Guzzoni, and the 230,000 men of the Italian 6th Army. They had been told by Mussolini in what was, even by his standards, a very silly speech, that the 'enemy were to be wiped out before breaking through inland', but both the Italian armed forces and the nation had lost enthusiasm for the war. Some Italian Divisions fought bravely against overwhelming odds and suffered heavy losses, but Montgomery's 8th Army took Syracuse and Augusta on 11 July without a shot being fired as both the garrisons had disappeared. By the time that Mussolini was overthrown on 24 July Italian resistance had caved in, but General Hube's Panzer Divisions still held the north-east corner of the island, frustrat-

Sicily landings – preparing a landing ground. An Army Airfield Construction Unit levelling machine at work.

ing Montgomery's plan to quickly seize Messina, and cut off their retreat.

On 1 August, 3201 were given orders to proceed to Palagonia. They struck camp the next morning and moved off in convoy, arriving at their destination at 16.00 hours. An hour later they were moving off again under orders to return to Cosimo aerodrome, this time to assist in servicing American light bombers. They arrived back at Cosimo on the morning of 3 August and here they stayed throughout the final phases of the operation. They set up camp and then relaxed until four squadrons of USAAF Mitchell bombers flew in on 5 August, complete with their own personnel. Two squadrons of Bostons came in on 9 August, and 3201 helped the ground crews with the servicing of aircraft until 24 August when orders were received for the unit to pack up and leave. By this time General Hube had withdrawn his Panzers from Messina and retreated into Italy and *Operation Bigot Husky* was successfully concluded with the whole of Sicily in Allied hands.

3230 SCU

3230 were formed in Palestine in April 1943 and had barely finished training when they were pitchforked into *Operation Bigot Husky,* sailing from Port Said in Egypt early in July. On 10 July they went ashore from landing craft at 07.00 at a beach-head that had been established by the 1st Battalion of the Hampshire Regiment on the southern tip of Sicily.

The landing of the SCU was unopposed — the Hampshires had sorted out the opposition — but their objective was the airfield at Pachino four miles from the beach. As heavy fighting was still going on inland they dug-in on a site allocated to the Airfields Group, just off the beach, to wait for orders to proceed. Twenty-five pound guns were firing from the site and the enemy was sniping back.

During the afternoon Sgt Gover made a recce of the camp surrounds and captured ten Italians, including an officer and an NCO, and marched them for two miles to a prisoner of war cage. Later in the day he captured another Italian officer, this time with the help of a party from the unit, and escorted him on the long walk to the cage. There were air raids on and off all night, bombs fell on the camp and a heavy anti-aircraft barrage made it desirable to keep one's head down. A piece of shrapnel hit Flt Sgt Roberts on the chest, but luckily for him it struck first a button and then a full breast pocket, so his wound was slight.

By the morning Italian resistance in the area had been overcome, and the unit left the campsite at 07.00 and marched through Pachino town to the airfield, which they found had been ploughed up. They camped on a salient overlooking the aerodrome where engineers and a Basuto unit were repairing runways and laying out belly-landing strips. Three of the unit's trucks arrived early in the afternoon and were used to ferry petrol from the beach back to the aerodrome. 3230's transport had been incorrectly loaded onto the SS *Joseph Alston* and the remainder of their vehicles were still on board the ship and consequently the transportation of fuel and ammunition from the beach-head to the airfield took much longer than was planned. However, several amphibious vehicles were pressed into service and by midnight there were 15,000 gallons of petrol and large quantities of oil and ammunition camouflaged in pits and dumps dispersed around the aerodrome.

While all this work was going on, a Spitfire of 72 Squadron, flown by Plt Off Keith, made a perfect landing on a ploughed-up runway. It was short of fuel and after a refuelling party had serviced and inspected the machine, Plt Off Keith took off again, this time from a nearby road. A little later two more aeroplanes came in, one very short of fuel, the other badly damaged by anti-aircraft fire. As they were being attended to, a bunch of ME 109Fs strafed the aircraft and airfield. Flt Lt Wainwright, 3230 Engineering Officer, who was standing by the aircraft, had two machine-gun bullets through his hat but was unhurt, LAC Hatson was wounded in the buttocks and an army officer and several dispatch riders were also hurt. The unit's Medical Officer and his staff showed great courage during the attack by driving round the airfield giving first-aid to the casualties. The army personnel were taken to the nearest Casualty Clearing Station (CCS) by the unit's transport and were later evacuated from the island. Shortly after the ME 109s had flown away Sqn Ldr Hill landed his Spitfire with a radiator damaged by low flying through a tree. The unit later heard that the ME 109s were all shot down by Spitfires.

Early in the morning on 12 July enemy aircraft attacked the harbour and the town but no bombs fell on the aerodrome. Five of 72 Squadron's Spitfires came in, were refuelled and inspected and returned to base. General Montgomery visited the aerodrome and the AOC, AVM Broadhurst, landed in a Spitfire. There were now 40,000 gallons of petrol and corresponding quantities of oil and ammunition in dumps around the airfield.

On 13 July one of 111 Squadron's Spitfires was making its approach when it was fired on by the airfield's anti-aircraft unit. After the pilot had complimented the gunners on their rotten shooting, he reported a success against a JU 88, although the rear gunner had fired a burst as his aircraft was going down, holing the Spitfire's rotor cylinder headplate.

By this time the runways had been repaired and in the afternoon the Spitfires of 92, 145 and 601 Squadrons of the RAF, and No 1 Squadron of the SAAF, all belonging to 244 Wing, arrived. They were serviced and re-armed and immediately began flying sorties from Pachino.

Since their own arrival at Pachino 3230 SCU had worked every day from dawn to dusk, often through the night, in very trying conditions. The four squadrons of Spitfires added to their workload and in addition there were many 'casuals': the twenty-four Spitfires of 93 and 243 Squadrons dropped in for fuel and ammunition and a damaged Kittyhawk of 112 Squadron that had been holed by flak called in for a check-up, taking off the next morning.

Cpl Guest was wounded in the shoulder, arm and hand on 14 July after a Sten-gun fell from a lorry and went off accidentally. He was taken to 21 CCS and an enquiry found that no-one was to blame. There was very little aerial activity by the Italians or Luftwaffe, and the Spitfires of 93, 72 and 243 Squadrons had all been serviced by 10.00.

On 15 July the Squadron personnel arrived and began work on their own aircraft, helped by a party from the SCU. All other unit personnel were busy either packing their equipment in the trucks ready for a move to Cassibile or looking after 'casuals'. Several DC 3 Dakotas were serviced the next day and there was some enemy activity at night.

On 17 July 1 and 2 Flights moved up to Cassibile to prepare the airfield, and petrol dumps were dug-in round dispersal points ready for the Spitfires of 244 Wing that were due next day. 3 and 4 Flights at Pachino serviced several 'casuals' and the aircraft of 417 Squadron, who then left for Cassibile. The AOC, AVM Broadhurst, flew in to Cassibile at 07.00 on 18 July and the aircraft of 244 Wing arrived at 08.00. All aircraft were refuelled, re-armed and dispersed by 13.00. The squadron's own ground crews arrived soon after that and the two Flights of 3230 drove back to Pachino. 3 and 4 Flights spent their day collecting bombs and ammunition from the beach in readiness for the Kittyhawks of 239 Wing that were expected in the morning.

There was a minor air attack that night that caused no damage. The Kittyhawks began landing at 10.30. 260, 250 and 112 Squadrons came in first, followed by 3 and 450 Squadrons of the RAAF, and they were directed to disperals and handed over to the squadron personnel. At 11.00 hours three squadrons from the 57th Pursuit Group USAAC came in from Malta and were serviced and bombed-up. Three Flights from 3230 SCU serviced more than sixty aircraft before they were handed over to the USAAC ground crews who were brought in from the beach at 16.00. The remaining Flight had been occupied with servicing the 'casuals', and with salvaging spare parts from two crashed Spitfires on the beach.

On 21 July the unit were allowed a 'stand-off', with the exception of a party required to service 'casuals' and to repair unserviceable aircraft that the squadrons had left behind when they moved on. For the next few days 3230 at Pachino were engaged on salvage and repair work. Flt Sgt Marshall's No 1 Flight spent a day at Syracuse repairing a crashed Spitfire, but by 28 July the R&SU took on the salvage work and there was little for the SCU to do. Enemy action in the area was non-existent and the unit felt that it was irksome to remain so far behind the lines, as they were trained Commandos and expected to be doing something useful close to the front line. Then came welcome news. The unit was to be attached to 329 Wing and as their Kitty-Bombers were comparatively short-range aircraft that was bound to mean a move in the desired direction.

On 1 August orders came for the unit to move forward to Agnone, a landing ground twelve miles south of Catania where fierce fighting was in progress as the XIV Panzer Corps under the command of General Hube held out against Montgomery's army, whose objective was Messina.

The majority of 3230s personnel and kit were in the advance party that left within two hours of the order's being received. They arrived at Agnone early in the evening, after a dusty journey over battered roads. Flt Lt Wainwright set up an office in a farmhouse, allocated out-houses to be used as a kitchen and dining hall and organised the bivouacs on a pleasant camp site near the beach. The constant rumble of the battle could be plainly heard and shells exploded near the landing ground.

Back on Pachino the rearguard under the SCU's CO, Flt Lt Haggar, cleared the camp site, serviced three Liberator bombers that had run short of fuel on their way home from bombing oil fields in Rumania and prepared for an early start next day.

In the morning the five squadrons of Kittyhawks landed at Agnone and the rearguard party moved up from Pachino to be welcomed early in the afternoon. No enemy aircraft were active in the area, but gun flashes and explosions could be seen and heard from the direction of Catania.

On 3 August the officer commanding 329 Wing defined the working arrangements for the SCU and parties of riggers, fitters and ancillary tradesmen were detailed to the squadrons.

The action against the enemy around Catania continued. During the night there were many explosions and fires could be seen around the town. Pilots returning from early morning Ops reported that the enemy was withdrawing to the north and that the explosions and fires were caused by the destruction of fuel and ammunition dumps. Nevertheless, explosions in the battle area went on all day and there was a heavy air-raid on Augusta, plainly visible from Agnone, ten miles away.

Catania fell to the 8th Army on 5 August and the unit was kept busy with the Kittyhawks as the squadrons were at full pressure harassing the Panzers as they withdrew towards Messina. The main body of the army was now seven miles beyond Catania, but the sounds of battle could still clearly be heard.

The unit's CO visited Catania shortly after it fell to the Allies and reported that a notice had been painted on a wall, in English. It read, 'Cheerio Tommy. It's been a pleasure fighting you; you've got guts. We are pulling out and you deserve this town'.

The remainder of the squadron's personnel arrived from Pachino on 6 August and once again the SCU had little work to do. NAAFI goods had been issued for the first time on 3 August, but were nothing to write home about. Although the enemy had left behind large stocks of beer, wine and spirits they had been sold off to the highest bidder and the NAAFI ration was one bottle of beer between two men per week! There was insufficient soap and other toiletries and the 'NAAFI Wallahs' were subjected to a chorus of abuse. To add to the men's miseries, the only mosquitos in the area were anopheline, not the type with Merlin engines, and the danger of malaria was such that on 7 August all ranks were ordered to take one Mepacrine tablet every day.

There were several accidents during the period. On 4 August an anti-aircraft gun being set up on the beach toppled over and killed one of the crew and three days later two soldiers lit a bonfire the beach over a mine and both were killed by the explosion. Then on 11 August a Baltimore crashed on take-off and the crew of three all lost their lives.

On the night of 11 August there was an intense air-raid which began at 22.00 and continued for at least an hour. The area was lit by flares, bombs fell on the airfield and its surroundings, casualties were heavy and fifteen Kittyhawks were damaged, most of them by falling shrapnel.

Italian invasion – RAF Servicing Commandos relaxing at the assembly area.

The anti-aircraft units kept up a constant barrage. Although delayed action bombs were dropped, the danger area was soon cleared and the damage to the runways was quickly repaired by the CREs.

Apart from that one night the time from 7 August was relatively quiet and a small stage was erected in the dining hall so that concerts could be given to entertain army and air force personnel, as there was nothing much to do at night. The first concert was held on 12 August and the unsuspected talents demonstrated by members of the SCU both surprised and delighted the audience.

On 13 August the CO, Flt Lt Haggar, together with Flt Sgt Squirrel, Sgt Jones and Sgt Kelly visited HQ and 3231 SCU. On the way back their jeep collided with a stolen Fiat car driven by a Private from the Royal Canadian Engineers. Both vehicles were written-off and Flt Lt Haggar, Sgt Kelly and the occupants of the Fiat were taken to the CCS. On the CO's return to camp on 16 August he was told that he had been promoted to Squadron Leader.

On 17 August Montgomery's army arrived at Messina and 3230's first taste of active duty was at an end.

3202 SCU

The early part of 1943 was a busy time for 3202. For the two months following the end of *Operation Torch* they were constantly employed on repairs and salvage work at several airfields in Algeria. Then, in March and April, they were back at 'Kings Cross' and Canrobert servicing the Mitchell bombers of the USAAF's 12th Bombardment Group and in early May the main body of the unit was at Medjez el Bab near Tunis, with a party at La Marsa on the Cap Bon Peninsula servicing a variety of aircraft for 242 Group Communications Flight.

By the middle of the month the entire unit was at La Marsa, and it was here that they received instructions to prepare their transport and equipment for a further operation.

On 26 May the unit received orders to proceed to Blida, near Algiers, and from there they went to Arzew, near Oran, for a battle training course that they could have taken in Tunisia. By 27 June, 3202 were in Tunis, having completed an unnecessary trip of some 2,000 miles in transport due for major overhauls and shortly to embark on a major operation.

In Tunis on 30 June 3202 received their orders for *Operation Bigot Husky* and the news that the CO, Flt Lt Wheadon, and WO Draycott had both been awarded MBE's, while Flt Off Hatton and LAC Valance had been Mentioned in Dispatches.

The unit spent the first week of July bivouacked in the luxury of a US Army Concentration Area. Here they spent their time waterproofing vehicles in preparation for the landings and collecting equipment and supplies through the 'proper channels', which proved to be an irksome task.

At 07.30 on 13 July the SCU embarked aboard three LCIs on the outskirts of La Goulette, and set sail on a flat calm sea, which was very much appreciated as LCIs were horribly uncomfortable in any kind of swell. The south-west coast of Sicily was sighted at dawn on 14 July. To avoid the minefields the LCIs approached the island at Licata and then proceeded down the coast to Gela, where General Bradley's troops of the US 7th Army had landed on the first day of *Operation Bigot Husky* and where the counter-attacking German armour and the Italian 'Livorno' Division had been very badly knocked about by five-inch shells from US Navy guns.

There was some difficulty in grounding in the LCIs, due to the shallow nature of the beach, but all three parties had been disembarked by 14.00 hours. FO Hatton, and his party, who were first ashore, marched into Gela to report the SCU's arrival to the RAF Embarkation Officer who was eventually located on another beach three miles from the town. 3202 were informed that their objective was the airfield at Biscari, fifteen miles east of Gala, where US Paratroops had landed in the first stage of the operation, but as it was still being shelled by Italian and German guns the unit bivouacked outside the town.

In the morning the Embarkation Officer was contacted once again and the airfield was declared safe but there was the usual problem of lack of transport. The unit's Bedford trucks were still at sea. Flg Off Hatton somehow 'found' four US Army trucks to transport personnel, petrol, oil and ammunition to Biscari. They arrived there at 11.30 and found the airfield a mess.

The next four days were spent in stocking up with fuel and ammunition while US Army engineers repaired the runways and dispersals. Sixteen unexploded bombs had to be disposed of and four dead US Paratroopers were found and buried. Flt Lt Wheadon arrived at Biscari on 17 July and immediately went to 324 Wing Headquarters at Cosimo a few miles away. On 18 July the engineers announced the airfield to be serviceable but word came from the XIIth Air Security Corps that it was not to be used and that no more supplies were to be transported to the airfield.

At 23.00 on 19 July Flt Lt Whiteley RAF EO turned up unexpectedly with orders from 324 Wing that 3202 were to move, without delay, to an aerodrome five miles east of Agrigento. Despite the lateness of the hour the unit packed and loaded up and were on the move for the thirty-five mile journey by 07.30 the next day.

By 11.30 on 20 July they were at Argrigento. The Spitfires of the 31st Fighter Group USAAF started to come in at 15.00 hours and although the Group's own

Italian invasion – RAF Servicing Commandos relaxing before zero hour.

ground crews were already at the airfield the unit serviced and refuelled the aircraft.

The following morning Colonel Ayling of the XIIth ASC gave orders for the unit to be ready to proceed northwards to Palermo by midday. They met with Col Ayling at Bivio, where they bivouacked for the night, setting off early the next morning to rendezvous with American army units, two miles north of Corleone, at 10.30. Col Ayling went ahead, promising to send word when it was safe for the unit to move on to Palermo. The orders came through eventually at 17.00 that they were to be ready to move off at 04.30 hours. Then, although they were ready, the order to advance did not come through for several hours and the unit finally arrived at Boccadifalco aerodrome, Palermo, at 11.00. No resistance was encountered, but the ammunition dumps were burning and the flying field was littered with burnt-out enemy aircraft and oil barrels. Flt Lt Wheadon inspected the aerodrome and allocated dispersals to the four sections of the SCU.

On 24 July the wrecked aircraft were removed and fuel, oil and ammunition dumps were made at the dispersals. Two squadrons of Spitfires of the 31st Fighter Group were expected to fly in at 15.00 hours but did not arrive, either on that day or the next. The SCU continued clearing up the aerodrome and at 20.00 an urgent order came from the 3rd Strategic Air Force for 3202 to move immediately to the airfield at Termini Imerese, a few miles to the east along the coast, but an hour later, when packing was well under way, the order was cancelled.

No Spitfires had arrived by nightfall on 26 July, but the SCU were kept very busy with the servicing and refuelling of passing transport aircraft. The Spitfires finally landed at 10.00 on 27 July and the work of refuelling and re-arming them began immediately. At 15.00 hours the CO was ordered to send two-thirds of the unit to Termini, and a detachment, under Flg Off Hatton, was on the way within two hours.

When Flt Lt Wheadon called on them next day he learned that no aircraft were expected at the aerodrome for several days, which meant that one-third of the unit were servicing two squadrons of Spitfires and a large number of transport aircraft, while the remaining two-thirds of the unit were twiddling their thumbs. In the meantime USAAF ground crews had arrived.

On 29 July a squadron of USAAF Spitfires belonging to the 52nd Coastal Group landed at 16.00 and the American ground crews took on the responsibilities of maintenance and servicing, leaving 3202 to undertake such major tasks as engine changes, forty-hour inspections and refuelling. Between 6,000 and 8,000 gallons of petrol were used every day throughout this period, all of it handled by the refuelling parties of the SCU.

During the first two weeks in August 1943 the detachment at Termini took on the servicing of the two squadrons of Spitfires of the 31st Fighter Group and engine changes, and air frame repairs for the US 52nd Coastal Group continued until the unit personnel at Boccadifalco were instructed to report to Termini.

As 3202 had received no communications from the Headquarters of the Desert Air Force and had no work to do, the CO went to DAF HQ in Syracuse to establish contact and to ask for further orders. He was told that on 4 August a signal had been sent, which he had not received, ordering the unit to return to No 2 Base Area, North Africa, for a refit even though heavy fighting still went on in the north-west corner of the island.

So ended 3202's somewhat unsatisfactory part in *Bigot Husky*. The unit sailed from Palermo for Bizerta, with the general feeling that through no fault of their own they had had no chance to fulfil their proper function in the operation.

3203 SCU

3203 SCU had arrived in French North Africa during the latter part of *Operation Torch* but had seen more action in the final onslaught on the Axis forces in Tunisia than either of the other SCUs.

Following the Allied victory 3203 were kept busy at captured airfields around Tunis, and had no opportunity for rest and relaxation before they were ordered to return to Blida, 700 hot, dusty miles away. They pitched camp at Blida at 11.00 on 2 June and spent the day unloading their equipment and overhauling vehicles. In the afternoon Flt Lt Webster, the CO of 3201 SCU, brought news that all three SCUs were to take part in a Combined Operations training programme at Port Aux Poules, near Oran.

The training, which included the American Assault Course at Arzew, route marches and weapons training, was completed by 15 June and on 18 June 3203 left Port Aux Poules and returned to Tunis in an MT Convoy. They arrived five days later, having covered a further 800 gruelling miles at the height of a hot summer.

On 26 June the unit were advised that they would be taking part in *Operation Bigot Husky* and that Tunis would be out of bounds. D-Day for the operation was 10 July, by which time 3203 were at the Arizona Assembly Area situated on the east coast of Tunisia between El Aquina and La Marsa. The COs of all RAF units scheduled for landings on D-Day plus four were summoned to a briefing at Tactical Air Force HQ, La Marsa, where Air Commodore Elmhurst gave a report of the progress of the invasion and stressed that, in the absence of orders, initiative should be used. Flt Lt Roberts was given a complete outline of the unit's function during *Operation Bigot Husky*, complete with maps. 3203 were to go in at Cent Beach, near Scoglitti and then proceed as directed by the Embarkation Unit to Cosimo to help 3201 prepare the aerodrome for four squadrons of Spitfires.

The unit was split up into parties for the voyage to Sicily. One party, made up of Flg Off Woodhead, Plt Off Ward and eighty-two assorted NCOs and airmen, left La Goulette aboard LCI 233 at 10.30 on 13 July, while Flt Lt Roberts with his party of fifty-seven other ranks and the unit's motor transport sailed from La Goulette at 07.00 on 15 July on board an LST.

FO Woodhead's party disembarked in two-and-a-half feet of water at 10.00 on 14 July and marched the twelve miles to Cosimo, arriving at 12.30. One party set up camp in an almond grove on the north side of the aerodrome while the other party went back to the beach in a captured German three-ton truck loaned to them by Flt Lt Webster to collect tools, rations and equipment.

At 08.30 the next day Flg Off Woodhead's party received the Spitfires of 111 Squadron and servicing began using only the tools that they carried with them and equipment left behind by the retreating Germans because the party's own equipment was in the unit's trucks which were still at sea. 3203's arrival on the island had not gone off as planned: both parties should have landed on D-Day plus four.

This separation of the SCUs from their transport and equipment had bedevilled all three units in both operations. In this instance, Flt Lt Robert's party and the vital trucks were not on shore in Sicily until 16 July and even then they arrived at Gela, not Scoglitti, due to problems in beaching and unloading their LST in too great a depth of water at the appointed beach. Due to further problems in unloading the trucks at a pontoon in Gela harbour, the equipment did not reach Cosimo until 09.00 on 18 July, four days late. Had there been intense activity by Axis combat aircraft during those four days Flg Off Woodhead's party could not have coped without the proper tools, so it was fortunate that at the time of the invasion there had been only 200 Italian and 300 or so German aircraft in the whole of Sicily and they had suffered heavy losses.

By 18 July there were five squadrons of Spitfires at Cosimo. 3203 continued servicing 72 and 111 Squadrons until their own ground crews took over on 22 July. The Spitfires were escorting bombers to their targets and flying strafing sorties without meeting opposition from the air. The chief problem was an epidemic of burst aircraft tyres caused by bomb splinters that were scattered everywhere. Fifteen new tyres were fitted in this period.

On 24 and 25 July the unit worked on forty-hour inspections on the Spitfires and routine maintenance on the equipment. Then, on 25 July, word came through that the whole of western Sicily was in the hands of the American 7th Army.

From 25 July to 2 August, 3203 at Cosimo acted as an R&SU. On 30 July they heard that 324 Wing HQ and the five Spitfire squadrons were to move on to Pachino and orders were received next day that 3203 were to move with 324 Wing. Flt Lt Roberts went to the Advance HQ of the Desert Air Force for instructions and was told that, due to the large number of aircraft under repair, 3203 were not to move until all work on 324 Wing's aircraft had been completed.

All unit personnel were at Pachino Satellite airfield by 4 August and contact was made with 324 Wing. Sqdn Ldr Le Petit of Admin gave orders that the unit were to carry out 40X and 40XX inspections for 72 Squadron in liaison with their Engineering Officer, Flg Off Paish.

There was some excitement on 4 August. An ME 109 left behind by the Lutfwaffe had been made serviceable and painted in British camouflage with RAF roundels on the fuselage and wings. One of the squadron pilots took off in it for a test flight and every Ack-Ack gun for miles opened up on him! A Spitfire went up, the pilot attempting to stop the AA fire by waggling his wings, but the gunners took no notice and in the general uproar the ME 109 landed in a hurry on the port leg of the undercarriage and the aircraft crashed.

During the days that followed, streams of Mitchell, Baltimore and Boston bombers were constantly flying overhead, collecting fighter escorts on their way to pound the Panzer units that still held the north-western corner of the island around Messina, which was the way to their escape to Italy.

The weather was extremely hot and malarial mosquitos were a perpetual pest. Two parties from the SCU carried out inspections as arranged, while others repaired damaged aircraft and changed engines when required to do so. One Mitchell and two Bostons suffering from engine trouble called in at Pachino on 9 August.

By 10 August the bomber offensive had slackened off. 3203 continued with inspections and repairs until 17 August when Montgomery's army took Messina, which marked the end of *Operation Bigot Husky.* The SCU then switched to R&SU work until they were sent to a new airfield site at Gerbini, near Catania. Here they received a signal, dated August, 'Commando units to be withdrawn and hold themselves in readiness to move on or after 1 September 1943'.

3232 SCU

3232, like 3230 SCU, was formed in the Middle East and had only recently completed training at Hadera, Palestine, when it was dispatched to Malta to take part in *Operation Bigot Husky.*

3232 sailed from Valetta harbour aboard an LST on 16 August 1943. It had been intended that the unit would be landed at Catania as their objective was the airfield at Gerbini and its satellites, but since the port and airfields were still in German

Italian invasion – Commando cooks brew up while waiting at the assembly area (3232 SCU).

hands they disembarked at Syracuse, complete with transport, on 17 July.

Syracuse was very busy, so to relieve congestion the Embarkation Officer sent them to a camp site at Priolo, near Augusta, where the CO made contact with 322 Wing. At 17.30 the next day the unit was directed to move to a new airfield on the south-west corner of Lake Lentini, to the north-west of Augusta. They moved off at 18.15 and took five hours to complete the ten-mile journey due to serious congestion on the roads as troops, armour and supplies moved up towards the front.

At dawn on 19 July the airfield was inspected. The Royal Engineers had levelled the main runway which, when finished, would measure 1,200 feet by eighty feet, running east-north-east by west-south-west. The unit's technical and refuelling equipment was unloaded and prepared for use in the dispersal areas. 1396 General Transport Company arrived with 20,000 gallons of aviation fuel and 2,000 gallons of engine-oil, which were dispersed in small dumps all around the airfield. Several of the unit's MT vehicles were sent to 121 MU, returning with 20mm, 0.303 and 0.5 ammunition which was stored in deep, dry ditches. In the afternoon Air Commodore Atcherley landed in a Stinson aircraft to inspect the airfield and it was decided that the runway would be usable as from dawn next day.

At 10.30 on 20 July two Spitfires made successful landings and the pilots reported that the surface of the runway, although loose on top and very dusty, was suitable for operations. Thirty-two Spitfires of 81 and 154 Squadrons began to land at 17.00 and were dispersed, refuelled and serviced and had their long-range petrol tanks removed. During the evening, personnel of 322 Wing ACP took over 322 Wing equipment and the Engineering Officers were shown the layout of dispersal areas and the positions of the fuel and ammunition dumps. A little later a DC 3 landed, carrying two jeeps and squadron personnel. The aircraft was unloaded in eleven minutes and loaded again immediately with twelve seriously wounded soldiers for evacuation to Malta. At 19.30 another DC 3 arrived with squadron pilots and mail.

All members of 3232 had been busy since their arrival at Lentini, being constantly at work preparing the airfield for operations with very little time to sleep but, when the squadron personnel took over, only half the SCU were needed at the airfield, so on 21 July the unit moved to a new camp site, half a mile from the recently completed runway and beside a small, clear stream which was not only pleasant but also extremely useful.

On 22 July a party from 3232 was detailed for a recce to explore the eastern part of the Catania Plain and to report on the condition of an airfield recently vacated by the Luftwaffe known as Gerbini Satellite No 7. This airfield lay immediately behind the 8th Army's side of the front line, just south of Catania, and was well within the reach of German guns.

The party consisted of one officer, one NCO and half-a-dozen other ranks (including Cpl Davies, a co-author of this history). They left the camp site in a three-ton Chevrolet truck, with enough supplies to last the day, and headed north along the Catania-Lentini road to the Primasole Bridge across the River Gornalunga.

During the night of 13-14 July two hundred British Airborne troops had been landed in the area to take the bridge — a steel box-frame construction some 400 feet in length which the Germans were intending to blow up once the retreating Panzers had pulled back across the river. The

Italian invasion – 3232 SCU await zero hour cutting up bread in the Commando assembly area on the Catania Plains at the foot of Mount Etna, Sicily.

Paratroopers took the bridge and removed the charges, but the Germans brought up reinforcements and tried, time after time, to regain possession. There were heavy losses on both sides and the Paratroopers eventually withdrew due to lack of ammunition. The 8th Army re-took the bridge on the morning of 17 July but, although it was intact, it was badly damaged and unsafe for heavy vehicles until it was repaired.

The recce party crossed the river by a pontoon bridge erected by the 8th Army, under fire, a quarter of a mile upstream. This area had been the scene of a fierce battle, where two German long-barrelled 88mm guns had been in action, firing armour-piercing shells at close range at the British tanks. The burnt-out hulks were strewn about, some with damaged tracks and some with turrets blown completely off. Wrecked trucks were scattered all around the area. Many soldiers had been buried where they died and the stench of death still hung about the battle-ground.

In a sober frame of mind the party drove on northwards in the direction of Catania. Vast quantities of military equipment had been left at the roadside and in the ditches by the retreating Germans and a steel helmet, a Mauser rifle and a full bandolier were picked up as souvenirs by one of the authors.

Cpl Davies was impressed by the Germans' skill in camouflage: what looked like a natural feature from a distance often turned out to be a pill-box, or a gun emplacement.

It was only possible to travel on this road to within two miles of the airfield at Catania. The badly damaged hangars could be seen through field glasses and 8th Army units were being shelled by German guns from strong positions on Mt Etna, to the north-west of the town.

After watching for a while the party drove away, and took the next road on the left, heading in a westerly direction until they came to the place where the Airborne troops had landed in the opening phase of *Operation Bigot Husky* which began on the

Sicily: Comiso Airfield. RAF Servicing Commandos going to service a Spitfire on a newly captured airfield.

night of 13-14 July. Abandoned Horsa gliders were scattered over a wide area. Some had landed safely but others had hit trees and other obstacles and many men had died without a shot being fired. Apart from themselves there was not a soul in sight and the silent, empty gliders and the recently dug graves made a desolate and lonely sight.

As they were near another German airfield, known as Gerbini Satellite No 6, the officer-in-charge decided that they should find the landing ground and check on its condition. They had travelled only a short distance when they saw the tail fin of a large aircraft protruding from a clump of trees, where it had gone in upside down. To their horror they found that it was a DC 3 Dakota, half burnt-out and full of the bodies of dead Airborne troops, that must have been shot down after releasing the Horsa glider that it had towed into the target area. The smell was overpowering and the only thing that they could do was to report the crash site and leave it to the Army to arrange a burial detail.

After that horrific incident the party soon discovered Gerbini No 6. It had been part of the original Combined Operations plan that several SCUs would take over the Gerbini airfields, but strong resistance from the Panzer units had held up the 8th Army and all the airfields were still in range of German guns. No 6 had obviously been bombed by Allied aircraft: the main runway was full of large bomb-craters, all the buildings had been badly damaged and unserviceable aircraft and equipment had been destroyed by the departing Germans. Having investigated this area the party moved on quickly, as shells were still falling on the airfield.

They then made their way, through the back lanes, to Gerbini No 7, which they found to be in a condition very similar to No 6, with the important difference that a great deal of serviceable German equipment had been left behind. The party appropriated a portable petrol/electric generator set in perfect order, at least a mile of telephone wire, three telephone receivers that would be useful on dispersal, and a quantity of tools. Cpl Davies had a further opportunity to admire German camouflage. What appeared to be a hayrick near the runway turned out to be a small control-tower, hangars had been dressed up to look like barns and a hut disguised the entrance to an underground network of air-raid shelters.

The most exciting find was a Gotha GO 145, a trainer biplane, many of which were in service with the Luftwaffe. The wings had been detached, but the aircraft seemed to be complete.

Gerbini No 7 was too knocked about to be of any use immediately, quite apart from the unpleasant fact that German shells were still falling on the airfield. Snipers were also firing at the recce party but in spite of these discouragements they stayed for several hours and collected many other useful pieces of good quality equipment. They then returned by the shortest route to the camp site at Lentini and rounded off a most interesting day with a very welcome evening meal.

Several days later Cpl Davies went to Gerbini No 7 once again, this time with a salvage party, and as a mobile workshop was at the airfield repairing damaged army trucks recovered from the battle area he took the opportunity to make some new wing bolts for the Gotha GO 145. Other members of the salvage unit checked the engine and the airframe while Cpl Davies and others re-attached the wings. One of the Spitfire pilots gave the Gotha a quick taxi run between the bomb craters on the runway. Having got so far it seemed a pity not to fly the aeroplane, so the pilot took off, flew a circuit of the aerodrome in a hail of small arms fire from Allied forces in the area and quickly landed before he was shot down!

On 23 July orders were received from

Sqn Ldr Belcher from the AHQ of the Desert Air Force to transport petrol from 121 MU to a new landing ground that was being constructed at Agnone. The vehicles were loaded and ready to move off when a signal was received cancelling the order. At 21.00 the CO received another signal ordering 3232 to pack up immediately and move to Agnone to service several squadrons of Spitfires due there at first light. The unit moved off from Lentini one hour later and after a very difficult journey they reached Agnone in the early hours.

Agnone had not been used before because it had been shelled by Panzer units of the German army from their positions on the south-eastern slopes of Mt Etna. They, in their turn, had been bombarded by heavy battleships standing off Catania, by waves of Allied bombers and by the guns of the 8th Army situated on the airfield.

3232's four Flights were located at the main dispersals and their equipment was unloaded and prepared for use. Petrol supplies had not arrived at 06.30 hours and the unit's transport was just about to leave for 121 MU to collect the fuel when an army petrol convoy arrived at 07.00 with 13,000 gallons, 700 gallons of engine oil and a small quantity of 20mm ammunition. During the afternoon the squadron commanders of No 1 Squadron USAAF and 417 Squadron RAF landed their Spitfires at Agnone to inspect the runway, and the Group Captain commanding 244 Wing arrived by air for an inspection of the runway. The Spitfire squadrons did not arrive and at 18.00 more orders came for the unit to move to a new landing ground known as Lentini West, to be in position there by midday the next day.

3232 moved from Agnone at 03.00 hours and arrived at their new location at 11.00 hours next day, 25 July, only to be told that their services were not required. After some discussion with 244 Wing and the Engineering Officers it was decided that the unit's tradesmen would be equally divided between 92, 145, 417 and 601 Squadrons to assist with servicing their Spitfires, but leaving sufficient personnel for a repair party.

Three Spitfires had been damaged in accidents whilst taxying and a fourth of 417 Squadron's aircraft had crash-landed on the aerodrome. The repair party spent the next two days swopping engines, wings and airscrews and eventually produced two serviceable aeroplanes from undamaged parts.

On 28 July the undercarriage of a Lockheed Hudson collapsed as it touched down on the airfield and 11 FSU were called in to remove the badly damaged aircraft which was obstructing the main runway. During the afternoon there was some sporadic sniping from the hills and a detachment of the RAF Regiment went out to put a stop to it.

There was little flying activity at Lentini West during the days that followed. The unit continued to assist the squadrons with daily maintenance, inspections and repairs. An Imprest Account was opened on 6 August, the Imprest holder being Flg Off Fallon. Two captured vehicles, a Fiat SPA three-ton truck and a Fiat 10 saloon, were brought into camp and made serviceable with salvaged parts. They were then taken on charge, and Retention Certificates were obtained.

At around 23.00 hours on 11 August there was an unexpected heavy air raid on Lentini East, Lentini West, Fransisco and Agnone airfields. The attack went on for half an hour, and was carried out by thirty or more German aircraft, including JU 88s. The Ack-Ack batteries around the airfield put up barrage, claiming five of the attackers, but there were many casualties. Twenty-nine airmen were killed and forty or fifty injured. Considerable damage was caused to aircraft on the ground, forty of them classified as Category 2 repairs, while a further eight were classed at

Category 3. 3232's camp site was situated between the two Lentini airfields, but the unit suffered no casualties or damage to equipment. When the air raid finished relief parties went to both the airfields to render first-aid, to help to put out fires and to move aircraft from dangerous positions.

After discussions with 244 Wing it was decided that the SCU should repair a total of eleven aircraft. This entailed two engine changes, three airscrew changes, several mainplane changes and an enormous amount of minor work in the repair of bullet holes and shrapnel damage. After tests, the aircraft still held on squadron charge were transferred. The remainder were either handed over to the R&SU or flown to North Africa for repairs. 3232 were still working on the Spitfires damaged in the air raid when Messina fell.

Sicily — RAF Servicing Commandos working in a trench testing and repairing radio equipment, whilst a Spitfire taxies out on a newly captured airfield.

3226

3226 SCU first saw the coast of Sicily at 07.00 on 19 July 1943 and early in the afternoon they went ashore from LCTs on a beach south of Augusta without their transport or equipment which, typically, was still somewhere at sea on board the *City of Newcastle*. The unit marched two miles inland to the RAF Assembly Area, which they found was open ground bounded by the road on one side and a vineyard on the other, with no facilities at all. As they had no tools they were unable to dig slit-trenches or latrines. Camouflage against air attacks was virtually impossible and dispersal was limited by the large number of units who were crammed into the area.

During the night there was a heavy air-raid on Allied shipping in Augusta harbour. The Ack-Ack barrage was intense, as was the hail of shrapnel but, although the unit felt somewhat exposed, nobody was hurt. 3226 kicked their heels at the Assembly Area for eleven days and every night there was an air raid. Bombs fell near the camp, but caused no casualties.

On 23 July Flt Lt Fairbairn visited AHQ Desert Air Force, at Lentini, to discover the location of the unit's transport and equipment and was told that it was still at Malta. The bomb-disposal section of the unit passed the time by collecting booby-traps, but although the area had not been cleared of mines, none were found. The unit were also at risk from malarial mosquitos: the mosquito nets and the quinine were still in the trucks at Malta and the unit suffered, but not silently. At last, on 30 July, the unit was advised that their transport was being landed some distance south of Syracuse and drivers were sent to the beach to pick it up.

On 2 August Flt Sgt Langton was injured in an accident in a Bedford truck and was taken off to hospital. Later in the day a signal was received directing 3226 to the airfield at Cassibile to work on the Beaufighters of 600 Squadron.

One section of the unit began working on the Beaufighters on 4 August. The CO, Flt Lt Fairbairn, received a document from AHQ DAF laying out the policy of employment and duties of Servicing Commando Units, 'as a general rule, one SCU is to be attached to each Wing, and is to have a working party in each squadron of that Wing'.

On 8 August the CO was summoned to DAF HQ at Lentini and was told that 3226 were to move to Lentini East to gain experience on Spitfires with squadrons of 322 Wing. The section employed on Beaufighters at Cassibile and a rearguard party were left behind and the remainder moved to Lentini East, arriving just in time to be caught up in the air raid on the airfields that took place on the night of 11 August and is described in the account of 3232 SCU. A large bomb fell into the middle of the camp site, but luckily it did not explode. The unit quickly moved to another camp site at a safe distance, while the bomb, which weighed 500kg and was buried twelve feet down, was dug up and defused.

Following the raid, five airmen were taken to hospital, but Cpl Montgomerie died in the ambulance. He was the only fatal casualty suffered by the SCUs involved in *Operation Bigot Husky*.

Owing to the extensive damage caused to aircraft by the air raid the unit were employed on repair work with No 11 FSU and the invasion of Sicily had been successfully completed before they had an opportunity to work on Spitfires.

3204 SCU

When the men of 3204 SCU sailed from Liverpool on 27 June 1943 aboard the SS *Ormonde* they had no knowledge of their destination and were not informed that they were to take part in *Operation Bigot Husky* until the convoy reached Algiers on

10 July. The convoy sailed again the same day, this time for Malta, and on the way 3204 were briefed for landing at Catania on D-Day plus six, 16 July, to proceed to Gerbini airfield where they were to work with 3232 SCU in the initial servicing of several squadrons of Spitfires.

On D-Day plus six, 3204 were still in Malta: *Operation Bigot Husky* was running behind schedule and it was not until 19 August that the unit landed at Augusta, where the convoy was attacked by dive bombers. Once ashore, the unit marched some distance to a transit area and Flg Off Renner of the Armament Section was slightly injured whilst disposing of a booby-trap. They hung about the transit area until the end of July.

The 22 and 28 July were memorable, the former for the reasons that Flg Off Renner was released from hospital and news came through that Mussolini had resigned, the latter for an air raid. There were air-raids on Augusta almost every night, but this one was severe and LAC Wise and AC 1 Cotterill were badly wounded in the legs by shrapnel and were evacuated to North Africa by ship.

On 30 July, 3204's transport and equipment were put ashore, and a detachment of twelve fitters and two electricians were detailed for Lentini airfield to service captured enemy equipment. The remaining personnel moved to another transit camp and on 8 August they were ordered to Lentini for forty-hour inspection work on the Spitfires of 152 and 154 Squadrons of 322 Wing. They were still at Lentini when the operation ended.

3231 SCU

There is little that can be said concerning 3231 SCU's involvement in *Operation Bigot Husky* as their records are extremely brief. Certainly they spent some time on Gozo helping to service Spitfires and other aircraft to provide an air 'umbrella' for the landings, and they did not leave the island until 23 July. They landed, complete with transport, from two LCTs and joined the 57th Fighter Group of the USAAF at Pachino South, where they found that there was no work for them to do.

On 1 August the unit were moved to Scordia, still with the 57th Fighter Group. Once again there was no work as the Group were at full strength. On 5 August the CO, Flt Lt Roach, was blown up by a land-mine and was evacuated to North Africa. By the time he returned to reassume command, *Operation Bigot Husky* had been over for some time.

Whilst the invasion of Sicily was a success and revealed Italy's inability to continue with the war, the deployment of the SCU had been less successful and clearly showed that there were serious deficiencies in the plans that had been made for shipping out the units' transport. Also, largely due to the enormous assumption that Catania and the Gerbini airfields would be captured early in the operation, only five of the eight SCUs involved had had the opportunity to make a useful contribution.

3225 SCU

3225 SCU saw very little active service, but while they were not involved in the invasion landings in North Africa and Italy they were held in reserve for *Operation Bigot Husky*. For that reason it seems logical that the unit's history should be recounted here.

3225 was formed at Old Sarum in July 1942 and, after a few months spent with R&SUs in the United Kingdom, the SCU embarked for service overseas and sailed from Liverpool aboard HMT *Otranto* on 15 March 1943, bound for the Middle East. They transferred to the HMT *Sobeiski* at Burban and docked at Port Twefik, Egypt, on 5 May and proceeded to RAF Kasfareet in the Canal Zone later the same day.

During May fifty-one of 3225's NCOs and men were posted to 3230, 3231 and 3232 SCUs. These units had been formed to take part in *Bigot Husky* and were under strength, due to a lack of volunteers.

No reasons were ever given for 3225's exclusion from the three major operations, but it seems likely that they were intended for deployment in the Dodecanese Archipelago should the need for them arise. In the event, only a small detachment from the unit saw service in that area and 3225, under the command of Flt Lt Hill, spent its time travelling between Egypt and Palestine assisting other units. They served at Kasfareet, Asluju, Hadera, Bilbeis, Haifa, Ramat David, St. Jean, Kabrit, Kilo 17 and Kilo 40 and small detachments spent short periods on the islands of Cyprus and Cos.

A detachment from 3225 did some particularly useful work at RAF Ramat David. Here they served the DC 3s of 217 and 267 Squadrons which were engaged in dropping paratroopers in support of Brigadier General Tinley's 234th Brigade who had been put ashore on Cos and Leros to help Italian units to hold out against the Germans. This half-hearted operation came to nothing when the Germans launched a strong attack and took the islands with heavy losses to both sides.

Another useful period was spent with 135 MU at Kilo 40, an airfield on the road to Alexandria in Egypt where 3225 prepared Hawker Hurricanes for the reserve aircraft pool at Helwan.

Several detachments went to Cos. Cpl Smith flew there on 18 September in one of 216 Squadron's DC 3 Dakotas to inspect an unserviceable DC 3 and to effect repairs if possible, in order that the aircraft could be flown home to base. The aircraft was second in a line-up of several similar machines, and Cpl Smith soon discovered that the generator and main battery cut-out had been removed as faulty. All other electrical equipment in the engine nacelle

Sicily — Mount Etna as seen by the crew of a Boston aircraft on a dawn operation.

was serviceable and he decided that if the battery leads were bolted up and insulated the aeroplane could be flown home safely — certainly the wisest course as the aircraft was a 'sitting duck'.

The captain, however, was definitely opposed to flying the aircraft unless it was 100 per cent serviceable, and Cpl Smith returned to the Dakota to take the numbers of the defective parts. He had removed the cover from the electrical panel from behind the first pilot's seat when there was the sound of gunfire, several loud explosions in the aircraft and he was showered with glass and bits of metal as three ME 109s strafed the line of DC 3s. Cpl Smith climbed out of the Dakota, very quickly, and realised that he had been extremely lucky as the side of the fuselage was full of holes and the centre section and the starboard engine were on fire, but as there was no fire-fighting gear nothing could be done except move the other aircraft. Luckily, two DC 3s had taken off before the Messerschmitts arrived. The aircraft in front was dragged away with the help of a few soldiers. The one behind had a large hole in the mainplane but the pilot decided that he would fly it back. The next aircraft in the line was well alight and the last one had considerable damage to its starboard engine. As there was no purpose to staying there any longer Cpl Smith hitched a lift to Ramat David in a Hudson.

A few days later the CO took off from Kasfareet to fly to Cos, also in a Hudson, but had to land at Ramat David due to engine trouble.

Sgt Savage went to Cos on 25 September to service a DC 3 Dakota. He was accompanied by LAC Barber from the unit and by Cpl Hall and LAC Whitaker of 216 Squadron. Sgt Savage, who was killed in a motorcycle accident in Palestine a few weeks later, left the following account:

> We took off from Ramat David in a Dakota at approximately 18.45. The trip to Cos was made mostly in the dark and was uneventful, and we arrived at 22.15. The aircraft to be serviced was a DC 3, number 778, which was dispersed about a mile from the landing strip, so we borrowed a jeep and made our way, with Flt Lt Cody, DFC of 216 Squadron, out to the aircraft.
>
> The dispersal was a wrecked farmhouse and its out-houses, surrounded by trees into which the aircraft had been backed. Work commenced immediately by the light of two hand torches. The magnetos were checked and found to be OK, so the engine was run up, but still maintained a 100 rpm mag-drop. The torches began to fade, so a wandering lead was fixed from the jeep battery to the inside of the nacelle of the starboard engine and the three bottom plugs were removed. These plugs were a problem and burnt our fingers as the engine was still hot. On the second run up the mag-drop was still present so all the plugs on the front bank of the engine were removed and replaced with new plugs that we had taken with us. The next run up was successful and a mag-drop of only 50 rpm was registered, so all tools and spares were packed into the aircraft and a Form 700 was made up to date and signed.
>
> We then started up the aircraft and I took the responsibility of guiding the pilot out to the strip. Just as the aircraft began to taxi one of my torches packed in and I took the pilot out on one torch. I then found the OC Aerodrome Control and we lit the flare-path and got into the aircraft, but when the pilot ran the engines up the magneto on the starboard engine almost cut so, after trying once more with the same result, I guided the Dakota back to the dispersal. As the jeep had gone

no light was available, so work was suspended until dawn.

Meanwhile I obtained an axe from the Dakota and we began to camouflage the aircraft with trees and bushes. This continued until approximately 05.00 hours when work was commenced on the magneto, which we changed. Around 07.00 hours Flt Lt Cody and his observer took on the job of scrounging food, and visited all the detachments on the aerodrome without having much success. The Flight Lieutenant then borrowed an army jeep and went off to town where he obtained some tins of sausages and steak and kidney. Whilst he was away I lit a fire and, being the only one with mess tins and utensils, prepared them for the feast. The one and only meal we had there went down very well and everyone was much more cheerful after the feed.

Work began again, but was soon disturbed by five JU 88s with escorting fighters that appeared from the direction of Turkey, flying at about 12,000 to 14,000 feet, and dropped bombs of various types, including anti personnel. When the enemy were sighted the party made for the nearest ditch, from whence I saw the first stick of bombs fall. While the Junkers were circling for a second run I nipped back to the DC 3 for my small pack and Form 700 and then put as much distance as possible between the aircraft and myself in the shortest possible time.

After the scare had died away I returned to the DC 3 accompanied by Cpl Hall, the two airmen failing to return. We carried on working on the magneto and we had not progressed far when a second wave of JU 88s appeared, so we belted off to our trench once more and stayed there while the aerodrome was plastered. The DC 3 came out unscathed, for which I think we could thank our camouflage, for the aircraft certainly looked more like an overgrown Aspidistra than an aeroplane, but several Spitfires on the strip had been written off.

Once more work commenced and a few minutes later the airmen returned so all my party was still intact. For the rest it was a case of getting the aircraft serviceable as soon as possible so that we could get on our way. Our job was finished at about 13.30 and all the gear was packed away while the pilot was sorting a piece of ground where he could take off. At 14.15 we began stripping off the camouflage, which took half an hour. We then all piled aboard, the engines were started and we were away by 15.00 hours. The pilot had found a 500-yard strip and by running up on the brakes we made it fairly easily. I took turns with the Sergeant Air Gunner in keeping watch out of the astrodome for German fighters, but we hedge-hopped all we could and only climbed to clear the mountains. We had an eventful trip and arrived back at Ramat David at 19.40 hours, where I reported verbally.

These excursions were the highlight of 3225's short existence, for although the unit hoped to be included in the campaign in Italy they never had the chance to put their commando training into practice. 3225 SCU was disbanded on 31 December 1943.

CHAPTER 4
Operation Avalanche — Italy

The conquest of Sicily left the Allies in control of many useful ports and airfields and very nicely placed for a limited assault on Italy where, following the fall of Mussolini, the new government were uncomfortably aware that they had quickly to decide upon a course of action: continuing the war would be unpopular, and would bring Italy into further painful and costly contact with the Allied forces; defecting from it would mean unpleasant conflict with the Germans; vacillation could bring on punishment from both these powerful and impatient parties.

Il Duce's downfall came as no surprise to Hitler and plans for such a contingency had been drawn up months before. When word reached him, at Rastenburg, on 25 July 1943, Hitler ordered that the four divisions of the XIV Panzers were to be withdrawn immediately from Sicily and that Rommel was to be in charge of an operation, code-named *Alarich,* intended to 'neutralise' the forces of his former allies if that proved necessary, for Hitler suspected that they would shortly be negotiating for an armistice with the Allied powers.

In this assumption Hitler was absolutely right. On 12 August 1943 Generals Montenari and Castellano met Eisenhower's Chief-of-Staff in Lisbon to discuss an armistice. While these talks were going on, Rommel moved his headquarters from Munich to Bologna and brought another eight divisions in from France in case they should be needed to deal with the Italians or an invasion by the Allies.

The armistice was signed, in secret, at Cassibile on 3 September, the day that Montgomery's 8th Army landed at Reggio di Calabria for a diversionary assault upon the toe of Italy. The Italians had been informed of the impending operation. There was no harm in telling them, even if they told the Germans — Field Marshal Kesselring expected an Allied landing at or near Salerno and Hitler had been advised. The Italians, however, had not been given any details and for reasons of security they had deliberately been misinformed about the date on which the main landings had been scheduled to take place.

The Italian negotiators were anxious that the world should not be told of the surrender until there were at least fifteen divisions of Allied troops in Italy to protect the major towns and population from reprisals by the Germans. At the time the Allies did not intend to occupy the whole of Italy, but merely to secure a bridgehead which would include the important aerodromes at Foggia and Naples, from which it would be possible to bomb the oilfields of Romania, and accordingly they were proposing to commit no more than five divisions to *Operation Avalanche.* However, it was eventually agreed that there would be sufficient airborne troops in Rome to protect the government and city when the announcement of the armistice was made on 12 September.

The Salerno landings actually took place on 9 September and the announcements of the armistice were made that evening. Eisenhower, who at Cassibile had said to Castellano that he looked upon him 'as a colleague', brusquely told the government

Italy – the first airmen to land in Italy. On the right Pl/Off W J Ives, who flies a Spitfire, landed at newly-captured Reggio di Calabria aerodrome where his aircraft was refuelled. He is photographed with Lt A Sachs from South Africa who was sent by his squadron to refuel Ives' aircraft. Their aircraft were serviced by 3232 SCU.

in Rome that unless they made a simultaneous announcement they would 'have no friends left'. This piece of cruel but justifiable deception cost many thousand lives, for within minutes of the broadcasts the German army and the Luftwaffe struck savagely at the Italian armed forces in the Balkans, the Dodecanese, in Sardinia and Corsica and out at sea as well as throughout Italy. The Allies were in no position to adopt an elevated moral tone about the German action: the British had done much the same thing, on a smaller scale, to the French fleet, and by this time they were too involved in *Operation Avalanche* to spare much thought for the misfortunes of their former enemies.

Since the withdrawal from Sicily to Italy the German war machine had put some effort into preparing its defences on the high ground south of Naples from the Tyrrenhian to the Adriatic Sea against invasion by the Allies and while the 8th Army's advance through the Province of Calabria had met with very slight resistance, as the LXXVI Panzer Corps had orders to fall back before them and not to get involved in any serious engagement, General Mark Clark's US 5th Army were soon in dire straits at Salerno.

The troops spearheading the invasion had gone ashore from their assault craft at 03.30 on 9 September, backed up by an impressive naval force that included seven aircraft carriers. The 5th Army landed to the south of the River Sele, with the British X Corps landed to the north on a twenty-five mile front. By nightfall the US 36th Division were five miles inland, but X Corps were still engaged in street fighting in Salerno, having met with stiff resistance from the 16th Panzers holding the high ground that overlooked the beaches. By 11 September the US 45th were ashore and fighting hard and General Clark's forces were eleven miles inland on a curving forty-five-mile front from Amalfi to Agropoli.

Now began the phase of *Operation Avalanche* that Mark Clark himself described as 'near disaster'. The LXXVI Corps had left the 1st Parachute Division and a small force of Panzers to hold up Montgomery's advance as best they could and had hurried north to help out Kesselring and Veitinghoff's 10th Army. On 12 September the Germans launched a counter-offensive that almost succeeded in cutting the invading force in half and although Clark threw in everything he had, including a regimental band and a smattering of cooks and orderlies, it was touch and go for several days. The German advance was stopped, eventually, only five miles from the beach, where it was pinned down by a concentrated and appalling barrage from a fleet of heavy warships laying close inshore.

Even so, the 5th Army lost almost 6,000 officers and men killed, missing or wounded and the battleship *Warspite,* the cruiser *Uganda* and the US battle cruiser *Savannah,* were all very badly damaged by the Luftwaffe's new and massive glider bombs that carried almost 800 lbs of high explosive and were radio-controlled. The German 10th Army finally withdrew from the battle for Salerno on 16 September when the 8th Army's 5th Division arrived at Agropoli.

By the end of September 1943 the Allies had, between them, 375,000 men and almost 50,000 vehicles in Italy, and amongst their number were the men and vehicles of the same eight RAF Servicing Commando Units that had taken part in *Operation Husky.* Three of the units landed at Salerno, four at Reggio di Calabria and one landed at Taranto. Strictly speaking, the landing at Reggio on 3 September came under an operation code-named *Baytown* while the Taranto landing on 9 September came under the heading of *Operation Slapstick,* but both landings were sideshows of *Operation Avalanche* and inextricably bound up with it.

3232 SCU

3232 was the first SCU to land in Italy. They had received their orders to stand by to move while they were repairing damaged Mustang aircraft at Francisco aerodrome in Sicily and on 29 August they were sent to an army Vehicle Mustering Point south of Catania to waterproof their vehicles in preparation for a seaborne landing. Here they experienced great difficulty in obtaining any information about their role in the invasion, as neither the 5th Division or the 1st Canadian Division of the 8th Army had instructions regarding the transportation or deployment of an SCU.

On 2 September orders came from Advanced Headquarters, Desert Air Force, that their objective was to be the airfield at Reggio di Calabria and that they were to embark aboard an LST at a beach south of Messina as soon as possible. The LST grounded at Reggio at 07.15 hours on 4 September without meeting any opposition and the personnel, complete with vehicles, were quickly disembarked onto a dry beach.

After a brief visit to an assembly area to de-waterproof their vehicles the unit drove to their objective. The surface of the airfield was extremely dry and stony with bomb craters everywhere. The runway had been mined with rows of bombs, the majority of which had not been detonated, and all the airfield buildings had been damaged in varying degrees.

While a bomb disposal squadron dealt with the bombs that had been buried in the runway and the Royal Engineers were bulldozing a landing strip 1,250 yards in length and 100 yards across, the SCU were busy laying out telephone lines and an emergency flare path beside the runway and making fuel and ammunition dumps at the dispersals. This work was greatly hampered by large numbers of Italian soldiers wishing to surrender, but by dusk the airfield was considered fit for use, provided pilots were careful and avoided the bomb craters when taxying to and from the landing strip or runway, which had now been cleared of bombs and stones.

The next morning a Light Ack-Ack Regiment arrived and were dispersed on the perimeter. General Montgomery came in, by road, to have a conference with Generals Alexander and de Gargon who landed in a brace of Fairchilds escorted by four Spitfires. More supplies of fuel and ammunition were brought up to the airfield and at 11.30 the two Fairchilds took off again, complete with Generals and their Spitfire escort.

From 6 to 11 September the unit serviced and refuelled some sixty aeroplanes in transit, mostly Spitfires and Warhawks, and changed the engine of a Spitfire. During this period a party from No 1 AAAU landed and set up an air evacuation centre for flying the wounded to Catania. This service was operational by 14 September.

On 12 September the CO and 9 and 10 Flights, which made up approximately half the unit, were sent to Vibo Valentia, ninety miles to the north of Reggio on the west coat of Calabria, which gives some indication of the rapidity of the advance towards Salerno. Here the party found the airfield serviceable but fit only as an emergency landing ground as the runway was very short. In the time that they were there only two aircraft landed. One was almost out of fuel, while the other one had engine trouble. On 17 September they

Italy – RAF Servicing Commandos work on a captured airfield assisted by an Italian peasant boy (3232 SCU). One of the authors, ex-Cpl J Davies, is carrying a jerry petrol can to help make up a petrol dump.

were ordered to pack up and move on to Cotrone, their stocks of fuel and ammunition being transferred by motor transports from 310 S&T Column.

While 9 and 10 Flights had been doing next to nothing at Vibo Valentia, the party left behind at Reggio had been extremely busy with Spitfires and Warhawks of the USAAF. On 15 September they serviced and refuelled four squadrons of aircraft as well as several DC 3s and in spare moments they began repairing a Warhawk with a collapsed undercarriage.

On 19 September the Reggio detachment rejoined the CO's party at Cotrone and here the unit stayed awaiting orders until 22 September when they were sent off to Cassano to assist No 7 SAAF Wing. It was a long journey, but they reached Cassano late in the afternoon next day, to find that the South Africans had moved on to Scanzana where 3232 eventually caught up with them at midday on 24 September, only to be told that the SAAF did not need their assistance.

On 25 September the CO called on the Advanced Headquarters of the Desert Air Force and was told to take his unit to the aerodrome at Lecce, on the heel of Italy, to form an Aircraft Pool with the help of 3230 SCU who were already there. The unit left Scanzana at 15.00 hours, camped near Taranto for the night and arrived at Lecce at 16.00 on 26 September to find that their new billets were some squalid wooden huts.

The situation at this aerodrome was rather difficult. The Italian Air Force was still in residence with fifty aircraft and in possession of the hangars and the barracks. Sqdn Ldr Haggar of 3230 SCU had been appointed to command the Pool and he informed the Station Commandante that he intended to requisition the hangars, the barracks and whatever else he needed. The Commandante replied politely that Air Commodore Fraser of the British Military Mission had informed him that no Italian buildings, equipment or aircraft would be requisitioned and the frustrated Squadron Leader had this confirmed, on the telephone, by the Air Commodore in person.

The situation was further strained by the arrival of an advance party from 416 Squadron USAAF who flew in to arrange accommodation for their Beaufighters and personnel. The angry Sqdn Ldr Haggar then borrowed someone's Baltimore and went off in it to plead his case at Allied Military Headquarters, where he was once more refused persmission to requisition anything, at least until the BMM had finished its discussions with the Italian authorities. Meanwhile the SCUs remained as lodgers on a captured aerodrome in unhygienic billets, while their erstwhile enemies enjoyed the excellent barracks and facilities.

On 28 September an advance party from No 4 ADMU arrived at Lecce with four aircraft and over the next few days a total of ninety-three more aircraft, mostly Kittyhawks and Spitfires, were received. All these aircraft had to be dispersed in areas where they would not inconvenience the Italian Air Force. A crashed Mosquito of Malta Command was found on the airfield and salvaged to await repairs by a Mosquito repair unit. One incoming Spitfire crashed forty miles from the aerodrome, and all its serviceable components had to be retrieved.

The aircraft fuel situation was most unsatisfactory. The nearest supply point was at Taranto, seventy miles away, and four lorries collected fuel for seven days. The Italians stated that they had no 100 Octane petrol and although it was widely believed that they had large stocks of fuel nothing could be done about it.

At this time the unit were still living in the huts which, they had discovered, had been an encampment for a detachment from the Luftwaffe, who must have loathed the huts as much as they did. This was too much and Sqdn Ldr Haggar protested strongly to the Commandante who grudgingly agreed to let the SCUs use two stone barrack blocks as their accommodation.

On 7 October the Desert Air Force moved their Advanced HQ up to Palazzo. Signal communications then broke down completely and a Hawker Hurricane was used to run a daily courier service.

Since 3232 had been based at Lecce, more and more aircraft had arrived to swell the Pool. By 8 October the airfield was already running out of room and when No 89 Fighter Group and No 115 Servicing Squadron, both of the USAAF, turned up with ninety twin-engined, twin-boom Lightning fighters there were almost 300 aircraft at the airfield. The Lightnings were to play a vital role as long-range escorts to the USAAF's Flying Fortresses that were operating from the ex-Luftwaffe airfields around Foggia, bombing strategic targets in Albania and Greece which had previously been out of reach, but their arrival posed a problem. The CO sent a message to Advanced HQ by the daily Hurricane to the effect that even a minor air raid on Lecce would be a costly business, as the aircraft were so tightly packed.

Ten days later Wg Cmdr Falconer of HQ DAF visited the airfield. He agreed with the CO about the presence of so many aircraft and made arrangements for the Lecce Pool to be restricted to a maximum of seventy machines and for the remainder to be transferred to the Bari Pool.

Later the same day the unit received a new establishment, dated 15 October 1943, to the effect that 3232 was to be reduced to a total of 124 officers and men and were to lose three of their three-ton trucks, leaving them very short of transport for petrol and equipment.

On 29 October one of the pool's Spitfires landed with a fault in its air system, overshot the runway and collided with a steam roller, killing one Italian civilian and seriously injuring two others. A court of enquiry was set up by 4 ADU.

Orders came through on 30 October that the unit was to move to Bari on the Adriatic Sea to help maintain RAF aircraft in conjunction with 3201 SCU. 3230 were to continue work at Lecce until their aircraft were transferred to Bari when they would be flown to their new location by pilots from 4 ADU.

3232 arrived at Bari, without incident, at 15.00 on 1 November to find their accommodation as primitive as usual. Some personnel were housed in old farm buildings, while others were to live in tents. The next day a larger farm building close to the dispersal area was requisitioned as the unit's cookhouse, dining room offices and sick quarters. The hangars and workshops had been badly damaged, so there were no facilities for working on the aircraft, and the RAF office, freight dispersal and equipment stores were in tents. 3232's task was to clear the airfield of all wreckage, patch up the buildings, look after the reserve pool of Kittyhawks and Spitfires and to prepare for the arrival of 117 MU who were to take over the airfield as soon as their personnel and technical equipment could be transported from North Africa.

The aircraft soon arrived from Lecce and the two SCUs were very busy. The dispersal area was extended to an olive grove on the south-east side of the airfield and, as time went on, more and more USAAF bombers and supply aircraft called in to refuel. Many VIPs were seen to come and go as a new Allied Headquarters was being set up in Bari, together with a new hospital to deal with all the casualties that were being flown in. There was enough work in the Bari area to justify employing Italian civilians who enjoyed their new prosperity, for in most parts of Southern Italy there were signs of unemployment, hunger and depression.

The volume of work at Bari Airfield varied considerably according to the intensity of the fighting as the Allies pushed

Italy — one of the first Hurricanes to land in Italy at Reggio di Calabria aerodrome, serviced by 3232 SCU, being refuelled by Cpl Mamwell on truck, left, Paddy Trimble on truck, Sam Armitage filling up, with Garrod on the leading edge, being watched by an aircrew pilot.

northwards towards Rome. Early in October there was a lull as the Allied forces rested along the Volturno/Termoli line, a few miles to the north of Naples, but demand for replacement aeroplanes increased dramatically later in the month when Montgomery's army forced a crossing of the Sangro River and the US 5th Army launched an assault on the heavily defended Gustav Line which followed the northern banks of the Garigliano and Rapido Rivers from the Tyrrenian Sea to cross the central mountains to the Adriatic coast north of the Sangro.

In fact, the squadron's demands for aircraft at short notice, particularly those for Spitfire Mk VIIIs, soon exceeded the supply being flown in from North Africa and the situation was exacerbated by the discovery of severe corrosion in the undercarriages of many Kittyhawks, due to poor maintenance over long periods at landing grounds in many places in Algeria, Tunisia and Sicily during Operations *Torch* and *Husky*.

By the beginning of December the weather had turned very cold and wet and as 3232's personnel were still wearing the lightweight kit in which they had landed at Reggio di Calabria extra boots and underclothing were issued, together with army greatcoats, no RAF coats being available.

The unit continued to maintain the aircraft in company with 3201 SCU and to assist with the establishment of 117 MU on a camp site near the dispersal area. The sub-pool at Lecce had by now closed down and all the aircraft were at Bari.

The farmhouse that housed the unit's dining room and cookhouse was on a slope and from the top of it one could clearly see the town of Bari and its harbour some two-and-a-half miles away to the south-east. In off-duty hours it was possible to walk down a pleasant track from the farmhouse to the town. A Malcolm Club had opened there in late November and had proved popular, with meals and drinks being served in civilised surroundings. The Opera House was open and the cinema was showing old Laurel and Hardy films with English subtitles. There was time for sport and the unit's team played several football matches, with varying success. Their great ambition was to defeat the Italian Air Force team who had a tremendous reputation in the area and were now regarded as being 'co-belligerents'.

At 19.35 on 2 December 1943 the Germans made an unexpected but effective air raid on shipping laying in Bari harbour. 3232's Cpl Davies was a witness to the air raid and remembers it most vividly:

> A large convoy had arrived only that day, but during the afternoon a high flying Luftwaffe reconnaissance aircraft was spotted over the area. Unfortunately the RAF had no high altitude aircraft available, with the Spitfires and Kittyhawks at Bari giving their best performance up to 14,000 feet or on ground strafing attacks, so trouble could be expected, because this kite could not be shot down.
>
> The Luftwaffe Commanders mustered all the available bombers in Northern Italy and surrounding countries to carry out this daring and most successful attack on this Allied target and we were just finishing our meal when someone shouted, 'There's an air raid, over Bari harbour'. We had all been trained not to stay in buildings during air raids and everybody grabbed their greatcoats and their steel helmets and ran up the hill behind the farmhouse to get a good view of the air raid. Flares were falling as we ran, bombs were exploding and we could hear the distinctive sound of German aircraft engines on full throttle as the bombers roared across the town at rooftop height, climbing steeply as they turned away.
>
> Crouching behind a rocky outcrop on the hilltop we could see wave after wave of JU 88s flying in very low across the sea to drop their high-explosives on the shipping in the harbour, with only light Ack-Ack fire and no night fighters to deter them. We watched in horror as an ammunition ship blew up. We found out later that it was the *John L Motley*. A mass of fire, it drifted with the wind, hit the jetty and exploded. The whole ship seemed to lift clear of the water before it disintegrated and sent a column of multi-coloured flame shooting to a thousand feet. Burning debris rained down on the other ships and on the houses in the old part of the town and a blast wave roared above our heads.
>
> Ten minutes later another ship, the *John Harvey*, blew up with even greater violence. The consequent display of fireworks was the most horrific that I'd ever seen and as the blast wave of the explosion rocked us I thought of all servicemen, and the Italian civilians, down there in the devastation. Some ships were burning fiercely, others were sinking and fires raged on the quayside, with buildings enveloped in a sheet of flame. A massive cloud of smoke rose high into the air and drifted out to sea.
>
> I had been bombed and strafed on several occasions and experienced Flying Bomb and V2 Rocket attacks on southern England, but the raid on Bari was the most appalling thing I'd every seen. Rescue parties were organised by the RAF, with many

> volunteers from my own unit, but I was on early morning duty dispatching fighter aircraft from the pool, and I remained behind. The stories that we heard from those who went down to the docks were frightening, and horrible, and that was one job I was glad I missed.

Over 100 JU 88s took part in the raid which only lasted twenty minutes. They lost two aircraft, but seventeen Allied ships lay on the bottom of the harbour and another eight were badly damaged. A thousand servicemen were dead, and another thousand wounded. There were no details of civilian casualties, but all hospital accommodation in the Bari area was packed with air-raid victims. In addition to the shipping losses and the carnage, 38,000 tons of valuable supplies were lost, which had untold repercussions on the Italian campaigns.

What Cpl Davies did not know was that the *John Harvey* was carrying two thousand mustard gas explosive shells, shipped from America, to be stored in special bomb dumps in case the Germans should use gas against the Allied forces. This was officially hushed up for years and even the Permanent Historical Records in the RAF Operations Books make no mention of the air raid on Bari harbour.

During the attack liquid mustard gas had seeped out of the shattered shell cases to mix with oil slicks on the water, and turned to vapour when this evil mixture was ignited. Men jumping from the burning boats or blown into the water were soon contaminated by the gas which, in serious cases, could cause fatal burns, or total blindness and even mild contamination could cause bad blistering, damaged eyesight or lifelong disability. The rescue teams were unaware of the presence of the mustard gas and many of them became contaminated. In all there were over 600 casualties and sixty-nine fatalities from contact with the American-made mustard gas, although the cargo of the *John Harvey* was not known or not revealed, and the injuries were put down to chemicals or toxic gases created by the fires.

None of 3232's rescue party were affected, but it was extremely fortunate for all personnel at Bari airfield that the wind was in the right direction to disperse the gases out to sea. Had it changed, the casualty figures would have been a great deal higher and 200 aircraft would have been unserviceable, thus presenting the Luftwaffe with an even bigger bonus.

The air raid put a stop to the pleasant afternoons in Bari. Within a short period the town was put out-of-bounds to all Allied personnel. The reasons given were danger from the toxic gases from the fires and the possibility of catching typhus. Years later Cpl Davies discovered the truth in a book called *Disaster at Bari* by Glenn Infield, which included the report made by Lt Col Stewart F Alexander, US Army Medical Corps, and a consultant in chemical warfare medicine, who was flown to Bari to verify the cause of the contamination.

During December there were high winds and heavy rain. Aircraft became bogged down in mud and the unit's tents were flooded. Spirits were not raised by the news that 3232 was to be placed under the immediate control of 117 MU as it had been hoped that the unit would be allowed to fulfil its proper function and take part in operations in the forward areas, but by Christmas Eve the struggle against Kesselring's defensive tactics had petered out in difficult terrain and arctic weather. Orders were received for the unit to proceed to England.

3232 sailed from Taranto to North Africa on 2 January and from there, via Algiers, to Liverpool. They were disbanded in Blackpool on 31 January 1944.

3202 SCU

3202's records have been damaged at some

Italy — RAF Servicing Commandos at Monte Corvino airfield near Salerno, with an Italian RO37 biplane.

time and are difficult to read and many of the dates are missing or illegible. However, from a study of the records of the other SCUs involved in *Avalanche* it seems more than probable that 3202 were the first Servicing Commando Unit to go ashore at the Salerno beach-head.

The unit had sailed from Bizerta, with their transport, in three LSTs early in September and by the evening of D-Day their convoy was at anchor off Salerno. Their records state that, 'Owing to the tactical situation it was not possible to disembark'. At 10.30 on the morning of 10 September the three LSTs were beached and the CO, Flt Lt Wheadon, went off to find the Embarkation Officer as no instructions had been received as to the SCU's objective. No information was available, so Flt Lt Wheadon used his own initiative and decided that Montecorvino airfield, at the centre of the beachhead, would make a good objective, being as it was close to the front line and was bound to be of use. In fact, due to strong resistance by the battle-hardened veterans of General von Vietinghoff's 10th Army, it was much too close to the front line to be of any use for several days. It was being shelled heavily when Flt Lt Wheadon went up to have a look at it and he delayed the start until next day.

In the morning Montecorvino airfield was still being shelled and just as heavily, but the unit moved in, expecting that the fighting and the shelling would soon move away. They began stocking up with oil and patrol and arranging Flight dispersals.

On the morning of 12 September two USAAF Lightning fighters bombed the airfield by mistake, and the only aircraft that came in to land immediately drew a hail of shells from German guns that wounded WO Geer and Cpl Fazackerley. Aircraftsman Edwards and Simpson were also injured later in the day by exploding shells.

By 18 September the unit was thoroughly frustrated, having received no orders and no aircraft and performed no useful task, except to provide target practice for a lot of German gunners, but on 19 September Wg Cdr George arrived with instructions that 3202 were to move on to Asa airfield, where they started work next day.

Here they carried out inspections on the Spitfires of the squadrons that were attached to 322 Wing until moving on again to Serretelle landing strip on 29 September, where there was work for only one-third of the unit. On 9 October they moved to Capodichino aerodrome to service 322 Wing's Spitfires. It took five hours to drive the forty miles as the roads were congested with 8th Army traffic and heavy armour heading north.

The first three nights at Capodichino were spent in tents, in heavy rain, but on 12 October they found billets in a school. During this period 3202 stacked 55,000 gallons of 100 octane fuel in dumps at the dispersals, major inspections and repairs were carried out for 322 Wing and three crashed aircraft were moved from the airfield in the absence of the FSU, or Forward Service Unit, whose job this should have been.

On 15 October 322 Wing moved out and 324 Wing moved in. Inspections and repairs were carried out, but were hampered by a lack of spares, especially propellers and header tanks. Squadron personnel came and took over on 17 October and from then until the beginning of November the unit were engaged in the difficult and unnecessarily dangerous activity of unloading and erecting heavy machinery for an incoming Maintenance Unit, without access to the proper gear which would have made the job much easier and a great deal safer.

On 3 November a signal came from Rear Headquarters of the Desert Air Force that transferred 3202 back to 322 Wing and ordered them to move to Gioia del Colle, a distance of 200 miles and away from the front line. Two days later the unit arrived at Gioia airfield to find that 322 Wing had no idea that they were coming and no real work for them.

Flt Lt Wheadon contacted the Headquarters of both the DAF and TAF but with no success, and for the remainder of November 3202 did odd jobs for other units. One day they picked up 500 Spitfire long-range tanks from Taranto Docks and a few days later they were at the docks again, this time for aircraft tyres for Gioia airfield and 135 Advanced Servicing Post (ASP). Meanwhile they trained, maintained their vehicles, did some forty-hour inspections and ferried lorries from Taranto Docks to Bari.

From the beginning of December the records are unreadable, but it appears that they were in the Foggia area later in the month where all their technical equipment was handed over to an ASP. The unit was disbanded on 31 December 1943.

3203 SCU

3203 was the second SCU to land at the Salerno beach-head. It was split into three parties under Flt Lt Roberts, the CO, Plt Off Carpenter and Plt Off Ward. All three parties sailed from Millazzo docks, Sicily, the first two, with the CO and Plt Off Carpenter on board left on the evening of 8 September and the third party followed on next day. Sqdn Ldr Tyrie, 324 Wing's Padre, was with the CO's party and by the afternoon of D-Day their LSTs were anchored off the British beaches at Salerno. The only excitement on the voyage had been provided by a submarine of the Italian Navy that had surfaced and surrendered. Warships were shelling, intermittently, and five large fires could be seen inland.

The two parties went in in very shallow water at Roger Beach by moonlight. All vehicles and personnel were directed to a de-waterproofing area and arrived there as an air raid started and a jeep was set on fire. The unit pitched their tents about a mile inland. Gunfire could plainly be heard and there were further air raids on the beach.

Reveille was at 06.30. The unit breakfasted and waited for Wg Cdr George to give them orders to proceed to Montecorvino airfield, but he returned to tell them that the airfield, which had first been recaptured by the Germans and then retaken by the Allied forces, was now too close to the front line and was still being shelled. A Spitfire had landed there during the morning and had received a direct hit. The unit was instructed to disperse their vehicles amongst the sand dunes and to wait for further orders. They had a pleasant lunch that included cabbage and marrow that they picked themselves. The weather was both fine and warm, and they relaxed all afternoon, watching the Lightnings, Kittyhawks and Spitfires that patrolled the skies above the beach-head, together with Mustangs fitted-out with long-range tanks. While they waited two Spitfires belly-landed on the beach. The pilots were unhurt and 3203 salvaged what they could for spares. There was a three-quarter moon that night and constant anti-aircraft fire gave little chance of proper sleep.

In the morning they were ordered to proceed to Roger airstrip, a new landing ground still under construction at Map Ref. N765205. The runway was 700 yards long and ten yards wide, running north-west – south-east. There were three batteries of British 25lb guns nearby that were attracting gunfire from enemy positions. Shells were passing overhead and bursting near the British guns. The unit's equipment was unloaded and as supplies of petrol were brought in dumps were laid around the airstrip.

Plt Off Ward and his twenty men disembarked at midday on 11 September after a slow and boring voyage. They were directed to report to Montecorvino aerodrome, but on the way they came across a couple of ditched trucks belonging to the unit and learned that 3203 were now at Roger airstrip. They arrived in time to say goodbye to Sqdn Ldr Tyrie who had been ordered to report to Wing HQ within the hour. He made his farewells and set off cheerfully on a motorcycle combination with no idea where Wing HQ was situated. The unit set up camp. The airstrip was almost ready and petrol and oil were both available, but no ammunition. No aircraft had arrived at dusk, when an artillery dual began between guns on either side of the airstrip.

At 22.00 the CO heard that German tanks had broken through inland of the airfield. 324 Wing, Air Formation Signals, the Airfield Construction Company and everybody else pulled out, heading for the beaches to the north-east of the airfield. 3203 advanced to the west side of the airfield and stood-to, with all available weapons, on a road beside the river bank. One of the unit's motorcycles was used to mount a DR service to collect battle orders from Brigade HQ. At 01.30 the DR brought the order to stand down.

For an hour from dawn a very heavy artillery barrage passed over the airfield. All kit and technical equipment was unloaded at the camp site and dispersal areas. An orderly room was set up in a truck and telephones were installed to the site of Wing HQ and to dispersals and most of the day was spent humping oil and petrol to dumps at the dispersals. At 10.30 the first aircraft arrived, one of 72 Squadron's Spitfires with a glycol coolant leak. While it was being repaired enemy shelling began again, with shells screaming over the southern end of the runway and bursting at sea. British artillery replied, and this went on till dusk, when there was a short air raid.

13 September saw the arrival of a considerable number of aircraft. The first

group to come in where the Spitfires of 72 Squadron, the first of which overshot the runway and finished up off the perimeter with its undercarriage in a ditch. The remainder landed safely and were looked after by No 3 Flight at dispersal, who removed and sealed the Spitfires' ninety-gallon jettison tanks and refuelled and serviced the aircraft as quickly as possible. 243 Squadron's Spitfires began arriving at 12.30 and were all safely down within ten minutes. Both squadrons were operational until darkness fell, with only one casualty, a Spitfire of 243 Squadron which made a belly-landing on the grass.

The Spitfires were joined during the day by twenty-four Seafires which had been displaced from Paestum airfield by fighter-bombers. The Seafires had been carrier-borne on D-Day, but had been land-based since the departure of their parent ship. After they had flown four or five sorties they were discovered to be long overdue for checks — most were low on coolant and hydraulic fluids and one flew the last sortie of the day with its wheels down due to the failure of the undercarriage selector gear.

Throughout the day, much to the annoyance of the pilots circling the airfield, a constant barrage of heavy shells passed over the dispersals, fired from the British artillery positions situated near the beach. During the afternoon the Air Liaison Officer of 324 Wing sent word that an Army Co-operation Taylorcraft machine was to be used at Roger airstrip for night observation and direction of this activity, so a flare-path had be laid out. At 19.45 another artillery duel began, with shells screaming across the airstrip. This was followed by an air raid and heavy anti-aircraft fire, with the British batteries firing off rounds at fifteen minute intervals for most of the night, during which the Taylorcraft stooged around reporting the results, eventually landing safely between two lines of red glim lamps in the early hours of 14 September, which proved to be another busy day: the German offensive was threatening the airstrip and the Allied beach-head was in danger of being cut in half. From first light, heavy, medium and fighter-bombers pounded the Germans and bombs could be seen bursting in the area of Battipaglia, about five miles from the airstrip. At 11.30 a detachment of tradesmen from 3202 SCU came in to help with servicing the Fleet Air Arm Seafires which flew two sorties, refuelled and took off again to fly to Sicily.

The work of refuelling and re-arming Spitfires went on constantly throughout the day. In the evening the artillery opened up again and warships laying off the coast joined in with their heavy guns until 01.30. Wave after wave of Wellingtons passed overhead to bomb the Battipaglia-Eboli area by the light of the full moon. Flares lit up the sky, the artillery kept up a heavy barrage and sleep was difficult it not impossible.

The weather continued hot and sticky, but cool at night. On 15 September 3203 kept the Spitfires in the air flying frequent sorties and moved their camp site to the north side of the airstrip, closer to the German lines. In the evening a force of USAAF B17s and B25s bombed the Battipaglia area and at 19.45 the British guns around the airstrip began a bombardment that went on all night.

On 16 September flying went on again all day. One of 43 Squadron's Spitfires crashed on landing and broke its back by somersaulting on the runway. The pilot was injured, but the aircraft was removed and the runway repaired within ten minutes. At 14.00 hours another Spitfire was in trouble when it overshot the runway, nosing-over in soft ground and bending its propeller. Shortly after it had been retrieved two damaged Lockheed Lightnings managed to land safely. Later in the afternoon there came a warning that German tanks had penetrated to within a mile of 3203's camp site, but no defensive action was called for from Servicing Commando Unit personnel. 43 Squadron had a successful day and shot down several FW 190s, but 72 Squadron lost a Spitfire, pilot missing presumed killed, when the aircraft went down some thirty miles north-east of Roger airstrip. All this activity was followed by another noisy night, with a stream of Allied bombers passing overhead and an intermittent artillery barrage that went on until dawn. In addition to the general uproar the Germans carried out three air raids, but no bombs hit the airfield.

The squadrons took off at dawn on 17 September and flew sorties throughout the day. At 09.30 one of the P38 Lightnings was made serviceable and left for home. The drama really began in the afternoon. First a fire started in the engine compartment and cockpit of a Spitfire piloted by 43 Squadron's CO on take off. He stopped the aircraft just in time and jumped out to help put out the fire. Then, in the early evening, a Flight Commander of 152 Squadron made an emergency landing in a damaged Spitfire without the benefit of either flaps or brakes. He was taken back to base at Asa on the unit's motorcycle while his aircraft was repaired by the SCU. Just as he was leaving shells fell on the north side of the airfield, causing casualties among No 11 FSU. This was followed by an air raid, most concentrated on the shipping at the beach, during which a Mustang fighter-bomber dive-bombed enemy positions immediately inland from Roger airstrip causing a terrific fire. A little later the artillery near the airfield opened up again, assisted by the warships, and the action continued at first light with another air raid on the beach and an attack at 07.30 by a group of FW 109s. Squadrons of 322 Wing operating from Asa airfield on an early sortie called in for fuel and

Italy — Vibo Valentia airfield, badly damaged by Allied bombing.

ammunition and at 08.45 the Mustangs were out again, making life unpleasant for the enemy some five miles to the east. The artillery were fairly quiet all day, firing only a few rounds.

There were two casualties that afternoon when aircraft overshot the runway. At 16.16 a USAAC DC 3 landed to deliver some cylinders of oxygen and sustained some damage, since the runway was rather short for the type. Then, less than an hour later, a Spitfire was damaged on take off. There were no injuries caused by either incident.

An intelligence bulletin was issued on 19 September which gave details of the Luftwaffe's new glider-bombers that had been used successfully against the Italian and Allied shipping.

Normal servicing went on at the usual hectic pace with additional attention paid to 11 Spitfires of 111 Squadron and a DC 3 which came in to deliver a load of plasma, landing and taking off without much difficulty, despite the too-short landing strip.

The military position improved during the day with the German troops abandoning their positions and withdrawing north to the area around Salerno, followed by the British artillery who took their noisy 25lb guns with them.

There were two incidents that day, although in neither case was the pilot injured. First one of 243 Squadron's aircraft crashed on take off and shortly afterwards one of 43 Squadron's Spitfires developed engine trouble as it came in to land. The pilot baled out and the aircraft dived into the ground a mile or so away, exploding on impact.

There was no enemy action in the area of Roger airfield that night, but heavy shell fire could be heard from the direction of Salerno.

On 20 September the weather was hot and humid. The squadrons had just completed their dawn patrols and had landed safely at 08.00 when half a dozen FW 190s dived in from the east and bombed the airfield, causing casualties among the crew of a Bofors gun on the perimeter.

Wg Cdr George, the RAF Liaison Officer with the 12th Air Security Corps USAAF, came in that day with instructions that 3203 were to look after the P51 Mustangs of the 31st Fighter Group USAAC at Montecorvino, starting the following day. 1 and 2 Flights were to service 307 Squadron and 3 and 4 Flights were to service 309, while 308 were to be cared for by their own USAAC ground crews. 3203's cookhouse and accommodation were to remain at Roger, with 'meals on wheels' being transported to them as required.

The trucks and equipment left Roger airfield at 07.20 the following morning and arrived safely with fuel and oil to set up dumps around dispersals. During the day thirty-three DC 3s arrived at Montecorvino to deliver USAAC ground crews and equipment and fifteen cylinders of oxygen for the SCU. 307 Squadron landed in the afternoon and were serviced by their Flights before they returned to Roger airfield, which was renamed Tusciana airfield that day.

Both on 21 and 22 September a dozen FW 190s bombed and strafed the Battipaglia-Salerno road and the beach area. The unit spent 22 September refuelling Mustangs as the USAAC had enough tradesmen at the airfield to cope with all the more demanding work.

During the next two days 93 and 111 Squadrons, based at Asa, operated from Montecorvino providing air cover for the US 5th Army's push on Naples. 3203 refuelled, re-armed and serviced their Spitfires until they returned to Asa on 24 September, leaving behind two Spitfire Mk IXs for repair work and an engine change.

From that date onwards it is the usual story of an SCU being used on various odd jobs. During the last days of September, which were very windy, with torrential rain, the.unit spent some time transporting fuel and oil from Tusciana to the landing strip at Battipaglia as the US Transportation convoy that had been expected to delivery fuel direct had not arrived,

No records exist for 3203 SCU for October 1943, but on 1 November they were at Tusciana helping 11 FSU to pack and dispatch aircraft components to Capodichino aerodrome near Naples. By 3 November there were only three Spitfires at the airfield, all requiring engine changes, but no replacement engines had arrived. On 5 November Flt Lt Roberts received orders that a detachment from the unit was to go to Capodichino to help 113 MU to establish an Emergency Repair Section (ERS).

When 3 Flight left for Capodichino on 8 November snow was falling on the mountains inland from Salerno, and work at Tusciana was curtailed by the appalling weather. The airfield was a sea of mud so all personnel who were not engaged on engine changes or repairs were transferred to making up the roads with hardcore, where the constant stream of military traffic had cut deep ruts during the heavy rain. For the remainder of the month the main body of the unit spent their time in maintenance and salvage work, with the occasional football match as light, if muddy, relaxation. During this period a detachment had been sent to Montecorvino to bring four aircraft back to base, but due to the waterlogged conditions they had great difficulty with the low loader.

At the beginning of December Tusciana was declared unserviceable, and all aircraft were grounded. By the middle of December 3203 were reunited at Capodichino and under one warm dry roof for the first time since January 1943. Here they assisted 113 MU and awaited orders to move north to take an active part in the assault upon the Gustav Line. 324 Wing had moved up to a landing ground on the coast between the Massico Ridge and the Volturno River, but the order to join them never came.

After a spate of embarkation orders and cancellations the unit embarked at Naples docks on 6 February for an unspecified destination. No definite date is available for the disbanding of 3203 SCU, but it is considered to have taken place in February 1944.

3226 SCU

3226 SCU sailed in convoy from Millazzo docks in Sicily on 10 September and were off the beaches south of Salerno on 11 September. Their LST was beached successfully after three attempts and the unit disembarked complete with transport at midday, moved off the beach to a de-waterproofing area and from there to an assembly area three-quarters of a mile inland.

Although they went ashore on D-Day plus two they found that heavy fighting was still in progress close at hand and shells from German guns were exploding on the beach and in the sea. 3226 quickly camouflaged their vehicles and dug slit trenches. This proved to be a very sensible precaution as in the afternoon the barrage was intensified and shells fell all around the unit as they waited there for orders. At 23.00 an artillery barrage nearby passed the word that an enemy attack was developing 1,000 yards or so down the main road. The unit quickly took up suitable positions and a DR was dispatched to patrol the road. Liaison was maintained with the artillery battery but the counter-attack fizzled out and the unit stood down at 04.00 hours.

All next morning there was heavy shelling from 75mm guns on the high ground inland from the beach. At 13.00 orders came through from the Beach Unit and 3226 moved off to Sugar Advanced Landing Ground. They put their tents up in an orchard and Flt Lt Fairbairn, the CO, inspected the runway, which was still under construction. There was an air-raid after dark, and sporadic shelling went on until the early hours. There was also some patrol activity some little distance to the north.

On 13 September Sugar ALG was renamed Asa and the CO was instructed by Wg Cdr George at 51st Divisional HQ that the airfield was to be operational as soon as it was ready. The SCU immediately began preparations to stock up with fuel and oil, although they experienced some difficulties. On that day and the next supplies were collected from the Petrol, Oil and Lubricant (POL) dump at Pontecagnano and the landing ground was ready to receive aircraft from 14 September. Although the unit had received a message from Beach Brick HQ that supplies of petrol were to be delivered to the airfield on 13 September no supplies actually arrived until 15 September and the unit had to spend the night unloading it and arranging dumps at the dispersals.

152, 232 and 242 Spitfire Squadrons of 322 Wing arrived at midday on 16 September, followed by two DC 3s which brought in some of the Wing's advance party. All three squadrons carried out one patrol that afternoon and two the following day. Eighteen of the aircraft were between fifteen and twenty hours overdue for inspections and all were found to be in bad condition.

Shells exploding at the airfield on the morning of 17 September caused no damage, but when the Luftwaffe bombed it again next day a good deal of damage was done. One Spitfire was burned out and several others damaged by bomb splinters and shrapnel, and one of the unit's Bedford trucks and a fire tender were set alight and totally destroyed. 3226 were finding that they could not keep up with the inspections and the overdue maintenance as well as servicing the Spitfires, so it was arranged that 3202 would come in from Montecorvino, where they were unemployed, to take over the inspections. They arrived on 20 September, followed the next day by advance parties of squadron personnel, and together they took over one Flight of each squadron.

On 23 September 3226 were sent to service 322 Wing at the airfield at Serretelle and set up their camp site in an orchard. The squadrons flew in on 24 September, but as their Spitfires were now being serviced by squadron personnel there was not much for the SCU to do other than a few inspections.

On 1 October the unit was transferred from the control of RAF Middle East HQ to HQ North West African Air Forces and Wg Cdr George gave orders that they were to clear Asa airfield of all petrol, oil and ammunition dumps and to transport it all to the airfields at Scafati and Pomigliano in the Naples area. 322 Wing moved to Capodichino on 4 October, but as they had no work for an SCU, the unit were instructed to stay behind at Serretelle to take over the reserve aircraft pool.

On 17 October the unit's billets at Serretelle were requisitioned by Americans and they moved to Portico to assist 11 FSU. By 3 November the unit had moved on again to Capodichino where they were to provide a duty crew for airfield duties and continue helping 11 FSU, but by 13 December all work was completed.

On 23 December the CO visited Rear HQ Desert Air Force where he was told that the unit were to be moved to another theatre of war. They were packed and standing by to move next day but no orders came. After a frustrating period of inactivity with hints of orders to move on, and cancellations of the orders when they came, 3226 SCU were disbanded at Portico on 31 January 1944.

3231 SCU

The CO of 3231 SCU was Flt Lt G C Loach and on the evidence available it seems he was a man of action rather than words. His records for the unit during *Operation Bigot Husky* are extremely brief and his records of 3231's involvement in *Operation Avalanche* are almost non-existent for, although they begin at the beginning and finish at the end, there is very little information in between. The following is all that is available.

The unit disembarked in the Taranto area on 16 September and spent a few days at Grottaglia servicing Spitfires for an RAAF squadron of 239 Wing. In October they spent a fortnight at Foggia preparing landing grounds for 244 Wing and from there they went to Gioia to establish a reserve pool of fighter aircraft for the DAF. During November they were at Canne, operating a forward landing ground and early in December they returned to Foggia to work there in conjunction with 51 R&SU. The main body of the unit went to Trigno landing ground on 12 December to service aircraft for 244 Wing, but returned to Foggia on 15 December.

Two days later a salvage party found a twin-engined ME 410 in the Sangro River and on 31 December 1943 the unit was disbanded.

3230 SCU

3230 sailed from Messina on the Naval Ferry Service and arrived at Reggio di Calabria on 20 September with orders to proceed to Cotronne airfield to establish a reserve fighter pool.

They pitched camp at the airfield at 14.00 next day, made enquiries regarding the supply of petrol and sent a signal to AHQ Desert Air Force to the effect that they would be ready to receive aircraft by 22 September. AHQ contacted Sqn Ldr Haggar, the CO, and told him that his instructions had been cancelled and the unit was to move on to a USAAF airfield some eighty miles away, nearer to the front, to service aircraft for the 57th Fighter Group.

The convoy left at dawn and after travelling all day they made camp at a small village on the coast. The Italian police called on the CO to warn him that the villagers were very short of food and would probably attempt to rob the trucks, but the night passed without incident and 3230 were on their way again next morning. They looked forward to finding a home, at least for a few days, as they had been constantly on the move since they left Agnone on 9 September.

The USAAF airfield was in open country, sixty miles north of Taranto. They arrived there on 23 September to find that they were not required to stay as the airfield was unserviceable and the 57th Fighter Group were moving forward. After a night spent beside the road, in the morning Flt Lt Wainwright, the Engineering Officer, reported on their difficulties to AHQ, who seemed unsympathetic, and told him that the unit should proceed with some urgency to Grottaglia to set up the reserve fighter pool.

They were hot and tired when they climbed down from their Chevrolet trucks at Grottaglia on 25 September to discover that the USAAF were already in possession and unwilling to make room for a nomadic SCU to set up a reserve fighter pool. Once more AHQ were contacted, and they wearily suggested that 3230 might like to try their luck at Lecce. Unfortunately, AHQ forgot to mention that the Italian Air Force were still very much ensconced at Lecce. In fact, they were still flying their aeroplanes, and 3230's arrival at the gates was looked upon as an unmannerly intrusion. The Commandante was so frosty that it crossed Sqdn Ldr Haggar's mind that perhaps the news of the capitulation had not yet reached him, but he eventually agreed, with some reluctance, that the SCU should move into some wooden huts that had been constructed for the Germans. 3232 SCU arrived later in the afternoon, and were also directed to the wooden huts.

There is little point in chronicling 3230's stay at Lecce in any detail, as their experiences at the airfield closely parallel those of 3232 SCU which have already been recounted, although it did strike them as odd to see Macchi 202s and Savioia 79s diving on the airfield without interference. While the unit were at Lecce work began on changing the Fascist markings on the aircraft to the Royalist insignia. Sqdn Ldr Haggar was posted to Egypt in October, and Flt Lt Wainwright assumed command. The posting had been following the unit around Italy, and by the time that he received it the Squadron Leader was unwell, and unfit to travel. When he finally departed on 20 October everybody was sad to see him go as he had been with the unit since its formation and was liked and respected by all the ranks.

At the beginning of November 3232 SCU had left for Bari, and 3204 SCU were drafted in to assist 3230 in winding up the pool and seeing that all the aircraft were transferred to Bari. Throughout their time at Lecce the unit had felt very strongly that although the job that they were doing was an essential one, it was disappointing to be so far from the front. Nevertheless, in spite of their eagerness for action they stayed on at Lecce until the unit was disbanded on 30 November 1943.

3201 SCU

3201 SCU slept in a Messina street and breakfasted in public before a crowd of envious Sicilians before embarking on 23 September for the voyage to Italy. By nightfall they had reached Siderno, thirty-seven miles from Reggio, and were off again next morning on their journey north, making good time until they were held up by an army convoy moving very slowly

L.A.C. Harold Worthington, 3232 SCU, studying a home-made contraption for making distilled water that was needed to top up aircraft batteries.

over the appalling surfaces. A halt was called ten miles beyond Strongoli and here the unit bedded down. By this time they had been living on forty-eight hour rations for two days and were craving for some proper food.

A start was made at 08.00 hours, but they were held up by the same convoy that had held them up the day before, unable to overtake on the narrow, battered roads and progress was slow and painful as they bumped and lurched along. When they camped that night outside the town of Amendolara they had covered no more than sixty-eight miles after ten hours in the trucks.

The unit's destination was the Montalbano airfield and they finally arrived at mid-morning on 26 September. While they set up camp Flt Lt Webster reported to Desert Air Force AHQ, only to be told that 3201 were to pack up and move on to Barletta airfield to assist the 79th Fighter Group of the USAAC with servicing their aircraft.

Rations were drawn and the unit left Montalbano at midday next day and made rapid progress. The roads were well kept and very good, except for a few treacherous tank traps near Altamura where the civilian population seemed particularly pleased to see them and where they bivouacked that night. Early the next morning they were on their way again, and reached Barletta at midday on 28 September.

The trucks were immediately unloaded and eight of them dispatched to Bari to collect petrol, oil, bombs and ammunition. The trucks returned at 21.00 hours and were dispersed along a cart track that skirted the camp site, but before the tents could be erected a violent thunderstorm broke out, followed by torrential rain.

The following morning the laden trucks were driven out to Pennypost airfield, six miles from Ceriglona on the Manfredonia road. Here they were unloaded and sent off again to Bari for another load of bombs and petrol in preparation for the expected USAAF aircraft, while the remainder of the unit spent the day drying out after the storm.

That afternoon Sgt Watkins and Sgt Shepherd were inspecting a dump of German bombs and mines. Sgt Watkins, the unit's bomb disposal expert, was demonstrating to two soldiers the correct procedure for defusing an antipersonnel device. Having dealt with the bomb he placed it on the ground and one of the soldiers picked it up and tossed it into the bomb compound where it exploded. Sgt Shepherd was badly injured with splinters in his chest, right leg and groin and the other three were slightly hurt. All were detained in hospital.

During the first week of October, 3201 moved camp to a new site near Pennypost and spent their time stocking the airfield with petrol, oil and ammunition that they collected from 121 MU situated at Ceriglona. There were frequent thunderstorms throughout this period, the airfield was waterlogged and insects, especially mosquitos, were a constant nuisance.

On 9 October the unit moved to Bari to service and refuel the aircraft of the TAFs Communications Flight. They arrived at 14.00 hours and set up camp opposite the airport entrance. Work began next day, and in the evening over half the unit attended a church service conducted in a deserted farmhouse by a padre from the TAFs HQ.

The unit remained at Bari throughout *Operation Avalanche* and thus found time for some recreation. In mid-October, 3201 presented a two-hour revue called 'All for the Boys'. Dr Ronald Martin remembers the occasion well:

> Surely now was the time to hold a Christmas concert. Experts and beginners were soon hard at work, and within a day or two it was all written and rehearsed.

A stage appeared in the barn, then curtains, then stage lighting (good engineers these 3201 men), then a whole area of seats, all in best quality wood, erected at top speed and without fuss. The concert blossomed, the Welsh choir went into training and our violinist from the Welsh National Orchestra regained his skills. Talent surfaced overnight and two Masters of Ceremonies were appointed to keep the 'House' in order and the party clean.

It was an astonishing success and 'Wild Bill' Webster, our CO, was pleased beyond belief. The show ran for three nights; there were no matinees. On the last night every officer for miles was invited as the CO's guest. He swelled with pride, and told everyone that we were first class chaps (he never told us that). 'Very resourceful', he said. 'Always rise to the occasion.'

In fact, everyone was very pleased except the Italian Air Force, for it seemed that one of Mussolini's mighty military hangars was missing from a nearby airfield. They said that it was made of wood, of the best quality, and must have been dismantled by a team of experts.

On 28 October, 3201 took over a sub-reserve pool of two dozen Spitfires from 3231 SCU, who were leaving Bari, and work began on nine unserviceable Spitfires, in addition to the servicing and refuelling of the Communications Flight. The mosquitos were very active, and all personnel were instructed to take precautions against malaria.

At the beginning of November 3201 were working as a DAF reserve aircraft pool in conjunction with 3232. All personnel were now wearing heavy battle-dress as the weather had deteriorated and was wet and cold. The health of the unit was pretty poor, with several cases of malaria and jaundice. In fact, sixteen per cent of the unit were in hospital, an unacceptably high figure. Work on the reserve aircraft pool continued throughout December when it was taken over by 117 MU, but 3201 stayed on working as a Flight of the MU.

The unit witnessed the air raid on Bari harbour that has been described so graphically by Cpl Davies of 3232.

On Christmas Day the unit worked all morning but the afternoon was free. The airmen's mess hall had been gaily decorated and even had a Christmas tree. Dinner began at 18.00 with the corporals serving and the officers and NCOs acting as waiters. Wine and fruit were plentiful and everybody thoroughly enjoyed their second Christmas with the SCU.

From Christmas into January high winds and heavy rain made it impossible for work to continue on the airfield. Early in the month 3201 received instructions from TAF HQ that they were to proceed in their own transport to the Naples area for embarkation via Montecorvino. Here they would be reunited with a detachment that they had originally left behind in Sicily with 600 Squadron, but who had been at Montecorvino since 1 October.

It proved to be a long and difficult cross-country journey. The first night the unit bivouacked on a bleak hillside to the east of Tolve in a strong cold wind and heavy rain which continued until the convoy reached the mountains. Then the rain turned to snow, and eventually became a blizzard that made the roads extremely dangerous.

With the exception of the Willys Jeep and one of the Bedford trucks, both of which had broken down up in the mountains and were not towed in until the early hours, 3201 arrived at Montecorvino at 17.00 hours on an unspecified day in January 1944. Most of the next day was spent in repacking the trucks for a sea voyage and repairing the two unserviceable vehicles. The CO contacted the Embarkation Officer at Salerno and spirits were high at the prospect of another job. The unit moved off in convoy at 07.50 the next morning, passed through Salerno and Pompeii and reached a rendezvous point at the Naples end of the Autostrada at 10.30 hours. After a wait of two-and-a-half hours a dispatch rider arrived to lead the convoy to the docks where 3201 discovered that they were bound for Corsica.

3204 SCU

3204 was the last SCU to become involved in *Avalanche* and their records of the operation are extremely brief. They landed at Reggio early in the morning on 24 October and were on their way to Gioia by 10.30. After four days on the road they arrived at Gioia airfield to find that there was no accommodation but they eventually found billets in a monastery eleven miles away.

On 28 October the CO, Flt Lt Gravill, reported to Rear Headquarters, Desert Air Force, and was told that the unit was on stand-down for seven days.

On 31 October two of the unit's officers were posted to AHQ, DAF, and attached to 3230 SCU at Lecce for the DAF's reserve aircraft pool.

After the week's leave at the monastery the unit moved into barracks on the airfield, only to be told by the Squadron Administration Officer of 322 Wing that he required the barracks for another squadron. 3204 moved out on 8 October with orders to proceed to Lecce, where it was impossible to find any accommodation, and the unit pitched their tents on rising ground just off the main road, almost two miles from the airfield.

At Lecce 3204 worked with 3230 SCU, helping them to clear the backlog of aircraft left behind when the reserve aircraft pool had moved to Bari. In all the unit was allocated thirty-two aircraft and two salvage jobs and remained at Lecce until January 1944.

On 4 January a signal was received from 214 Group HQ requesting that the CO report to them, in person, with details of the unit's personnel and vehicles. Flt Lt Gravill left by road next day and returned on 7 January with orders that the unit was to move to Bari, where it was to be split up: Two officers and one hundred men were to remain with the reserve aircraft pool at Bari, while one officer and eighty men were to be detached to work in conjunction with 117 MU at Catania in Sicily.

This order proved to be the beginning of the end for 3204 SCU. The unit moved to Bari on 9 and 10 January, and two days later Flt Lt Gravill was detached to HQ 214 Group for engineering duties. On 17 January B Flight left for Reggio to embark for Sicily and the unit was disbanded on 31 January 1944.

CHAPTER 5
Operation Thursday — Burma

Before Brigadier Orde Wingate and his Chindits crossed the River Chindwin into Burma in February 1943 morale amongst the British, Indian and Ghurka troops in India was in the doldrums. Although they had numerical superiority they had been soundly beaten by the Japanese and driven out of Burma, thousands had died from malaria, dysentery and other causes unrelated to the enemy, the loyalty of the Indian element of the Allied army had been seriously undermined by subversion from the Indian Independence League and the legend of Japanese invincibility in jungle warfare was gaining ground in the malaise.

Wingate and his Long Range Penetration Group, which was sometimes called his Private Army, remained in Burma for some months, blowing up the Mandalay-Myitkyina railway in many places and generally harrying the Japanese. The expedition had no strategic value and was a costly business in terms of human life as one-third of the force were lost, but Wingate had proved that the Japanese were not invincible, which was of great importance for moral, and Wingate was rewarded by a promotion to Major-General.

During his first Chindit operation Wingate had earmarked several sites along the Irrawaddy that would be suitable as strongholds, each with its own airstrip for supplying a larger force of Chindits and for flying the sick and wounded back to India. These sites, that had been designated as Broadway, Piccadilly and Chowringhee, paved the way for *Operation Thursday*, in which Brigadier Calvert's brigade would be airlifted to the strongholds and then fight their way northwards to join up with Brigadier Ferguson's brigade who were then to march into northern Burma, at Ledo, through appalling country. The object of the operation was to cut off the supplies to the Japanese 18th Division opposing General 'Vinegar Joe' Stilwell's Chinese army that was advancing on Myitkyina, and to Mataguchi's army besieging the Allied force at Imphal.

Plans for the operation were formulated in August 1943 with the full support of Lord Mountbatten and the Americans who formed a special group known as the Air Commando, under Col Philip Cochran, a USAAF fighter ace. The group was to be comprised of several squadrons of P51 Mustangs long-range fighter bombers operating in conjunction with squadrons of the RAF's 3rd Tactical Air Force. It would also be equipped with DC 3 Dakota transport aircraft and with gliders that would take the first wave of Chindits and an Aerodrome Construction Company into Burma. The RAF also supplied other smaller units to support this operation, amongst which was No 1 Servicing Party trained along similar lines to the SCUs.

During July and August 1943 one hundred officers, NCOs and airmen had been assembling at a small grass airfield that has now become an international airport on the outskirts of Bombay. Here they were formed into units to be known as Nos 1, 2 and 3 Servicing Parties, the establishment of each being one junior officer and thirty other ranks of various specific trades. After training in Bombay, each Servicing

Burma – a recalcitrant Missouri mule objects to his first air trip as Wingate's troops and supplies are loaded into a transport plane.

Party was issued with three Chevrolet three-ton trucks, one jeep, one 500-gallon petrol bowser and, in addition to the usual tools and spares, each unit was issued with a set of shear-legs, which were indispensable for changing aircraft engines at remote airstrips.

The first phase of *Operation Thursday* began on Sunday 5 March, when fifty-four Dakotas towing gliders took off from airfields in Indian for the 200-mile night-flight to Broadway. Thirty-seven of them landed in the target area and eight in friendly Chindwin territory, but nine gliders landed in an area held by the Japanese, although most of the occupants made their way safely to the Allied lines.

Broadway airstrip was operational only twenty-four hours after the first glider had touched down, and within two days of D-Day 3,000 combat troops and their equipment had been airlifted in. Chowringhee was ready three days later, enabling a further build-up of men and materials to support the task force, but Piccadilly was abandoned when aerial reconnaissance revealed that it had been obstructed by felled trees. Three other airstrips were soon constructed at locations known as Blackpool, White City and Aberdeen.

Major-General Wingate was killed when the aircraft in which he was flying crashed into a hill near Broadway. After his death *Operation Thursday* was reviewed and was considered not to be having much effect on the flow of reinforcements and supplies to the Japanese at Imphal, so his force was sent north to assist General Stilwell. Nevertheless, with the exception of a five-day period when the Japanese attacked the airstrip, Broadway continued to supply the Chindits and to air-lift the wounded back to India until the airstrip was abandoned at the end of May.

Glider crews sort the towropes ready to hook to gliders and tug planes for the take-off to 'Broadway', the rendezvous behind the Japanese lines for Allied troops operating in Burma.

Men of No 1 Servicing Party were on board the last Dakota to fly out of Broadway. So far as can be ascertained there are no official histories of the Servicing Parties, and it is therefore extremely fortunate that Sqn Ldr Brown, who served at Broadway as a Sergeant Fitter, has supplied the following account of his experiences with the unit, together with some notes on the activities of Servicing Parties Nos 2 and 3.

No 1 SERVICING PARTY

In February 1944 Mataguchi opened his offensive in the Arakan with a tactical surprise. 7th Indian Divisional HQ was overrun and XV Corps was surrounded in what became known as the Admin Box battle. No 1 Servicing Party was moved up to Ramu, which is just north of Cox's Bazaar in the Arakan. Spitfires of 81 Squadron operated from a forward airstrip at Ramu and members of our SP had their first opportunity of refuelling and re-arming aircraft and carrying out daily inspection on those aircraft that stayed overnight. There were no exciting incidents from our point of view. The Japanese had little or no air support in this battle. The Admin Box, manned by a heterogeneous garrison of forward and rear area troops, stood firm and were supplied completely from the air. This was made possible by the complete air superiority of the Spitfires that had very recently arrived. The 14th Army won their first victory here, and the Japanese suffered their first defeat since December 1941 and lost 65,000 men.

From Ramu, No 1 SP moved north, to Jennie, I think. From here I and six others were detached for a move to Burma. Air transport seats were difficult to come by in the days that led up to the new offensive. However, we eventually finished up at Imphal, under the orders of Sqn Ldr Vaughan-Edmunds, the Senior Technical Officer of 221 Group. I think it was some time during the first days of April 1944 that we moved to Burma. A night flight from Tulhal airstrip to Broadway by Dakota! We were followed a few days later by the rest of No 1 SP. I think that there were twenty-six of us at Broadway at this time.

Our role at Broadway was entirely different from the original concept of the Servicing Commandos. Here our main task was receiving and dispatching Dakotas of the Troop Carrier Command. Always night-time activities. Three or four times a week the odd 'Dak' would bring supplies and take back the sick and wounded; these included the wounded from Brigadier Calvert's columns that had taken over a large area around the area code-named White City. The wounded were brought to Broadway by tree-top hopping Stinson L1 and L5 aircraft. They were cared for at a dug-in Field Dressing Station and placed aboard the first available Dakota bound for India.

All Dakota movements to and from Broadway were performed at night. Our flare path was a string of lights fed by a petrol-engined generator. Some flare path lights were once

U.S. planes landed Allied troops behind Japanese lines in Burma. In this picture Allied soldiers fight off Japanese snipers who are unsuccessfully trying to prevent American combat engineers from constructing an airfield behind enemy lines in North Central Burma.

extinguished by the Japanese, which put paid to flying for the rest of the night.

81 Squadron had moved six Spitfires into Broadway complete with mobile early warning radar. They lost three of these aircraft in an air battle with a large number of Zeros — the Japanese would bring up a large Fighter Wing for a few days at a time. 81 Squadron lost a fourth Spitfire before it could gain height on take off. Both the remaining Spitfires were shot-up on the ground. One was a write-off and the other had a bullet-holed engine and a fuselage fuel tank with a hole made by a cannon shell, or flak, in its upper surface. We removed the engine and replaced it with the engine from the write-off, using the shear-legs, and produced a special made dip-stick for the damaged fuel tank to prevent overfilling and overflowing at intermediate stations on its way back to base in India. It was flown out of Broadway by Sqdn Ldr Jacobs.

There was much activity one night when four Horsa gliders were towed in loaded with armoured vehicles for use at White City. The American glider crews dropped them like 'hot potatoes', then boarded the Dakota 'tugs' and hopped it. They had done a good job landing them on the darkened airstrip. We unloaded the gliders, one being somewhat difficult as it was caught up in our barbed wire, and booby trapped, defence perimeter. Anyway, they were all unloaded OK and disposed of somewhere in the jungle the next day.

We had a crashed American B25 bomber aircraft just off the strip. Sqn Ldr Vaughan-Edmunds begged us to try to recover one of the engines, to replace one on a B25 that 221 Group had 'won' somewhere or other. We obliged, thanks to the shear-legs, and made an engine stand for it out of old ammo boxes. Loading that onto a transport aircraft at night with the assistance of a platoon of Ghurkhas is another memory.

I think the most memorable, and difficult, task was carrying out out the sharp-end of the operation laid on to fly out Brigadier Ferguson's column, who marched into northern Burma. They had fought battles and suffered many casualties and much sickness. Their astonishment when they marched into our fortress at Broadway to find a few airmen preparing things to fly them back to India was morale boosting. Again it was done at night. It took a few days, as we were dependent on the weather. I was responsible for loading four reluctant mules, plus ten Chindits, onto certain suitably prepared Dakotas.

Another sergeant loaded wounded and equipment, while another loaded men, twenty-five per aircraft. Although all this was done in the run-up to the monsoon with electrical storms and heavy rain the operation was a complete success. Some of the aircrew did not relish carrying mules and needed some encouragement; more about that some other time.

We had the odd scare, but rations were our real problem. Mainly American K rations, augmented, perhaps twice a week, by good old British bully-beef and hard-tack biscuits, with *tea*. The K rations included coffee! After two or three weeks most men had some form of dysentery. We were allowed a fire to brew-up at dawn stand-to and dusk stand-down — full stop. Mepacrin anti-malaria tablets were mandatory of course.

All activity and conversation was in a quiet manner and at night all activity and orders were subdued. We were all issued with silk neckerchief maps of Burma and small button type compasses, in case of dispersal action.

I think it must have been the end of May 1944 when, at dawn one morning, No 1 Servicing Party boarded a Dakota bound for Sylhet in India. Probably the very last Dakota to leave Broadway.

REHABILITATION

Mepacrin subdues malaria. When it ceases to be taken the dormant malaria takes over. The first day at Sylhet saw half a dozen hospital cases from our own small unit, so we moved to Shillong, a hill station for the Pemacrin treatment — malaria curse. From there, three or four weeks later, to Rhumbergram in Assam. From there I was posted to No 3 Servicing Party.

No 2 SERVICING PARTY

No 2 Servicing Party never seemed to 'get off the ground', as far as I remember. I think they were used mainly in a support role, as a personnel reserve. I never heard of them after the training phase.

No 3 SERVICING PARTY

I joined No 3 Servicing Party at the Imphal airstrip. Here again No 3 had acted as a reception, refuelling, minor servicing and dispatch unit for the troop transport Dakotas and the odd Commando transport aircraft which was a little larger than a Dakota. The Imphal airstrip and the nearby strip at Tulihal had remained open to enable the supply and reinforcement of units of the 14th Army fighting in Manipur State. I do not know when No 3 SP had moved to Imphal, or when they moved away, because after some weeks I joined No 11 SQD at Tamu.

For the record, the CO of No 3 SP was Flg Off P H E R Dunn, a splendid, serious-minded and dedicated young officer. The NCO I/C was Flt Sgt Jack Lock.

Later I received a Chindit badge as worn by the army units forming the Long Range Penetration Group known as the Chindits, together with a covering letter of appreciation from Brigadier Lentacque, the successor to Wingate who was killed flying from Broadway to India. A nice thought, I think. I still have it, the letter that is.

Sqn Ldr F L Brown

CHAPTER 6
Operation Overlord — Northern France

The invasion of Europe, code-named *Operation Overlord,* has been so well documented that it would be superflous to do more than refresh the reader's memory with a brief outline of its history.

Plans for *Overlord,* originally known as *Round-up,* were laid at the Trident Conference in Washington in 1943 and, following a year of complex preparations, the invasion actually began on the morning of 6 June 1944. The Germans had been successfully encouraged to assume that the landing would take place in the Pas de Calais area of Northern France, but in fact the beaches chosen by the Allies lay between Le Havre and Cherbourg, some distance to the west.

At 02.00 hours on D-Day troops of the 82nd and 101st American Airborne Division and the British 6th Airborne Division were dropped by parachute and glider on objectives several miles inland and consolidated their positions in the extreme east and west of the invasion area, in spite of heavy losses. Warships and aircraft began pounding the beaches at 03.00 hours and at 06.30 the first troops went ashore, the American Western Task Force on beaches code-named Utah and Omaha and the British Eastern Task Force on beaches code-named Gold, Juno and Sword.

In round figures, 3,000,000 men, 4,100 transport vessels, 1,200 warships and 10,000 aircraft were involved in *Overlord,* but by the end of the first day the Allies had not achieved all their objectives. The US 1st Infantry Division had been pinned down for hours on Omaha, firstly because air attacks had failed to pulverise the beach defences and secondly because their amphibious tank support, launched three miles from shore, had been swamped and sunk in the rough seas. Nevertheless, the Allied armies had breached the *Atlantic Wall* and established a secure beach-head.

The weather, the German High Command and the French Resistance all made their contributions to the success of the invasion. The unseasonable high winds and heavy rain, that had caused General Eisenhower and his commanders many anxious hours, had grounded the Luftwaffe who would otherwise have seen the huge armada assembled off the Isle of Wight. The Germans were convinced that the invasion could not possibly take place in such conditions, although they guessed that it was imminent.

The Germans, in fact, were in some disarray. Rommel, commanding the armies in Northern France and the Low Countries, expected the invasion to occur only when high tide coincided with the dawn, although nobody knew where and he and Field Marshal von Rundstedt had disagreed on what to do about it when it did occur. Von Rundstedt, Commander-in-Chief West, whose 15th Army was on the alert too far to the east, favoured keeping beach defences to a minimum with a strong force centrally situated and ready to rush off at a moment's notice to repel the landings, wherever they took place. The Luftwaffe only had 400 aircraft in the area and it was Rommel's view that Allied air superiority would certainly ensure that von Runstedt's force would be defeated before it could oppose the landings, so he

RAF Servicing Commandos, who arrived on the first airstrip in France, watch a bulldozer at work.

advocated that the invaders should be defeated on the beaches before too many of them came ashore. Hitler believed, as the Allies had intended, that thirty divisions were concentrated on the Kentish coast poised for a Channel crossing, and his solution to the generals' difference of opinion was to come down firmly for a compromise that emasculated both proposals. One week after D-Day he was still insisting that the landings were a clever decoy and forbidding Rommel to use the eighteen divisions of von Rundstedt's 15th Army, because he expected the invasion proper to take place at the Pas de Calais.

The contribution made by the French Resistance movement, at great danger to themselves, is easier to understand. According to Lt-Col E Bauer in his fascinating book, *The History of World War II*, 'No military operation was ever based on such comprehensive intelligence as *Overlord*': that intelligence was supplied by the French. The invading forces were equipped with maps accurately marked with the positions of all fortifications in the invasion area, complete with detailed lists of ordnance from heavy artillery to machine guns. The Allies were also very well informed by carrier pigeon and by other means of the strength and disposition of the German armies.

Six SCUs had been formed in April 1943 to take part in *Operation Overlord*, and all six were in Normandy within a week of D-Day. 3205, 3207, 3209 and 3210 went ashore the day after the initial landings, with 3206 and 3208 disembarking one week later. They were allocated to the various groups of the 2nd Tactical Air Force. HQ Group included a Photo Reconnaissance Unit, and a Met Flight, No 2 Group was equipped with light and medium bombers, 83 and 84 Groups with fighters and fighter bombers, while 85 Group had specially prepared Spitfires, Tempests and Mosquitos for fast reconnaissance.

In order that the Tactical Air Force could make the best use of its aerial superiority, the Airfield Construction Companies of the Royal Engineers began building forward airstrips as soon as the beach-head had been consolidated, moving forward with the army to pre-selected sites. Within hours of the arrival of their bulldozers and excavators these sites were cleared and levelled and a carpet of steel mesh laid down to form the runways and dispersal areas. While these airstrips were being constructed, Army Transport Units brought in lorry loads of petrol, oil, bombs, ammunition and other essential equipment and supplies. During the first two months of the invasion the Royal Engineers constructed twenty-five such airfields, some complete with hangars and servicing facilities, between Bayeux and the coastline north of Caen.

The SCUs served at the majority of these forward airstrips but, with the exception of brief and personal accounts, there are no records of 3207 and 3209's involvement in *Operation Overlord*. Nevertheless, we know that 3207 was the first SCU to land in Normandy and we will begin this history with a look at their activities.

3207 SCU

3207 sailed from Gosport Hard on D-Day, complete with vehicles, on board an unspecified number of LCIs and an American landing ship. According to notes supplied by Sgt K J Hurst, the LCIs landed on Gold beach between Ver sur Mer and Grave sur Mer in the early hours of D-Day plus one. They had tried to go ashore at night on D-Day but had drowned two vehicles. On landing they drove through a minefield to Bazenville B2 ALG.

At B2 they serviced Hurricanes, the Spitfires of 'Johnnie' Johnson's squadron and Typhoons. Their next move was to Esquay sur Selle No 122 Airfield on the Bayeux-Caen road where they serviced the same aircraft plus a few Mustangs. Here they were bombed and strafed by FW 190s, but only suffered a few minor casualties. By this time the invasion was progressing well so the unit were pulled back to Meauvanes to assist a FRU to prepare damaged aircraft for shipment to the United Kingdom for repairs. They also recovered crashed aircraft and were employed to bury Allied dead, some of them from the Hampshire Regiment, as the minefields were cleared.

After eight weeks in France 3207 were relieved by 3206 and 3208 SCUs, and returned to the United Kingdom via the Mulberry harbour at Arromanches. They landed in the Portsmouth area, and drove to Littlehampton to assist 83 and 84 Groups' support units to prepare aircraft and equipment for shipment into France. Eventually they were sent back to Old Sarum to disband and reform in 3207 and 3205 SCUs for duty in the Far East, and from Old Sarum they were sent to West Kirby, Cheshire, to prepare for service overseas.

Ex-Fitter Armourer E Nuttal 631027 wrote the following description of the voyage to France on D-Day, and his subsequent experiences with 3207:

> For the last few weeks before the invasion, we were at various camps in the south of England. About a week before D-Day we were under canvas near Petersfield in Hampshire, then we moved to Gosport on D-Day and we embarked from there at six o'clock that evening. Our unit was split up into three sections, two small groups went on board LCIs and the remainder of us, including myself, crossed the channel on an American landing ship. For us it was almost a pleasure trip. We arrived off the coast

of France during the night and we dropped anchor waiting for the dawn. When it did come we moved a little further inshore towards Mulberry harbour. We were attacked by German aircraft but the American crew put up a pretty good barrage with their Pom-poms. We did not suffer any casualties, but we lost Jack Croft who was on one of the LCIs. They were torpedoed round about midnight and of course in complete darkness nobody could do much in the way of rescue for fear of giving away our own positions. While we were waiting to go ashore at Arromanches the battle cruisers *Rodney* and *Renown* were firing salvoes of shells at a big German tank battalion about seven miles inland, as they were apparently putting up a big resistance to our forces. I'll never forget the *Renown* as she passed quite close to us — she let off a broadside and the blast and heat from those sixteen-inch guns were awe-inspiring.

France — Normandy landings. A mobile crane removing a four-bladed propeller from a Spitfire.

We actually went ashore about eight o'clock in the morning. This would be D-Day plus one. We got all our trucks ashore and the jeeps, but when we got off the beach onto the road, one of the trucks broke down. Water had got into the engine. I believe it was repaired later on. We went to an Emergency Landing Ground about three miles inland which had been laid by the Royal Engineers. From there we refuelled and re-armed Spitfires and Hurricanes of various squadrons that were coming over from the south of England.

We were, of course, under canvas during our stay in Normandy. I remember that we got some unwelcome comments from some of the local villagers when we first arrived. You see, we were the first British RAF personnel they had seen and of course we were wearing RAF blue and everything was covered in dust. As a result our uniforms looked just like the German grey uniforms. I distinctly remember as we went through the first little French village a group of women could be heard quite plainly shouting 'La Bosche, Le Bosche', which we learned later was French for 'The Germans'. However, later on, when they got to know who we were, they were quite friendly. On the anniversary of the Bastille Day we had quite a nice time in the village. It was the first time it had been celebrated since 1939 and the local people had quite a fête on the village green. We got a team together and played an army eleven at football, much to the enjoyment of the locals.

A Cpl Howard and myself went for a stroll one day along the coast road right into Caen, which had only just been recaptured from the Germans. We wondered why everything was so quiet and deserted. We returned by a different route further inland and suddenly a shell flew overhead and exploded in a field about a hundred yards away. A bit further up the road we came across an army unit near the railway station and they told us we were under German tank fire. So needless to say we did not hang about for long. I could not help noticing how cool and unconcerned those army boys were. Some of them were having a shower under the water-tower that would normally be used for re-filling the engines on the railway, and all the time shells were coming over at about five-minute intervals.

We returned to Southampton in August 1944 after being in Normandy for about two months. We came back on a merchant ship. After disembarking we boarded a train at Southampton and journeyed up to Warrington where we rested. Then we were split up together with members of four other Commando units and made up to strength again. I believe some of the older members were left out. I was twenty-four years old at the time, my RAF trade was a Fitter Armourer.

Mr Nuttal's remarks about the RAF blue uniform are interesting. Originally the SCUs had worn army battle-dress, in khaki, with RAF blue badges and RAF-style rank insignias, army boots and webbing, with RAF blue forage caps, or berets and RAF cap badges. Just before the six SCUs embarked for France the khaki battle-dress was withdrawn and replaced with Air Force blues. Due to discolouration caused by unavoidable and constant contact with lubricants and dust, the blue soon looked very like the grey/green worn by the German army. This was not only embarrassing but downright dangerous in forward zones where soldiers had a natural tendency to shoot at anyone resembling an enemy.

Mr Nuttal also mentioned an incident in which Jack Croft was killed. The following is taken from an account by ex-Airframe Fitter S J Revell of the voyage to France aboard the LCI that was torpedoed:

> When darkness came the only noise was engine noise from the craft and the splash of water. I settled down on the kit on the back of the three-tonner and dozed. About 01.30 I roused and had a look around the convoy. Each vessel was making its own bow wave and leaving a trail with a slight phosphorescent glow. No one had given us any orders — still no briefing, so I decided I would load ten rounds into the magazine of my rifle before settling down on the kit to doze again.
>
> Then it happened — one hell of a bang and a cascade of water followed by flame and shouts of pain. One of the 20mm Oerlikons on the poop of our craft fired a few short bursts and then stopped as I climbed over the tailboard of the three-tonner and up onto the poop. Looking for'ard the craft was fairly well illuminated by flames which were spreading and increasing in intensity. The LCT slowed down and I think the engines were stopped. There was obvious heavy damage on the starboard side about midships. The convoy obviously sailed on. A torpedo had struck us launched from a surface craft — an 'R' boat or an 'E' boat, causing the damage and resulting in a fire which very quickly enveloped the vehicles in the area, generating heat which was felt throughout the

France — Normandy Landings. Recovery of belly-flop Spitfire.

craft. The Coles crane jib glowed, it seemed white hot and began to sag. The forward part of the LCT began to yaw, pivoting about the weakened area. An MTB appeared eventually and took off personnel from the for'ard end before moving out of the way as the for'ard end of the LCT began to break away. I don't know how many got off before the MTB then came round and approached from the stern and on the starboard side. Our craft was pretty low in the water and the fire was still burning. I think it was realised early on that trying to control the fire was out of the question and it was essential to get as many as possible off the for'ard end. The MTB slowed down and was just about hove to on the starboard side, under control about midships but the relative movement in all three planes between us and the MTB was such that getting across the gap to the MTB was a gamble to say the least. A rope was passed from the MTB and made fast aboard us, which helped to keep the separation distance under control to some extent. One or two took the chance of crossing on the rope which meant that, as it sagged, they took a ducking but fortunately no one was crushed as the two vessels came together in the swell. At this point a few more jumped aboard the MTB. One of the first I saw go was the Canadian Wing Commander Medical Officer followed shortly after by the other officers.

About this time I saw fellows coming back from the midships area and climb up onto the poop. One of them, approached me who I failed to recognise until he spoke. It was Jimmy Wright, an armourer from 'B' (Yellow) Flight of 3207, badly burned and with shoulder and arm injuries. He was wearing a balaclava helmet which had been some protection but much of the skin of his face was hanging off but fortunately his eyes seemed undamaged. I found a French Canadian Medical Orderly and brought him to see Jim. He took a quick look, made some remark about not being able to help and took the next opportunity to get across to the MTB. Mick Ryan had been with me throughout and we managed to get Jim into the shelter of one of the gun positions on the poop. The Skipper and the rest of his crew mustered on the poop and the MTB cast off. The risk of damage to the MTB and the need for it to pursue its own duties meant she couldn't stay and so we were left to our own devices. The for'ard end finally broke away whilst the rest of the hulk continued to burn though the flames were subdued. As the craft settled lower in the water wreckage went overboard. The Skipper and crew discharged their responsibilities by destroying what needed to be destroyed and then broke out the rum, passing a mugfull round to warm us up, as by this time we were wet and cold.

We wrapped Jimmy Wright in blankets and gave him a swig and a cigarette whenever he felt like it. Came the dawn and we were well down in the water. The poop remained above water but its deck was awash at times. There seemed to be nothing in sight from our position for sometime, until a couple of Lockheed Lightnings flew low overhead and shortly after we saw a small craft approaching. It turned out to be a United States Coastguard cutter which came alongside. We passed Jimmy Wright over and then scrambled over ourselves.

3205 SCU

3205 arrived at the Concentration Area at RAF Old Sarum at 13.00 hours on 31 May

1944, and here they waterproofed their vehicles and rested until moving to the Marshalling Area at Fareham on 2 June. At Fareham the officers were briefed and given maps and sealed instructions for *Operation Overload*. Rations for three days were issued and French currency was exchanged for Sterling. 3205's five officers and 176 other ranks sailed for Normandy from Gosport Hards at 11.00 hours on D-Day aboard four LCTs and disembarked near Ver sur Mer between 08.00 and 19.00 hours on D-Day plus one.

Sailing with them were twenty, three-ton Bedford trucks, two 350-gallon Bedford water tenders, two 15cwt Bedfords, one jeep and four motorcycles. The crews of the LCTs seemed anxious to unload and get out to sea again and two of the three-tonners and all the technical equipment and kit that they contained were lost when the doors of the LCT were opened too far off the beach and the trucks were unloaded in deep water. The occupants all swam ashore, but LACs Clark and Millard were slightly injured when their truck was blown-up by a land mine on the beach at Ver sur Mer.

Once all personnel and vehicles had been accounted for, a unit HQ was formed near Ver sur Mer, about a mile from B3 landing strip. Slit trenches were dug and the first night ashore was nightmarish as a large German force just north of Caen was shelling the invasion area although there was very little opposition from the Luftwaffe.

On 8 June, 3205 unloaded all their technical equipment at B3 and spent the whole of the next day transporting petrol, oil and lubricants (POL), bombs, rockets and cannon and machine gun ammunition from the main beach to the landing strip near St Croix. 3209 and 3210 SCUs were also at B3 and while 3205 were making petrol, oil and ammunition dumps at the

France — Normandy landings — erecting a temporary hangar.

disperals, they were preparing to receive the aircraft. It was not long before sixteen squadrons were using B3 landing strip and the three units were servicing Spitfires, Hurricanes, Typhoons, Lightnings, Thunderbolts, Mustangs, Air Observation Platform Austers and DC 3 Dakotas flying in equipment and supplies.

The build-up at B3 did not go unnoticed by the Germans. The area was shelled at night and bombed and strafed in daylight hours, but these attacks inflicted little damage. Life at B3 had its lighter moments when unexpected things were done, for example, the airstrip was very bumpy and needed to be flattened, but no heavy roller was available. Somehow an enterprising airman produced a steam roller from an unknown source and soon had the runway levelled — in between aircraft landing and taking off!

Due to the lack of tents the aircrew were flying back to England every evening and some of them returned one morning with drop tanks full of beer. Unfortunately the tanks had not been properly cleaned out and although the beer was very welcome, it tasted strongly of high-octane fuel, so smoking and drinking at the same time was not advised. The aircrew also brought back drop tanks full of fresh bread, butter and untainted bottled beer, which was shared with the army units bivouacked around the airstrip before moving to the front.

By 11 June sufficient tentage was available for the pilots to stay in France and this meant a dawn to dusk work schedule for the SCUs. Servicing was carried on well into the night by the light of electric light bulbs wired up to battery starter trolleys or aircraft batteries and, in order that such night work could continue without attracting the attention of the Luftwaffe or the enemy artillery, a large covered area was improvised from a framework draped with tent fly sheets, ground sheets and tarpaulins.

The pilots appreciated the hard work put in by the SCUs and on the first Sunday after D-Day a Spitfire flew low over the disperals and dropped a parcel. This contained the News of the World and other Sunday papers, and personnel of the three units at B3 landing ground were able to read about the first Allied aircraft to land in Normandy, and how they were refuelled by RAF SCUs!

In the absence of petrol bowsers at forward landing grounds, refuelling was carried out from jerry cans through a large funnel jammed into the aircraft's filler hole, a practice that led to overfilling and the dangerous and wasteful spillage of aviation fuel. 3205's ingenous Engineering Warrant Officer devised a quicker, safer and less wasteful process by mounting a 44-gallon drum with a hand pump and a hose and nozzle complete with filter on a trolley that could be pushed from one aircraft to another, the ground crews taking it in turns to keep the drum topped up with petrol and turn the handle of the pump.

12 June was an eventful day at B3, for the Supreme Commander, Allied Forces, visited the landing ground. Cpl Harthill of 3205 remembers the occasion well:

> At about 11.00am a Flying Fortress approached the airstrip from the direction of the sea, with a wing of fighter planes as escort. The Fortress landed, but not the escort, and it taxyed down the taxying strip towards the dispersal point operated by 3205. We had no word from the Control Caravan on what was happening, so assumed the Fortress had some kind of technical trouble. I went towards it and waved it into a clearing on the opposite side of the taxying strip to our dispersal area. When it came to a halt, I looked up towards the cockpit and was amazed to see the face of the Second-in-Command, Allied Forces,

> Air Marshal Tedder. The crew door at the rear of the Fortress opened, a crew member came out and after a very short delay out jumped the C-in-C, General Eisenhower. He was followed a little later by Air Marshal Tedder. From nowhere, either two or three jeeps came tearing down the taxying strip, with an armed guard on each and Eisenhower and Tedder climbed into them and off they went in the direction they had come from. The whole operation must have been very secret, because I said to one of the crew 'That was Eisenhower, wasn't it?' 'No', the crewman said, half smiling, 'It was another five star general'. There was not one photographer, newsreel man or reporter in sight and when they all returned about three o'clock in the afternoon, the same again. With the minimum of fuss, they all climbed into the Fortress, and I waved it to go along the taxying strip and go the reverse way it had come in. It then took off. One of the American crew told one of our lads that they had gone to have a conference with General Montgomery.

AVM L O Brown, DSO, DFC, Grp Capt A C Malan, DSO, DFC and the AOC of 84 Group also landed at B3 on 12 June. In addition to their aircraft 3205 re-armed and refuelled thirty-six Spitfires, one Typhoon, four Mustangs and a Lockheed Lightning from three separate squadrons.

Due to intensive use, coupled with a hot, dry summer, the landing ground soon began to suffer from excessive wear and every aircraft movement created clouds of dry white dust. To assist the pilots, who were almost blinded by the dust clouds, the SCUs supplied two 'guides', one sitting on each aircraft wing tip, to direct pilots to the runway or from the runway to dispersal. The clouds of dust also caused engine problems and the SCUs got the job of fitting desert air filters to all the engine air intakes.

Early on 13 June a Halifax Bomber ran out of fuel on the way home from a raid on Germany and landed at B3. 3205 partly refuelled the aircraft with 800 gallons of petrol. This was probably the first bomber to be refuelled in Europe and it was all done from jerry cans passed up onto a lorry, and from there into the high wing of the Halifax. During the day 3205 re-armed and refuelled seventy-seven Spitfires, one Mustang, two Thunderbolts and four Typhoons, some of the Spitfires belonging to 341 Squadron, the first Free French squadron to operate in France. 13 June was the day that the first German V-1 flying bombs were launched on London.

By this time Rommel was convinced that Germany had lost the war but heavy fighting still went on in Normandy for, despite his pessimism, he was determined to resist the Allies for as long as possible to strengthen Germany's position at any future peace conference, although neither Hitler or the Allies were ready for negotiations.

At B3 work continued on a frantic level, but on 15 June, 3205 handed over their responsibilities to the RCAF and moved to B4 landing ground near Beny-sur-Mer, a few miles to the east and even further from the sea than Ver sur Mer. At B4, 3205 serviced the Spitfires, and rocket-firing Typhoons of 181 and 245 Squadrons before handing over to 126 Wing of the RCAF at 12.00 hours on 18 June, although the unit's armament officer and a few armourers stayed behind to instruct 126 Wing personnel in making-up and loading rockets.

On 19 June that unit moved to Villier-le-Sec adjacent to an advanced party of 401 Advanced Servicing Post to rest and re-equip with Typhoon spares. 3205 camped in an orchard where a German antipersonnel device exploded, seriously wounding LAC Farquhar who was admitted to the

Casualty Clearing Station with leg injuries and evacuated to the United Kingdom on 20 June. AC Barker was also wounded in this incident. He was detained overnight, but was passed fit for light duties the next day.

19 June also saw a severe storm that destroyed the second prefrabricated Mulberry harbour that was being set up on Omaha beach. The first Mulberry harbour already operational in the British sector was badly damaged and the storm sank hundreds of landing craft with the loss of many thousands of tons of supplies, which created a serious shortage of weapons and ammunition for the American 1st Army and held up the assault on Cherbourg, the Allies main objective.

Wet weather in the second half of June and throughout July drastically curtailed the amount of sorties that could be flown by the aircraft of the TAF to support the front-line troops. This inability to exploit their massive aerial supremacy, coupled with difficult terrain and the undoubted superiority of the German Panther and Tiger tanks over the under-armed and comparatively flimsy and inflammable American and British armour, hampered the Allied effort to break out of the beachhead. The excellence of the artillery went some way to redress the balance, but it was not until the fall of Caen on 9 July, followed a few days later by the fall of Cherbourg, that the final victory over Germany began in earnest.

In the meantime, 3205 had moved from Villier-le-Sec to B10 landing ground near Plumetot, a few miles north of Caen, where Montgomery's army was still engaging a strong force of German armour lured into the area in a costly, but successful, diversionary tactic, although the town should have fallen into Allied hands on D-Day.

3205 were only briefly at B10, refuelling

France — Normany landings — Flying Control at work at a landing strip.

and re-arming Spitfires of 310, 312 and 313 Squadrons and on 1 July they moved to St Croix Grand Tonne, on the main road from Bayeux to Caen to assist 403 R&SU in the collection of crashed aircraft. It was here that Cpl Attwood was seriously injured in an explosion that occurred in A Section's camp lines on the evening of 5 July. He was taken to No 10 Army Casualty Clearing Station and from there to No 20 Army General Hospital, but four days later he was transferred from the dangerously ill list to the seriously ill list and evacuated to the United Kingdom by sea.

The unit's involvement in *Operation Overlord* petered out at St Croix Grand Tonne. During July one sergeant, two corporals and fourteen armourers were sent to B15 landing ground at Ryes to assist 3208 with armament maintenance and the re-arming, of 193, 197 and 257 Typhoon Squadrons, one senior NCO, fourteen other ranks and two Bedford trucks were detached to No 404 Advanced Servicing Post at Tour-en-Bessin and one sergeant and six fitters were detached to 404 ASP to de-waterproof and overhaul that unit's motor transport.

By 23 July the unit was once more united and had returned to Plumetot. From there they moved to the RAF Assembly Area at Buhot and embarked for the United Kingdom on 30 July. They disembarked *en route* for No 83 Group Support Unit at RAF Bognor Regis.

At the end of September 1944, 3205 moved from Bognor Regis to RAF Old Sarum and all ranks were granted fourteen days embarkation leave. In October all NCO and Aircraftsmen in Demobilisation Groups 1-28 not compelled to continue serving with the unit in India or the Far East were posted to No 2 Personnel Dispatch Centre at Morecambe, the majority of their replacements coming from 3209 and 3210. On 25 October 3205 were sent to No 1 PDC at RAF West Kirby for final preparation for service overseas and on 2 November they embarked at Liverpool and sailed for India.

3209 SCU

Very little information is available concerning 3209's part in *Operation Overlord*. We know that they served at B3 landing ground, St Croix and at B4 Beny-sur-Mer, at B10 Plumetot and at Villier-le-Sec. The following account by ex-LAC J F Craig is the only existing record of 3209 SCU's exploits in Normandy:

> We were taken to the LSTs, this was the evening of June 5th. After embarkation, we moved off towards the French mainland — Normandy. On nearing the landing area, we anchored about a mile from the beach, a warship was sending salvoes to support the invading regiments. The noise was crushing, tanks could be seen quite clearly in the open spaces. We landed with our vehicles on D-Day plus one, it may have been D-Day plus two, I am not sure. We established our HQ close to a village, Villier-le-Sec. An airstrip was laid down by the REs and we were servicing, which was mainly refuelling and re-arming, in a day or so. We were on 'K' rations, some of the pilots brought bread over in their wing compartments which was very acceptable indeed. Although we wore khaki, this was changed back before we left England. This is so similar to German Green at a distance that it was hazardous in a combat zone, someone had blundered. On occasions we were visited by enemy aircraft who showered quantities of small anti-personnel bombs, but our casualties were very light indeed. We had taken precautions to dig small depressions in our tents about twelve inches deep, this was very effective being just below ground level, quite successful.

France: Normandy landings – LAC T Langley and Flt Lt C E Wood, CO 3209 SCU.

I am sure there are so many incidents happy and otherwise, but it is hard to call to mind after so long a time. However, as the front was moving away from us all the time, it was not long before our stint was up. I think we were in Normandy about ten weeks, it was decided to repatriate 3209 to the United Kingdom.

3210 SCU

The following account of the unit's role in *Overlord* was written by the Officer Commanding 3210 throughout the operation:

> The morning of 6 June 1944 found us embarking at our port, and looking forward eagerly to whatever lay ahead. We saw many wonderful sights, but the outstanding memory is the endless stream of shipping going to, and returning from, the invasion beaches, for this was D-Day.
>
> Our trip lasted twenty-four hours. We stayed off-shore until the tide was right, and eventually made a dry landing at approximately 11.00 hours on D-Day plus one. The unit had been split up into three parties, and there was a little anxiety as to the safety of one party. This unit had been responsible for 3205 SCU and detachments from 126 Wing and 4519 R&SU, together with its own personnel and vehicles on the passage to the continent. The pyrotechnic display on the first night was brilliant. We camped at Ver-sur-Mer on the edge of B3 landing ground which was our objective.
>
> The next morning we moved to St Croix-sur-Mer, which was on the

other side of the strip and was, apparently, our correct location. In the middle of the morning it was a great relief to see Flg Off Hannaford and the remainder of the unit arriving at our camping site. On checking over we found that we still had all our personnel, but had lost one three-ton Bedford and one 15cwt Bedford and all the stores and equipment thereon. About ten men lost their personal equipment whilst trying to disembark. The Germans gave us a very hectic night.

9 June was the day of days, for soon after dawn a squadron of aircraft arrived at our strip, which meant that we had the honour to receive the first Allied aircraft to land in Normandy. By now we had learnt to dig ourselves in as we knew what to expect each night from the enemy.

For a day or two things settled down to the routine of servicing aircraft, until the night of 12 June when things got pretty hot. During the day Cpl Fennel was hit by a small piece of shrapnel, and the mail arrived.

On 15 June we moved to B4 landing ground at Beny-sur-Mer, where the ground crew comprised 3205 and the usual attachments, in addition to ourselves. We dug in for the night and the next morning the squadrons arrived. It was interesting to note that flying continued from B4 although there was a German 'strong point' still operative within a few hundred yards.

On 18 June, 126 Airfield arrived and took over all servicing, while we eagerly awaited our next move to a forward landing strip. Two days later we moved to B9 landing ground at Lantheuil but, as usual, we had to wait for the landing ground to be completed. Pay arrived next day, and for a short while the airmen considered themselves as being almost millionaires on receiving a month's pay in Francs.

On 24 June Air Commodore Montgomery visited us at 06.00 hours and told us that we were to be operative immediately. Naturally, we were delighted at this news and had a very busy day. 26 June was another busy day, and brought the good news that LAC Warren had been Mentioned in Despatches — London Gazette No 36544, dated 8 June 1944. The weather appears to have broken.

On the evening of 27 June Sqdn Ldr Betts, the deputy Padre of 2nd TAF, conducted a very good open-air service, followed by Holy Communion. This was greatly appreciated by the men. Three days later No 143 Airfield took over B9 landing ground and we moved to B7, situated at Martragny, to assist 405 R&SU to repair and salvage aircraft. The barrage put up in this sector was terrific.

To sum up, it can be said the men carried out all duties expected of them in a manner which does credit to the unit, but it must be recorded that they could have coped with at least three times as much work and were disappointed that more could not be found for them. Admittedly, the weather had a strong bearing on this matter, but each man, over a period of months, had trained himself to work flat out for days on end and naturally there is always the sense of frustration when the quantity of work falls below expectations. Flt Lt A O'Malley received from Air Commodore Montgomery a copy of a letter sent by Wg Cdr Hodson of 126 Wing, congratulating the unit and its Commanding Officer on its efficiency and keenness.

A historic month, but WE CAN DO MORE.

On 1 July parties of men were sent to work at the American A1 and A2 airstrips. This was salvage work detailed by the OC of 405 R&SU. Other sections were working at B7, on repairs and salvage with 405 R&SU.

On July 3 Sqdn Ldr Boggs of 83 Group (Main) visited the CO and asked for a technical report on the work of the unit since its arrival in Normandy. This was drawn up by the CO and delivered to Sqdn Ldr Boggs. It was unfortunate that this officer slipped when leaving the Orderly Room wagon, causing damage to his knee. He had suffered from a misplaced cartilage and this accident brought on a recurrence of the trouble.

On 6 July work was found with 85 Group's Heavy Glider Repair Unit on gliders in the Benouville district. This consisted of cannibilisation of these machines, and work proceeded quite well, despite occasional shelling and attacks by enemy aircraft. After several days' work was suspended as the enemy shelled the position each time they saw a completed glider being moved to a sheltered position.

The 14 July was a notable day, as we opened our NAAFI canteen, including serving beer and spirits, and the evening was completed by a sing-song, a joint effort between our own unit and the ambulance drivers of the MACC.

Two days later we moved to B12 landing ground at Ellon, just north of Tilly-sur-Meulles. We had difficulty with our camp site and had to make a hurried change of location. This proved fortunate, because that evening there was heavy shelling from the Germans and the original site

France: Normandy landings – a Spitfire and Typhoon returning from a sortie at an airstrip. An airman on the wing is guiding the the pilot.

received direct hits, killing three men and injuring several others. Twelve airfield personnel and a number of aircraft were hit by shrapnel.

There was a considerable amount of work repairing the damaged aircraft. B12 gradually became quieter as the front line advanced. The amount of work available to the unit became less and less and finally on 28 July the unit received a warning to be prepared to return to the United Kingdom at forty-eight hours' notice.

29 July was spent in preparing trucks for the voyage, and certain equipment was sent to the ASPs. Several unit photographs were taken. At 18.30 hours the unit was moved to the No 1 RAF Assembly Area at Buhot where we stayed the night. Most of our money was changed from currency to sterling and the balance of the Personnel Social Institute, or PSI, fund amounting to 14,644 Francs was handed to Flt Lt Swann and the Wing Commander I/C Accounts. The accountant officer had tried to reach us all day, but was delayed owing to the enormous 'push' that was taking place that day, hence the cash settlement in the Assembly Area. He stated that the remainder of the Francs which the airmen carried would be changed in the United Kingdom.

On 06.30 hours on 30 July we proceeded to the beach and, together with 3209 SCU, we were shipped aboard LST 360 by 07.00 hours. The 'Port' was transformed out of all recognition to what it looked like seven weeks ago and the organisation was excellent. At 07.30 hours the Americans on board this craft were serving breakfast to officers and men. The craft left the quay at 13.50 and stayed out in the bay for half an hour. It was a sad moment for us all, who felt that we had started a job and not had the pleasure, and the honour, of seeing it to a successful conclusion.

After a very quiet voyage and several excellent meals we arrived at Stokes Bay at 07.05 hours on 31 July. We were escorted together with 3209 SCU to the marshalling area, and at 14.00 the convoy proceeded to 84 Group Support Unit at Thruxton, where we arrived at 17.00 hours. The camp was set up and it was strange when the camp settled down for the night in the quiet stillness of the English countryside on a summer's evening.

To sum up, the highlights of the month were, firstly, the work done on British aircraft found in the American Sector, where there were upwards of forty-six aircraft, some not reported. This unit detached small parties, each complete with tools and domestic gear, to effect on-site repairs where possible, or alternatively to dismantle aircraft for transportation to the R&SUs. Personnel employed on this work had to proceed cautiously at first, as it was reported that the Americans were apt to shoot at the sight of a blue uniform. Covered with dust the RAF blue looked not unlike the enemy's field grey. An order was later issued authorising the wearing of khaki battle dress by SCUs based in France, followed later by a Group order, in signal form, making the wearing of collars and ties compulsory for work and walking out by all ranks in France.

Secondly, the work on the salvaging of Horsa and Hamilcar gliders which occupied the unit during a period when no strips were available. Upwards of 300 of these gliders were located in the Benouville area, the major portion of them being across

France: Normandy landings – Servicing Commandos line up for a meal.

the River Orme, on a very thinly held sector of the front. Under Wing Commander White — who had only one warrant officer, and two sergeants of his unit — 3210 personnel put in some valuable salvage work, despite occasional shelling and ground strafing by the enemy and once being bombed by USAAF Marauders. Eventually, however, the glider personnel arrived and 3210 Commando Unit moved to B12 landing ground at Ellon with 405 R&SU.

Thirdly, owing to the speed with which airfield personnel were moved to France and the limited area available, plus the fact that all six SCUs were in the theatre of operations, there was insufficient work for all the units. This unit was employed to capacity only during the early part of the operation and the CO, Flt Lt O'Malley, was prepared to take on anything from tank repairs to ambulance driving to keep the men busy and their morale high.

Health was excellent, there being only one case of long-standing gastric trouble, one broken leg and two cases of neurosis in the whole unit. These were all promptly evacuated. Food etc, was good, and welfare facilities, shows etc speedily organised.

The general feeling of the unit was of pride in having operated the first airfield on the continent, and of regret that we were unable to see the conclusion of the campaign.

Signed: Flt Lt A O'Malley Commanding 3210 Servicing Commando Unit.

3208 SCU

3208 landed in Normandy on 16 June 1944 and immediately drove to B7 landing ground some miles inland near the main Bayeux-Caen road. They found the landing ground to be unfinished, which seemed to indicate that the unit would not be operational for several days. The following morning instructions came from Air Commodore Montgomery that half the unit should go to B3 landing ground, to help out for one day.

B7 was completed by 24 June and 3208 began to service a squadron of Mustangs which returned to the United Kingdom that evening. The CO attended a conference at Group HQ and was told to take the unit to B8 landing ground next day. The servicing of aircraft continued at B7 until the airfield personnel arrived at 14.00 hours when the unit moved to B8 at Sommervieu. The airfield personnel were contacted and arrangements were made for the unit to service three squadrons who were arriving the next day, 26 June, but the weather was unsuitable for flying and the operation was cancelled.

By 29 June the weather had improved sufficiently for 3208 to be called upon to service forty DC 3 Dakotas and a squadron of Mustangs. Daily inspections were also carried out on the Mustangs and instructions were received for the unit to move their camp site to the opposite side of the airfield. By 09.30 the following morning all personnel and vehicles were at the new location, tents were erected and the camp was in working order. During the afternoon all personnel were engaged on airfield duties.

From 2–7 July, 3208 assisted 93 FSP in the loading and unloading of Dakota transport aircraft, but at 11.30 on 7 July they were ordered to move off to B15 landing ground, at Ryes, by 14.00 hours, where camp was pitched. During the evening the unit helped in the stocking of the airfield in preparation for the arrival of three Typhoon squadrons.

The Typhoons of 193, 197 and 257 Squadrons of 146 Wing arrived early in the afternoon on 8 July. They were bombed up and refuelled, but the weather was unsuitable for operations and the aircraft were de-bombed and left for the United Kingdom at 20.00 hours. They were scheduled to return at 05.00 hours next morning, but were delayed by weather until 10.00 hours. The aircraft were bombed up and refuelled once more, but the weather delayed the operation until 20.00 hours when 16 of them took off to attack enemy positions, only to find their targets were obscured by cloud, so the bombs were dropped into the sea. Daily inspections were carried out and the aircraft stayed the night at B15.

At dawn next day, twenty aircraft took part in an attack on ground targets around Caen and at 08.00 hours 193 Squadron flew an abortive sortie. Two hours later eight Typhoons successfully attacked more targets in the area of Caen, but the weather then closed in and all three squadrons took off for the United Kingdom at 20.00 hours that evening.

This was very much the pattern of operations for the next few days, with the aircraft flying to and from their base in the United Kingdom and operations sometimes flown and sometimes cancelled. On 13 July, 257 Squadron destroyed two ME 109s and damaged five other aircraft, but lost two aircraft and their pilots and had two more aircraft badly damaged.

On 15 July, 3208 were moved to B3 landing ground at St Croix-sur-Mer, but the unsettled weather continued to interfere with flying for the remainder of the month. Nevertheless, enough sorties were flown when visibility allowed to keep 3208 extremely busy. The high light of July was Winston Churchill's visit to B3. It was regarded as a great occasion, and his informal address was greeted with enthusiasm by all ranks.

On 30 July the Typhoons of 266 Squadron were handed over to the Airfield Servicing Echelon and the unit received instructions to return to B15 for a brief rest period. On 5 August, 3208 was transferred to 84 Group and moved to B10 landing ground next day to service the Mustangs and Typhoons of 268 Squadron. The aircraft flew in at 16.00 hours, and as they were not required for operations for the remainder of the day, daily inspections were carried out.

In addition to their thirteen Mustangs and eleven Typhoons, 268 Squadron had four Spitfires equipped for photographic reconnaissance. On 11, 12 and 13 August all these aircraft flew many sorties, with satisfactory results. In the afternoon of 13 August, 3208 and the aircraft of 268 Squadron were moved to B4 landing ground. One of the unit's Bedford trucks caught fire on the journey and was burnt out, together with the contents. One of the Typhoons was also damaged, by anti-aircraft fire, and was abandoned at B10.

On 14 August, 268 Squadron flew thirty-six sorties from B4 and one Mustang crashed on take off. Thirty-four sorties were flown next day before the aircraft were handed over to the Airfield Servicing Echelon. Approximately half the unit moved to B17, at 21.00 hours. The remainder of the unit followed on 16 August and spent a considerable amount of time cleaning the domestic site and waging war on flies, only to be moved to B14 at Colomby two days later, at short notice, to service and refuel Dakotas. The unit arrived at B14 within two hours of the receipt of the movement order to find that the operation for which they had been urgently required had been postponed. Group HQ ordered the unit to move on again to B16 to service two squadrons of Spitfires that were due to arrive from the United Kingdom and the unit spent 19 August preparing for their arrival. Due to bad weather only one squadron of Spitfires and one squadron of Typhoons landed and were refuelled, taking off again for base when the weather cleared.

The Spitfires of 66 and 127 Squadrons of 132 Wing arrived at 13.00 hours next day, and were handed over to airfield personnel at 18.00 hours on 21 August.

On 22 August, 3208 were directed to return to B17 to service aircraft belonging to 135 Wing, but the aircraft never arrived and on 26 August a detachment from the unit was sent to A12 landing ground to service aircraft of the TAFs Communications Flight.

At 23.00 hours on 31 August the main body of the unit was ordered to transfer to B29, some sixty miles away, and to be there by 14.00 hours next day ready to receive the aircraft which did not arrive. On 2 September the unit learned that they were not required. On 6 September the unit was directed to B37, about 100 miles away, where they were joined by the detachment from A12 and on 9 September they were moved to Vendeville Aerodrome, near Lille, another 100 miles away, to service aircraft for 145 Wing that would be landing there at midday on 10 September.

3208 arrived on time, only to be told that 145 were not expected until the following day, but while they were digesting this information the aircraft of 131 Wing began to land and 3208 were immediately operational. The unit worked on 131 Wing's aircraft until the airfield personnel arrived on 12 September, when it was arranged that 3208 would take on the servicing of all aircraft visiting the aerodrome. They remained at Vendeville and spent several days unloading petrol from several hundred USAAF Liberators until 27 September when they were sent to B58 at Melsbroeck, Belgium, to service aircraft operating on the Roulement system.

Throughout October and November, HQ and one other Flight remained at Melsbroeck while detachments were sent to B56, Evere, and B70. Personnel at all three airfields were engaged on the servicing of a variety of visiting aircraft, including Spitfires, Mustangs, Typhoons and Mosquitos.

During the first week of December the weather, which had been variable, improved and personnel at each of the

France: Normandy landings – Servicing Commandos playing cards during a lull while others bomb-up a Mustang fighter-bomber.

locations were kept busy with a constant flow of aeroplanes of assorted types. For example, on 8 December eighty-six Spitfires and nine Mustangs landed at B58 after completing operations and were refuelled and serviced. Eleven of these aircraft required wheel changes and thirty remained at the aerodrome overnight, intending to return to the United Kingdom the next day, although in the event a resurgence of bad weather prevented their departure until the morning of 10 December.

On 18 December the detachment at B70 was sent to B71, Coxyde, to provide emergency landing facilities for fighter and communications aircraft, but by the end of the month they had seen no activity of any kind, although preparations had been made. Throughout this period personnel at B58 had been fully occupied with visiting aircraft, including night-flying Mosquitos, while the detachment at B56 continued with the servicing of the TAF Communications Squadron.

The New Year started badly at B58 with an early morning air raid carried out by German fighters. This did little damage, but from a study of their records it would seem that the air raid was the most exciting thing that happened to 3208 Servicing Commando in the first two months of 1945! Routine servicing went on at B56, B58 and B71, with flying restricted by bad weather at all three landing grounds.

In March there was a change of pace, when twenty-seven airmen and one sergeant were withdrawn from B71 and returned to Melsbroeck. Later in the month a detachment of thirty-four airmen, led by Flt Sgt Bond and Sgt Brooks, were sent to B75 landing ground at Nivelles to prepare Dakotas for airborne invasion of Germany across the Rhine.

By 27 March, 3208 were reunited at B58. Two days later, twenty airmen were posted to 427 Repair and Refuel Unit at B89, Mill (Holland) and on 31 March the unit was disbanded, with no ceremony or commendation other than a few words from the CO.

3206 SCU

3206 sailed from Gosport Hards on 14 June 1944 and were assembled at B6 landing ground at Coulombs in Normandy by 15.00 hours next day to find that the Germans were still in occupation of a wood only two miles from the airfield. 16 June was spent in collecting and unloading ammunition, with the help of a detachment from the Pioneers and an advance party of 124 Airfield personnel.

Typhoons from 121 Airfield flew in next day, as their landing grounds were under shell fire, and almost impossible to operate. Four ME 109s strafed B6 at 14.00 hours and a Pioneer and three members of the airfield advance party were slightly injured. A big tank battle went on throughout the day about two miles from the airfield and great efforts were made to build up a stock of rockets for the 'tank busting' Typhoons.

The weather was very good and all three squadrons were operational on Panzer blitzing, but dust created problems with visibility and two Typhoons crashed before they could take off. B party of 124 AF and a new detachment of the Pioneers arrived and on 19 June the remainder of 124 AF turned up, flown in by Dakotas. They took over the servicing at 17.00 hours and 3206 were unemployed.

By 21 June all equipment had been collected from the airfield and the unit was standing by to move. Late in the afternoon instruction came for the unit to proceed to B8, Sommervieu, north east of Bayeux, where camp was pitched at 21.00 hours and a meal prepared. The following day was spent in stocking up with POL and ammunition. The weather was ideal for flying, but the only aircraft to arrive was a badly damaged USAAF Marauder which had been hit by flak whilst raiding Caen. The bombs were taken off the aircraft and an American salvage party was contacted and requested to remove it from the airfield.

When the pre-stocking of B8 was practically complete the CO was informed by 83 Group that it would operate only as an emergency landing strip as it was too close to the German lines and likely to be shelled. Very little worth recording happened at B8 during the last week of June: a Thunderbolt landed at the strip after being shot up, a sergeant was put under open arrest for indiscretions in his correspondence, a corporal was arrested for looting a French house, a Mustang was shot down near the airfield by five ME 109s just before the weather changed and seriously curtailed all flying, and someone built a portable machine for disinfecting blankets.

128 Airfield personnel arrived in groups throughout the week, and they took over at B8 on 3 July when 3206 moved on to 406 ASP, Brecy. B Squadron left at 10.00 with the CO and Flg Off White with A Squadron moved off one hour later. Brecy was less than two miles from B8, but due to military traffic jams and the bad state of the roads brought on by wear and heavy rain the journey took all morning.

It was still raining heavily next day and the camp site, which was in an orchard, rapidly became a sea of mud. A lorry was sent out to pick up rubble from an army dump, but the crew came back empty handed as road repairs had top priority. 3206 had hardly settled in when they received instructions to move back to B8. The order came at 13.30 on 7 July, and by late afternoon the unit had set up their new camp and were preparing rockets in readiness for two squadrons of Typhoons due in at daybreak.

164 and 185 Squadrons of 136 AF arrived from the United Kingdom at 06.30 hours and flew several Ops. Cigarettes were purchased from the Daily Inventory Depot

(DID) as the NAAFI was not due until D-Day plus 37. Wg Cmdr Collins and six RAF Regiment personnel arrived, also from the United Kingdom, as an advance party of 136 AF, and the Typhoons flew back to the United Kingdom that evening.

By 11 July many of the men were suffering from constipation due to the hard nature of the Compo rations which seem only to be satisfactory for a week or two. After five weeks on Compo rations the men complained that they were tired and had no energy, but medical supplies were running low and replenishment was difficult. The Typhoons went on commuting from their base in southern England. Few sorties were flown due to the bad weather but Sqdn Ldr Scarlett of 183 Squadron was killed on operations on 12 July.

There now followed a period of indecision. Instructions were received that the unit was to move to B12, Ellon, as soon as possible, but when the CO and Flg Off White visiting the landing ground they found it was unfinished, even though 136 Airfield advance party was already there with orders to assist the SCU and eventually to take over. Eight hundred rockets were prepared and transported to B12 before the move was cancelled. There were rumours that 3206 were to go to B7, but 83 Group then announced that a reorganisation would take place on a four-squadron basis and the unit was instructed to remain at B8 and assist the R&SU should they require assistance.

On 17 July the CO went to B10 landing ground to look for work but none was available, but 3206 then found employment at B8 with the Typhoons of 164 and 264 Squadrons. The Typhoons flew forty sorties on 18 July at a cost of one aircraft with flak damage, and the unit changed an engine on another aircraft with a piston failure.

Visibility next day was poor and there was no flying until the evening: eight Typhoons went out, but only five returned. The missing aircraft had been shot down by ME 109s. At 20.00 hours there was a roll-call and it was found that members of the unit were absent from the camp without permission, which could have been quite serious if a new squadron had suddenly arrived.

Heavy rain stopped flying for the next few days and the landing strip, roads and camp area were flooded. The unit received instructions to move on to B7, Martragny, but found that it was not possible to pack up their equipment whilst working ankle deep in mud.

At B7 they were to service the Typhoons of 164 and 183 Squadrons, due in on 22 July. The unit was on time, but 183 Squadron were delayed until 25 July. Fortunately their arrival coincided with a period of settled weather and the Typhoons flew many sorties during the next two days, which kept the armourers at full stretch preparing rockets.

The servicing echelons of the two squadrons arrived at B7 on 26 and 27 July and 3206 moved off to B10, Plumetot. Traffic density was such that a half-mile journey often took an hour and, due to the overcrowded roads, the unit's vehicles left B7 at four-minute intervals, the last one arriving at 13.45. 3206 set up camp in the middle of the cornfield, the only site that could be found due to the high concentration of troops around the area.

The unit started working on the Mk IX Spitfires of 302, 303 and 317 Squadrons on 29 July. The weather was fine, the American offensive was going well and the three squadrons and the SCU were hard at it from dawn to dusk, when the Spitfires flew back to southern England, to return next morning. On 31 July alone the Spitfires flew 100 sorties. One was shot down behind the German lines, but it was thought that the Polish pilot might be safe. During the day a flying bomb was seen, heading towards Germany. All personnel

France: Normandy landings – a group of RAF Servicing Commandos resting at their mobile workshop in a cornfield.

were now on full field rations to their immense relief.

The good weather continued for the first few days of August and the squadrons made the most of the good weather. At midday on 4 August they were handed over to the ground crews of 1313 airfield and the unit moved to B18 next day to receive the aircraft of 126 AF moving from B4. The unit arrived at 15.30 and found a pleasant camp site in an orchard. They also found the landing ground unfinished but the construction crews completed it that evening.

6 August was spent unloading petrol and dispersing it around the airfield. The trucks were cleaned, all their equipment checked and the weather was ideal for flying, but no aircraft came.

On 7 August A3 Section went to B2 to service the AOC's Spitfires and a movement order was received stating that the unit was to move to B6 in four days' time to service aircraft of 137 Squadron of Air Defence Great Britain. The CO went to 83 Group and returned with the news that the unit might be moving to B19 instead. Some time on that day a Boston crash landed on the airfield, but nobody was hurt.

Notable events of 8 August were the arrival of the mail and the explosion of six land mines in a nearby field, which showered the camp site with earth and debris. On 9 August the unit moved to B19, Bruceels, to service the aircraft of 124 AF. The unit arrived at 14.30 to find construction work was still in progress. Camp was pitched, the dispersals were inspected and then word came through that 124 AF were not coming after all.

3206 took a few days rest at B19, and held a sports day and a social evening. On 13 August B Squadron was sent on detachment to B6, Coulomb, to service 137 Squadron, and on 18 August the remainder of the unit moved to B16, Sequeville en Bessin, where camp was set up in an orchard amid a cloud of flies. Here the unit was allocated to two Norwegian Spitfire Squadrons which were busily engaged in harrying the German 7th and 5th Armies surrounded at Falaise. Servicing began on 21 August and was handed over to the servicing echelon of 132 Airfield who were flown in by Dakotas on 23 August. On 24 August the unit returned to B19, where they were joined by B Squadron, directly from Coulomb.

After a short break, A party left B19 for B24 at St Andre de Leuvre, arriving there at 00.00 on 26 August, while B party followed on next day. Here, once again, an SCU became an odd-job unit, mostly engaged in transporting aircraft spares and general convoy duties. LAC Lansdowne had a motorcycle accident near Beauvais and was taken off to hospital and the next day, 11 September, the main body of the unit was en route for Belgium, leaving fifty drivers and three trucks behind in France.

3206 halted overnight at Vitny and arrived at B55, Maelsbrook, on 13 September, where they prepared the airfield, which was never used. Orders were given for them to move to B60, Grimbergen, but the move was cancelled on the day that the fifty-five drivers and three trucks rejoined the unit. Later a detachment was sent to B60 to service aeroplanes of 133 Wing. Small parties also went to B56, Evere, to service aircraft of the TAFs Communications Squadron, to No 4 Dump, Dieste, and to B58, Malsbroeck, to recover aircraft engines, instruments and other valuable components from crashed Thunderbolts, Dakotas, Flying Fortresses and Liberators. They also recovered Hengist and Horsa gliders that had been used in the invasion.

On 10 October, 3206 moved to B82 to service Hawker Tempests for 125 Wing and A/C Fineran crashed his Bedford lorry on the way. He was unhurt but the lorry was burnt out. On 15 October the unit moved again, this time to B78 at Eindhoven. With the cold weather coming on, the Allied advance was slowing down and due to the bad weather there was very little flying. 3206 were keen to find some winter quarters and on 29 October they moved into the Old Mill at Dieste to work with 409 R&SU.

The unit settled to a routine of work throughout November and a detachment was sent off to the aircraft dump at Hertogenbosch for salvage work, returning to Dieste of 14 November. On 1 December, 3206 began intensive ground training under RAF Regiment instructors. This went on until Christmas, although detachments were sent off from time to time to assist 122 Wing and 419 R&SU. On 27 December all detachments were recalled and the unit moved to Y32, Ophoven, and were established under canvas at that landing ground by 30 December.

At Y32, 3206 were very much involved in providing air cover for the Allied forces in their attempt to stem the German counter-offensive launched in the Ardennes, known by the Americans as the Battle of the Bulge. This had begun before dawn on 16 December when eight Panzer Divisions, taking advantage of low cloud and snow that prevented aerial reconnaissance, unexpectedly attacked the American VIII Corps, causing great confusion in the Allied ranks. This savage battle was the beginning of Hitler's last attempt to throw the Allies out of Europe and it might well have succeeded had not the German tanks run short of fuel.

In support of the offensive, the Luftwaffe launched a series of attacks on Allied airfields and on 1 January 1945 thirty German aircraft attacked Y32, injuring three members of the SCU and causing a great deal of damage. During the first few days of January the unit was kept busy servicing Typhoons for 609 Squadron at Y32 and a detachment was sent to Y39,

France: Normandy landings – a rocket projectile workshop in a cornfield adjoining a landing strip.

Asche, to service nine Typhoons belonging to 198 Squadron which had been forced down at that airfield by bad weather. The detachment was welcomed at Y39 by USAAF personnel shooting at them because they had mistaken the RAF blue uniforms for German grey. Luckily nobody was injured in this incident. The detachment carried out daily inspections on the Typhoons and returned to Y32 on 3 January. On 4 January a party from 123 Wing took over from the unit.

3206 remained at Y32 servicing visiting aircraft and doing odd jobs for 125 Wing and 409 R&SU until the main part of the unit was moved back to Dieste at the end of January to fit urgent 'mods' to British aircraft. A small detachment was left behind at Y32 to clear the site.

The unit was at Dieste for the final months of its stay in Europe and much useful work was done, although all personnel were disappointed not to be deployed in the assault on Germany, as they had hoped. They were called upon to use their skills on a wide diversity of jobs on all sorts of aircraft, from Austers through to Lancasters, and in March a small detachment spent a morning at Maelsbrook with a Flight of Gloster Meteors. Detachments from the SCU also assisted REME tradesmen in the repair and servicing of tanks and other heavy vehicles fitted with American aircraft engines including a Wright Whirlwind initially installed in a 'Crocodile'.

After three months at Dieste 3206 were ordered back to the United Kingdom and left for Ostend on 23 April where their vehicles were handed over to 73 MTLRU. They sailed from Ostend on an LST and arrived at Gravesend later in the day. After being delayed by fog, they disembarked at Tilbury on 25 April 1945 and were taken to the Transit Camp at Hornchurch. From Hornchurch they went by road and rail to

13 OTU at Harwell, where they were absorbed into that unit.

Like 3208, 3206 was never officially disbanded and its members were allowed to disappear into other branches of the RAF with no recognition from the authorities for all their hard work and dedication to their SCU.

COPY OF SIGNAL RECEIVED FROM THE AIR OFFICER, COMMANDING No. 83 GROUP.

To. :– 3210 SERVICING COMMANDO.

FROM :– No. 83 GROUP, MAIN H.Q. Signal No. 0.216 28 July 1944

TO O.C. FROM A.O.C. (.) I WISH TO THANK YOU AND ALL RANKS OF No. 3210 SERVICING COMMANDO FOR THE FINE EFFORTS YOU HAVE ALL PUT UP IN SUPPORT OF THE INVASION OF EUROPE (.) BOTH I AND MY STAFF ARE GRATEFUL FOR YOUR LOYAL AND SUCCESSFUL WORK, AND WE REGRET MUCH THAT YOU SHOULD NOW HAVE TO LEAVE US (.) WE KNOW THAT YOU HAVE OFTEN WISHED FOR MORE WORK THAN HAS BEEN GIVEN YOU (.) THIS REFLECTS GREAT CREDIT ON YOUR ENTHUSIASM, ESPRIT DE CORPS AND EFFICIENCY (.) THE BEST OF LUCK FOR THE FUTURE (.)

Signed A. H. MONTGOMERY A/CDRE. T.O.O. 282000B.

CHAPTER 7
Operation Dragoon — Southern France

The invasion of southern France, as originally conceived, was named *Operation Anvil* and was intended to precede *Operation Overlord* in northern France. Renamed *Dragoon* the operation was put back to coincide with D-Day, but due to a shortage of landing craft it was put back once again and eventually took place on 15 August 1944 between Hyeres and Cannes.

The planning of *Dragoon* had caused some disagreement between the American and British leaders. The American view was that the invasion would open up the port of Marseilles and bring German divisions down from northern France, thus weakening resistance to *Operation Overlord,* whereas the British viewed *Dragoon* as something of a sideshow and would have much preferred to commit all available resources to the Italian campaign.

There were eight German divisions defending 400 miles of coastline from Menton to Cerbère. The Luftwaffe could muster fewer than 200 aircraft and the German naval force was equipped with a few E-boats and U-boats.

The Allied invasion force consisted of 1,000 ships, including five battleships, nine aircraft carriers, twenty-five cruisers, 100 or more destroyers and troop transports and almost 500 landing craft. The transports and landing craft carried the US 7th Army, which included the French II Corps, and air support was provided by 2,000 aircraft of the US 12th Air Force.

The invasion was anticipated although massive air attacks had been mounted around Genoa to mislead the enemy, but on 15 August over 4,000 sorties were flown by Allied aircraft in the invasion area and four-engined bombers did their very best to neutralize the beach defences and communications. At 07.00 on D-Day an Anglo-American parachute division was dropped some miles inland to secure the Argens valley, and by the evening the Allies had 60,000 troops ashore. Losses amounted to 300 dead, most of whom were killed by mines.

The US 36th Division headed west to Cannes and Nice and north to link up with the airborne troops at Le Muy, before advancing towards Gap. The US 3rd and 45th Divisions made for Avignon, while the French contingent under the command of the volatile General de Latre de Tassigny advanced on Toulon and Marseilles. Only the 3rd Division met with serious resistance, at Agay, and by the evening of the second day the invasion was considered to be a day ahead of schedule.

However, *Operation Dragoon* brought no immediate relief to the Allied armies heavily engaged in Normandy and it soon became apparent to the German High Command that General Alexander had contributed a quarter of his army to the landing in southern France, relieving the pressure on the German forces in Italy and allowing them to transfer two divisions to the Western Front.

Although the reinforcement of the hard-pressed German army in the north was contrary to the objectives of *Dragoon,* it was a complete success in other ways. The first link-up with General Patton's 3rd Army took place at Sombernon, near Dijon, on 11 September, while other elements of the invasion force headed north west for Belfort and the River Rhine for the assault on Germany.

3201 was the only SCU to take part in *Operation Dragoon,* but when they sailed from Naples, bound for Corsica after *Operation Bigot Husky,* the invasion of southern France was some months in the future.

The unit landed at Bastia on 11 January 1944 after a nerveracking but uneventful voyage via the minefields off Sardinia and Elba. The harbour was very small and was cluttered up with sunken shipping and their LST proved difficult to dock, but all personnel and vehicles were ashore by early afternoon.

After a few days at Borgo airfield with no work to do while they waited for the arrival of a squadron of Mustang fighter bombers, the unit struck camp on 16 January and moved south, on convoy, along the coast road heading for Ghisonaccia. All road and rail bridges had been destroyed and substitutes were being constructed by army engineers, but some of the crossings were very tricky and slowed down their progress. At Ghisonaccia they set up camp near the site of what had been a German AA battery. There were many unexploded German Teller and S mines in the area and all personnel were warned to keep strictly to the roads. Moreover, the nearby village was placed out of bounds because of typhus.

The unit were still waiting for the aircraft. During this period they filled their time with camouflaging tents and taking the hot sulphurous waters at the local Roman baths.

One squadron of Mustangs arrived on 19 January at 10.00. They were refuelled, re-armed and serviced and flew two missions in two groups of eight aircraft, later in the day, losing one Mustang over enemy territory. Upon their return they were refuelled and re-armed in preparation for dawn operations. After the operation the aircraft all returned to Italy. The unit hung about, waiting for another squadron of Mustangs due in on 21 January, but the flight was cancelled.

On 12 March, 3201 were still waiting for the Mustangs, and their enforced idleness and inexplicable non-arrival of their mail was affecting morale, but on 23 March news came that they were to move to Alto to service the Spitfires of 322 Wing.

Work began at Alto on 2 April with the arrival of the Spitfires. The squadron's own ground crews arrived at Alto ten days later, but some members of the unit went on working with the squadron, while others checked and serviced the equipment in preparation for another move. On 17 April twelve fitters and a complete Flight set-up were loaned to 237 Squadron as their equipment had been mislaid in transit and on 23 April personnel began assisting 108 R&SU.

On 26 April, 3201 were moved to Borgo airfield to service Spitfires for a Free French squadron, No 328 MACAF, who were expected any day. In the event work continued with 108 R&SU as the Free French did not turn up until early May.

On 12 May, in moonlight and clear weather, twenty German aircraft made a low-level attack upon Poretta airfield, raking the aircraft and squadron domestic sites with cannon and machine-gun fire and dropping antipersonnel bombs. Approximately eighteen aircraft were rendered unserviceable, with ten completely written off and thirty so badly damaged that they were beyond repair on site. As a result all 3201's airframe and engine fitters were recalled from Borgo, although the armourers and electricians remained with the Free French squadron, an work began at Poretta airfield on repairing the aircraft damaged in the raid. In fifteen days engine fitters removed twenty-nine aero engines and installed four, while the airframe fitters carried out extensive repairs and stripped mainplanes and tail units. All this work was accomplished in the normal working day from 07.45 to 19.00.

During the remaining days of May a small detachment went to 135 ASP to operate a mobile oxygen plant until the regular crew arrived from Italy, and every week the unit sent six men to act as drivers, barmen and waiters at the Officers and Aircrew Rest Camp at Marina D'Albo.

Nothing much occurred in June. Repairs and routine servicing of Spitfires continued at Poretta. The DAF Dance Band gave a concert. A leave camp was opened north of Bastia, and a team of boxers from the unit went one night to 322 Wing's HQ to take part in a tournament, where they won three bouts. LAC Strange was told that he had been awarded the British Empire Medal and Cpl Cooper heard that he had been Mentioned in Despatches. LAC Roethenbaugh was involved in a motorcycle accident with a Free French ambulance, suffering a fractured jaw and arm and skull injuries. Training was given in the action and firing of the Bofors gun and at 20.00 hours on 30 June there was a film show of operational combats and strafing sorties against the enemy in Italy, which went down very well.

On 12 July, 3201 moved on again to the main aerodrome at Calvi, where they were to service Hurricanes and Spitfires of squadrons attached to 324 Wing. The runway was very short at Calvi and that, combined with a strong prevailing cross-wind, made it a tricky place to land a Mk IX Spitfire. On 20 and 21 July eight aircraft crashed on landing and although they were repairable two of them could not be dealt with on site. Work on these damaged Spitfires continued throughout the remainder of the month.

It was at Calvi aerodrome, in August, that the unit heard of the landings on the Riviera, and while the news was greeted with enthusiasm, there was also surprise and disappointment that they had not been sent in with the invasion force. In fact, RAF personnel of 202 Group had been entrusted with the task for which the Servicing Commandos had been formed, to organise the captured airfields for the Allied squadrons in order to provide front-line air support for the American and French divisions as they advanced through France.

3201 went ashore at St Maxims on 1 September 1944, by which time the fighting had moved some miles away, with the US 36th Division nearing Annecy and the US 45th Division and the French II Corps approaching Lyon. The unit landed on Delta beach at 07.45 and by early afternoon they were on their way to Aix and enjoying the drive because the roads were in good condition, unlike those in Corsica. They camped overnight near Brignoles and set off again the next day for Marignane airfield, via Aix.

The billets at the airfield were in an estate of detached houses which had been used as barracks by the Germans. They were the most luxurious accommodation ever used by the unit. On site was a large wooden building with a stage and good facilities for cooking. This became the airmen's mess and facilitated a number of social events. There were several parties. The first, early in September, was a great success, even though the mess was so crowded that it was impossible to dance. By 10 September, the date of the next, that problem had been solved by a decision to make it 'by invitation only'. In addition, an open-air cafe was set up outside one entrance to the mess, which was much appreciated by the men, as was the hot-water shower which was constructed out of materials of German origin by 11 September.

Other events included a service held by 202 Group's padre, Sqn Ldr Scott, to commemorate the Battle of Britain, and a dinner dance, both held in the mess on 18 September, and football matches against the local team, Marignane, both of which the unit won, the first 3-1 and the second 4-1.

The main body of work involved the receipt of crashed Spitfires and wrecked Merlin engines for crating up to be shipped out to Base MU. The first Spitfire fuselages arrived early in September and were off-loaded in a requisitioned hangar. Also during that week Flt Lt Webster, Sgt Berry and twenty men set off to forage for abandoned German transport, but although they went as far north as Lyon and Grenoble they were unsuccessful because other units had already scoured the countryside.

By 22 September almost all the damaged aircraft had been crated up, and the unit's work at Marignane was all but over. Later in the week the unit football team played against another local team and a Wing Commander from Field Intelligence brought a captured German jet-propulsion power egg to the airfield to be crated up and shipped to England.

At the end of the month word came that 3201 would soon be leaving France and were to return to Italy. This news caused some despondency. A move had been expected, but it had been hoped that *Operation Dragoon* was the last stage, or last stage but one, in the journey home.

On 1 October Sqn Ldr Scott held a Harvest Festival service in the airmen's mess. The mess was decorated with vegetables and fruit and the service was well attended. On 2 October responsibility for the Aircraft Salvage Park was handed over to 108 R&SU at midday and on 3 October the unit was on stand-by ready to leave France, having prepared and crated thirty Spitfires, one Hurricane, one Fairchild Argus II and a Beaufighter.

3201's convoy left Marignane for the Assembly Area at Septimes at midday on 5 October. It had been raining heavily all night and the Assembly Area was ankle deep in mud. It rained heavily again that night and all of the next day. A more unsuitable site could hardly have been chosen. By 7 October conditions had deteriorated very badly — the area was waterlogged and ankle deep in mud.

Two days later the unit left in convoy for Marseilles and was caught up in a traffic jam along the way. At the docks the unit was split up. One officer and forty-five other ranks with bed rolls and small kit were loaded aboard LST 256, while the rest of the unit and the vehicles were loaded onto LST 501. They lay off Marseilles all the next day, and eventually sailed at 09.00 on 11 October, passing through the Straits of Bonifacio between Sardinia and Corsica to anchor off the harbour at Leghorn on 12 October. They sailed again next day for Naples and disembarked at Nisida at 13.00 on 15 October at the same quay from which they sailed for Corsica nine months before. The convoy formed up and proceeded to Gragnano where billets had been reserved in the spaghetti factory. On 15 October the CO, Flt Lt Webster, visited 214 Group and received instructions for the disbanding of the unit.

'Wild Bill' Webster, as the CO was known throughout the unit, wrote the following brief summary of its history:

> The unit has, in its two and a half years existence, been misused on so many occasions, I expected the men to welcome the break up. However, contrary to expectations, the majority seemed to wish to carry on.
>
> This was the 'Original Commando Unit' formed in the UK. I have commanded it throughout its existence, and would offer the following information on the tasks on which the unit has been employed during its existence.
>
> The first operation, the invasion of North Africa, was carried out with success by 3202 SC and this unit operating as shown previously in Form 540. Their means of communication made such highly mobile units

indispensable in a rapid advance through difficult country and for a period of five weeks this unit kept a complete Spitfire Wing operational in Tunisia, supporting the 1st Army.

The completion of this task, when squadron personnel arrived, left the unit without work and it was withdrawn to the Algiers area. From this time on it was never employed in its true capacity, except for the invasion of Sicily. This I believe was due entirely to lack of knowledge as to what the units could do, and were capable of doing well. It was, in my opinion, that an adverse opinion was being formed of their capabilities. This unit was engaged in the invasion of Sicily. They landed on D-Day, and went to Cosimo airfield on its capture and were ready to receive a Spitfire Wing. Nevertheless, the Wing was not sent in until the arrival of the Wing's own ground crews.

In conclusion, in view of my experience in command of this unit, throughout I was convinced that splendid service could have been rendered by it and other units in other theatres, e.g. to service the aircraft used to supply General Wingate's Chindits in Burma, or the operations in the Aegean Sea. The employment of such a unit in an island campaign offers great possibilities, saving the movement of large numbers of transports; for instance, the operations carried out on the Adriatic seaboard during 1943. The Pacific War I feel sure could find operations in which it could claim a valuable part, if these units were re-established in equipment to meet the requirements of that theatre of war.

3201 ceased to exist on 30 October 1944.

CHAPTER 8
India to Java

Territorial ambitions and the Chinese threat to Japanese supremacy in Asia were at the roots of Japan's involvement in World War II. In 1931 the Japanese had overrun Manchuria. Two years later they annexed Jehol, between Manchuria and China, and in 1937 they invaded China, occupying most of the major ports and huge areas of Chinese territory.

It was the Tripartite Pact between Germany, Japan and Italy, coupled with the non-aggression pact with Russia and the occupation of French Indo-China, that brought about American trade sanctions and an embargo on oil exports to Japan, and it was these sanctions that precipitated the Japanese attack on the US Pacific Fleet laying at Pearl Harbour, Hawaii, on 7 December 1941 — a surprise attack that should not have come as a surprise.

By May of 1942 the Japanese had occupied the Philippines, Burma, Malaya and the oil-producing Dutch East Indies, as well as being entrenched on numerous Pacific Islands. In spite of these successes, made easier by the unpreparedness of the US and the Allied preoccupation with the European war, the Japanese had no illusions that they could win a lengthy struggle with the Allies. Instead, they pinned their hope of victory on establishing themselves so firmly in their new and self-supporting Empire that even if the Allies were to win the war in Europe, which at the time did seem unlikely, they would feel that it was hardly worth the trouble of attempting to dislodge the conquerors of most of the Pacific and the whole of South-East Asia. Even the Americans themselves wondered whether it would be the British attitude once Hitler and Mussolini had been overcome.

The overwhelming run of victories by the Japanese armed forces had been helped by massive ignorance, both in Whitehall and in Washington, of the strength and formidable efficiency of Japan's war machine. For instance, the Mitsubishi 'Zero' was the equal of almost any Allied fighter aircraft and was superior to most of them, yet Air Vice Marshal Pulford RAF, the AOC Far East, declared that the ponderous and portly Brewster Buffalo, which the USAAF and RAF already knew was no match for an ME 109, was quite good enough for the defence of Singapore. Between them, the Japanese Army and Navy Air Services could must some 4,000 aircraft, the Imperial Army amounted to fifty-one divisions, the Navy was both modern and extremely powerful and the men of all four branches were dedicated and superbly trained.

The turning point of Allied fortunes in the conflict with the Japanese came on 13 April 1942, when a force of sixteen twin-engined Mitchell bombers (named after Billy Mitchell, a crusading US Army officer who was court marshalled for his strong belief in the value of air power) took off from the deck of the aircraft carrier *Hornet* and, led by Lt Col James H Doolittle, dropped a few tons of bombs on Tokyo and two other towns.

This minor air raid, which caused little damage, had a profound effect on the Japanese. After all, the Emperor himself had been exposed to danger and that

Malaya — RAF at Penang — line-up of Dakota DC3's at Bayan Lepas, Penang. They formed first of the mass flights to arrive at the airfield.

brought humiliation on the navy. The government, the armed forces and the population were determined that such a thing should not occur again and in order to extend the perimeter of their defences they single-mindedly embarked upon a programme of territorial expansion that overstretched Japan's resouces and would have led, eventually, to its defeat in any event even despite the use of the atomic bomb.

The immediate response to the raid on Tokyo was to advance upon Hawaii, this time to totally destroy the American Pacific Fleet. To that end the Japanese proposed to occupy Midway and the Aleutian Islands and, while that was going on, the 4th Fleet, in collaboration with the army, was to invade Port Moresby and to extend their occupation of the Solomon Islands, thus cutting off Australia, which one faction of the High Command in Tokyo was anxious to invade, from aid from the US.

The Americans, who had cracked codes used by the Japanese, were well informed about these plans and from this intelligence there followed the Battle of the Coral Sea and the Battle of Midway. The former battle resulted in a strategic victory for the US Navy and the latter in the end of Japanese supremacy at sea and there then began the slow and bloody process of re-taking the strategic islands and advancing on Japan.

While the defence of the Pacific was, by the terms of an agreement between Washington and London, America's responsibility, South East Asia was, to a large extent, a British problem and by 1943 morale amongst the troops was very low.

Hong Kong had fallen in December

1941. The Japanese invasion of Malaya and the loss of Singapore, described by Churchill as the worst disaster in British military history, was all over by early February 1942 and this catastrophe was quickly followed by the invasion of the Dutch East Indies where the defending force of American, British, Dutch and Australian troops soon succumbed to overwhelming odds. This humiliation was followed in its turn by the loss of Burma.

However, during 1942, preparations were begun to drive the Japanese from Burma and a steady stream of men, aircraft and equipment arrived in India. Amongst the aircraft were DC 3 Dakotas for the transport squadrons, Hurricane Mk Is, Blenheim Mk Vs, Vultee Vengeance dive-bombers and Curtis Warhawks. The Vengeances were used against the enemy's airfields whilst the Hurricanes and Warhawks began to take effect against Japanese air strikes.

At the end of 1942 the Japanese Army Air Force carried out night raids on Bengal and caused heavy casualties amongst the civilian population of Calcutta, but in January 1943 a squadron of Beaufighters arrived from Britain to discourage the night raiders followed by several squadrons of Spitfire Mk Vs. By the end of January the Spitfires had shot down forty-four Japanese aircraft for the loss of seven Spitfires and five pilots.

Throughout the year the build-up of Eastern Air Command continued. Two hundred airfields and fifty radar stations were constructed. Later marks of Spitfire were brought in and by December 1943 the RAF was making inroads into Japanese air cover. From these and other preparations it was obvious enough to the Japanese that an offensive was in the offing and, in order to pre-empt it, three divisions were ordered to prepare for the invasion of India, code-named *Operation U-GO* and timed for early March.

Happily, the Japanese had not yet realised that the Allies had access to their coded messages and General Slim, commanding the 14th Army, was expecting the invasion where it actually took place, on the Plain of Manipur. In the event General Mataguchi's 15th Army advanced so rapidly that the defenders were taken by surprise and by the end of March the garrisons at Kohima and Imphal were surrounded and cut off. The beleaguered garrisons had several airstrips and were supplied by air, a feat made possible by the squadrons of Spitfires who had rapidly deprived Mataguchi's army of its air support. Kohima was relieved on 3 June and Imphal, which had been reinforced by air, was relieved nineteen days later.

The British and Indian divisions suffered almost 17,000 casualties in these two battles, the great majority of whom were struck down by disease. The Japanese who, thanks to Allied air superiority, had received no reinforcements, had suffered from starvation, even more severely from disease and had lost 65,000 men in the campaign. The survivors straggled back towards the Chindwin with the British in pursuit, to report their failure to an unsympathetic High Command.

The follow up to this resounding Allied victory began in mid-November, and was code-named *Operation Capital.* It included the British 14th Army and XV Corps and General Stilwell's Northern Combat Area Command which consisted of five Chinese divisions. Early in December bridgeheads had been established in Japanese-held territory across the River Chindwin. The original objective of the operation had been to capture Mandalay and the area to the west of the Irrawaddy, but Stilwell's force made better progress than expected, and General Slim soon devised a better plan which he named *Extended Capital.*

Operations planned for Burma had to be approved by planners in Calcutta and Ceylon, by Chiefs-of-Staff in London, Combined Chiefs-of-Staff in Washington

Java – ground crews servicing Thunderbolts at Batavia.

and finally by Chiang Kai-shek, but in order to take advantage of the situation Slim had no option but to go ahead without approval. In essence *Extended Capital* entailed an advance to Mandalay, via Kalewa and Yeu, by XXXIII Corps under the command of General Stopford, while Major-General Rees's 19th Indian Division, which had never been in action before the operation, was to cross the Irrawaddy and advance along the river-bank to Mandalay. The second phase of *Extended Capital* involved Lieutenant-General Messervy's IV Corps moving south to cross the Irrawaddy at Pakokku immediately below the confluence of the Irrawaddy and the Chindwin and to advance due east to take the important road and rail communications centre of Meiktila.

Once the 260,000 troops of General Slim's 14th Army had crossed the Irrawaddy it was necessary for them to be supplied from airfields on the coast of Burma because they would be beyond reasonable reach of the airfields at Imphal and Agatarla, and for the airfields and port at Chittagong to be developed. Plans were made to renew operations in the Arakan and to take the airfield at Akyab, from which the Japanese launched air strikes on Chittagong, Calcutta and the Ramree Islands where airfields could be quickly built. Akyab fell on 2 January without a shot being fired and the Japanese on Ramree succumbed on 17 January to a massive operation involving battleships and Liberator bombers.

Slim's use of transport aircraft to supply his army was the key to his success in Burma and by January 1945 the Allies were in a position to dominate the skies. The Japanese could muster some seventy serviceable aircraft of all types, while the RAF had eight-nine heavy bombers, more than 500 fighters and fighter bombers, 110 transport aircraft and thirty-six aircraft adapted for reconnaissance. In addition, the USAAF had forty heavy bombers, almost 100 medium bombers, in excess of 200 fighters and fighter bombers, nearly 300 transport aircraft and sixty-seven reconnaissance aircraft.

During December 1944 and early January 1945 the four surviving Servicing Commando Units were drafted into India to help maintain this aerial armada. 3205, 3207, 3209 and 3210 had been withdrawn from *Operation Overlord* just as the Allies were breaking out of Normandy and had returned, dejectedly, to the UK and an uncertain future. 3205 and 3207 had been sent to 83 GSU at Bognor Regis, while 3209 and 3210 were sent to Thruxton to work with 84 GSU. At both locations they had spent their time in modifying and preparing aircraft for despatch to France and half expecting to receive the news that the units were to be disbanded, but on 30 September the commanding officers were ordered to attend a special conference set up by the Air Ministry. There they were told that the Servicing Commandos would shortly be transferred to South East Asia Air Command.

3205 and 3207 soon received their orders to join SEAAC in India as rapidly as possible and vacancies were quickly filled by posting the appropriate ranks and tradesmen from 3209 and 3210, the gaps left in the latter units being filled at a more leisurely pace, and in the usual way, which delayed both SCUs at Andover until the last week in November while the new recruits were trained.

Meanwhile, 3205 and 3207 had sailed from Liverpool on 2 November, arriving in Bombay on 4 December after an uneventful voyage in perfect weather. All ranks became eligible for the Japanese Campaign Allowance as from that day. As both units disembarked on the same day and proceeded to the Base Reception Camp at RAF Worli, we will begin with an account of 3205's part in the Japanese campaign.

3205 SCU

On 10 December 1944, 3205 SCU began a laborious and lengthy journey across the continent of India, amid the heat, mosquitos and the flies by lorry and by train to Chittagong and then on to join 903 Wing at Patanga. Here they collected their equipment from 92 ASP and 67 Squadron, and Flt Lt Fenton, the CO of the unit, was made up to Acting Squadron Leader while Flg Off Cummins, the unit's Adjutant, was appointed Acting Flight Lieutenant. They spent Christmas at Patanga, moving out on 3 January 1945 for the advanced landing ground at Akyab, which had been captured from the Japanese the day before without a fight.

3205's road convoy carried the servicing equipment, fifty tons of 100 Octane fuel, ten tons of 20mm cannon and 0.303 machine gun ammunition, oil, oyxgen and glycol, in addition to the unit personnel and all their kit. After a long hot drive they arrived at Foul Point on the tip of the Mayu Peninsula early the next morning to embark aboard their LCMs. After a short voyage across the estuary they disembarked on Akyab Island the same evening.

The next few days were spent in transporting their supplies from the beach to the Island Main Air Strip in five three-tonners, which was all the transport that they had at their disposal due to the limited amount of shipping space available for their landings on Akyab.

On 8 January five Spitfire Mk VIIIs of 67 Squadron, led by Sqdn Ldr Day, arrived at the air strip at 11.30 and flew fourteen sorties against the Japanese. They flew a further thirteen sorties the next day and in the afternoon six of the Mk VIIIs were 'scrambled' and intercepted half a dozen Japanese aircraft, shooting down five of them but sustaining only slight damage to one Spitfire. At 15.30 eight more of 67 Squadron's Spitfires arrived in addition to two Dakotas, two Vultee Vengeances, one Lockheed Hudson and one Harvard, all of which were serviced and refuelled.

On 10 January 67 Squadron flew sixteen sorties without loss. The SCU provided an escort and a bearer party for the funeral at Akyab cemetery of WO John Horan, who had been the air gunner of a RNZAF Sea Otter shot down by the Japanese three miles from the landing ground. During the day the unit serviced and refuelled two Vultee Vengeances, one Sea Otter, four Dakotas carrying 20,000lb of signalling equipment and a Lockheed Hudson with military passengers, all this in addition to servicing the busy Spitfires. At 16.00 a USAAF Super Fortress landed with two seized engines.

On 11 January the Spitfires flew more than twenty sorties. Air Commodore The Earl of Bandon, the AOC of 224 Group, arrived and departed two hours later in a Piper aircraft and Capt Graham of 231 Squadron landed his Catalina flying boat in the afternoon, searching for the crew of the Super Fortress.

This exhausting level of activity was maintained until the end of the first week in February, with the Spitfires of 67 Squadron flying an average of twenty sorties every day and expending enormous quantities of fuel and ammunition. A

RAF Singapore — first ex-POWs flown out of Singapore.

Singapore — Servicing Commandos and RAF regiment officers at Kaliang.

detachment of Hurricanes from 2 Squadron and a detachment of Spitfires from 8 Squadron came in on 26 January to be joined a few days later by detachments of Beaufighters from 89 and 176 Squadrons. There was also a constant stream of visiting aircraft in need of fuel and servicing. In this respect 27 January was typical with two Norsemen, twenty-five L5s, ten Dakotas, four Tiger Moths, one Harvard, one Beachcraft, one Lightning, one Hudson and one stray Beaufighter calling in at Akyab Main Air Strip.

During this period Air Marshal Sir Guy Garrod, the Allied Air Commander-in-Chief South East Asia Command, visited the air strip to address all officers and other ranks to compliment them on their efforts. More relaxing entertainment was provided by the open-air camp cinema, showing such classics as 'The Yellow Canary', 'The White Cliffs of Dover' and 'This Happy Breed'.

On 1 February LAC Swallow fell into the river and was drowned. His body was recovered and he was buried in Akyab cemetery with full military honours at 10.00 next day. All personnel not on essential duties were present and the unit provided a firing party and a trumpeter.

A few days later technical responsibility for the servicing and maintenance of the Hurricanes of 2 Squadron and the Beaufighters of 89 Squadron passed to the CTO of 903 Wing and 7067 Servicing Echelon, so on 10 February 3205 SCU sailed from Akyab Island to Foul Point, with orders to proceed to Double Moorings, Chittagong.

They arrived at No 5 Personnel Transit Camp at Chittagong on 11 February, collected ten Fordson and Chevrolet three-ton trucks, one 4 x 4 Desert Type Utility vehicle and four motorcycles and moved on to Double Moorings on 13 February.

The unit remained at Double Moorings until 16 June, occupying their time with overhauling their motor vehicles. Although detachments were occasionally sent for short periods to other airfields for specific tasks, the unit was, for the most part, unemployed, and in order to boost morale a monsoon pool was cleared of weeds, water snakes and other undesirables and turned into a swimming and water polo pool, the MO passing it safe as soon as it was chlorinated.

On 15 June Sqn Ldr Fenton, the CO of the unit, visited HQ, RAF Burma and BAFSEA to discuss back-up requirements for certain types of fighter aircraft which the unit might be required to service in future operations and next day they received the order for a move to RAF Kalyan by train from Chittagong. The advance party arrived at Kalyan railway station on 20 June, where the RAF's Railway Transport Officer directed them to the RAF station at Santa Cruz and on 22 June the main body of the unit arrived at Santa Cruz to hear the news that they were to take part in the invasion of Malaya, code-named *Operation Zipper*.

On 9 July Flt Sgt Wilson flew to BAFSEA HQ in New Dehli with a list of technical requirements for the forthcoming operation and WO Stride flew to Colombo the next day to liaise with the Flag Officer, Air East Indies, regarding the technical equipment and spares required for servicing twenty-four Seafires and twenty-four Hellcats for seven days and to advise on the trades and ranks required to DI these aeroplanes on ferry craft during the voyage immediately prior to *Operation Zipper*. On 11 July several members of the unit were sent to spend a week with 89 Squadron at Baigaichi to gain experience on their Mosquitos. On 13 July Flt Sgt Evans flew to Vizagapatam to collect the spares and equipment necessary for the operation of eight Thunderbolts for seven days, and on 21 July one sergeant and three corporals went on detachment to RNAS Tambaram to gain experience on the servicing of Seafires and Hellcats.

On 31 July unit strength stood at five officers, three warrant officers, fourteen senior NCOs and 157 other ranks. They had been issued with new motor vehicles for the forthcoming operation and these were pre-loaded and delivered to No 1 Mobile Waterpoofing Unit at RAF Juhu. The vehicles were waterproofed within the week, and were sent, with one driver only to each vehicle, to the Marshalling Area in Bombay in readiness for embarkation for Malaya.

On 6 August the first atomic bomb was dropped on Hiroshima, followed by the second bomb on Nagasaki, but news of these events was not conveyed to the Allied forces in India and Burma and on 31 August the unit sailed from Bombay for Morib in Malaya with the unit's transport and twenty-five drivers aboard the MT ships and the remainder of the unit on board HMS *Orduna*.

While 3205 were still at sea, Japan's new Foreign Minister had signed the official document of Japanese surrender on board the battleship *Missouri* and General MacArthur had accepted the surrender. World War II was over, although it was not officially announced until 2 September.

The unit disembarked at Morib on 10 September and immediately drove to Kelanang airstrip where they arrived late in the afternoon. The next day they serviced twenty Spitfires, seven L5s and four Dakotas. The officers were presented to Lord Mountbatten, the Supreme Commander South East Asia, to Air Commodore Sir Keith Park, the AOC-in-C, and to Air Vice Marshal The Earl of Bandon, the AOC of 224 Group. The Supremo and the AOC-in-C each addressed a parade of all ranks of the unit. General Slim landed at Kelanang on 14 September and it was later learned that these high-ranking officers were in Malaya for the surrender of all Japanese armed forces in the South East

Asia area at a ceremony to take place in Singapore.

Also on 14 September an advance party of 3205 consisting of Flt Lt Cummins and forty other ranks was sent by air to Kalang, the main airport of Singapore, by arrangement with HQ 903 Wing, only to be transferred to RAF Tengah by arrangement with 902 Wing, where they were joined, at intervals, by other members of the unit.

On 21 September, 3205 were given orders to move, immediately, to Singapore Main Airport, and the CO returned to Kelanang to organise the movement of personnel and transport still remaining in the area, but four days later the unit were ordered to move once again, this time to RAF Seletar.

At Seletar the unit looked after the thirty-two Mosquitos of 84 and 110 Squadrons and later in the month they also took on the responsibility of servicing the eighteen Spitfires of 11 Squadron and 17 Squadron. The servicing of all four squadrons continued throughout October and November. In the middle of October a small detachment went to service Thunderbolts for 905 Wing at Kuala Lumpur but a relaxed atmosphere prevailed. There was time for sport. Several soccer matches took place between the Flights and other local units. The Japanese had stored thousands of tins of paint in the swimming pool, and once these had been removed 3205 organised a number of aquatic sports events.

On 1 December 1945, 3205 were ordered to proceed, with their transport and equipment, to Batavia, Java, where they were to act temporarily as an R&SU. On 6 December the advance party left Singapore aboard HMT *Saiween* and one week later the whole unit, apart from a small detachment left behind at RAF Seletar, was at Kemajoran where they repaired the

Burma — men reloading a Hurricane's cannons.

Thunderbolts of 81 Squadron and the Mosquitos of 84 Squadron. They stayed there until 16 January when they moved their billets to Batavia after severe flooding at Kemajoran, although repairs continued at the airfield. A small party was sent to Semerang to salvage crashed Dakotas, and a detachment went to Medan, Sumatra, to service and refuel Dakotas bringing troops and supplies into Sumatra, and flying back to Singapore with Allied prisoners of war, many of them near death due to ill-treatment by the Japanese.

During February all detachments were recalled to the unit at Batavia following a Disbanding Order received on the first day of the month. Fifty-three NCOs and men were posted to Singapore to fill vacancies in other units. Letters of appreciation and good wishes for the future from the AOC and the Station Commander of Kemajoran were read out at the formal Unit Disbandment Parade. Sadly, Sqn Ldr Fenton was on leave in the UK when the Disbanding Order had arrived and was not on hand to say goodbye. 3205 SCU was officially disbanded on 28 February 1946.

3207 SCU

Throughout this history of the Servicing Commandos the authors have, at times, been hampered by the loss of the Official Records. In this case not only do we have the records with their wealth of details, but we also have an evocative account of the part the unit played in the Japanese Campaign in South East Asia. This account was written by Ken Hurst who served as a Sergeant in 3207 SCU and we will use his words as frequently as possible to exploit the opportunity to present both the official and the unofficial point of view.

The Official Record states that the unit, comprising three officers and 170 other ranks, embarked from the UK for India.

Java — RAF taking over Japanese aircraft at Kalidjat aerodrome.

The journey was made in perfect weather, with no incidents. According to Ken Hurst, the unit, 'embarked at Liverpool on the SS *Otranto* HMT C12 of 22,000 tons which was supposed to travel out in a fast convoy. Sailed at night for Glasgow, where we were stormbound for a few days, with double anchors down. In recovering our anchors they fouled up, and it took so long to untangle them we missed the fast convoy. We became Commodore ship of a slower convoy, which included ammo ships, and several Union Castle boats including one full of WRNS, ATS and WAAFs. Lived in the forward hold, mess deck N1.'

The remainder of the voyage was uneventful and the unit docked at Bombay on 4 December 1944. They were sent to Worli Transit Camp just outside Bombay, where they were under the direct control of RAF Worli and treated as a draft rather than a unit. No reference was ever made to the CO and very little information was given to him regarding future moves.

On 16 December the move to Tamu by rail and road commenced. The first stage of the journey to Manmad was made in reserved coaches. On arrival these coaches were transferred to a troop train under the command of Lt Lewis RASC, who was in charge of 600 Indian troops. Arrangements for feeding of the troops was haphazard. The unofficial version of the journey bears this out:

> There was the typical cockup, and though they eventually found room for us on the train we had no rations. We were sent to a warehouse stacked with tinned food; we took what we thought we would require, only to find that most of the tins were blown. At first we threw them away, but later on we retrieved what food we could from them. We even had to resort to flogging kit at the wayside stops to get food from the native population, mainly eggs, chickens and fruit. It was not long before we had sickness, mainly the runs, and malaria. We crossed the Ganges and Bhrampaputra. It was here we met up with an Indian unit who gave us their left-over curry and chappaties. Never knew food could taste so good. At last we came to Dimapur Road Transit Camp which was being prepared as a rest centre for troops over Christmas. On Christmas Eve we reached a base in Imphal and were told our journey was over for the time being. On Christmas Day we relaxed and washed our clothes and ourselves, only to find that at lunchtime, before we had a chance to eat our Christmas dinner, we were loaded onto trucks driven by Indians and taken over steep mountain roads to Tamu, just inside the Burmese border. The trucks belonged to 999 Line of Communication, and they just happened to have a gap in their loading schedule, hence our sudden move. All we had for Christmas dinner was one small can of Armour's bully beef and a packet of dry biscuits, between twenty-eight of us. When we got to Tamu they were not expecting us and had eaten all their grub. We got what was left over, which was precious little, and kipped down where we could.

The next day the unit was taken back across the border to the disused airstrip at Palel. Here they assisted 363 MU with repairs to motor transport and sixty men were sent to Comila to pick up vehicles for the MU. On 28 January another party of twenty-five went to Calcutta to collect six Jeeps and trailers for the unit, and on 1 February the Jeeps and trailers, one Ford truck and twenty-six men of A Section went off to Kalemyo, by road, while the remainder of A Section and HQ Section went by air.

On 3 February C Flight was flown to Ombauik to help with servicing of Hurricanes of 113 Squadron, while D Flight moved to Tabinguang to assist 607 Squadron in servicing their Spitfires. After a few days at Kalemyo HQ, A Section moved to Ywadon to assist with the Hurricanes of 60 Squadron, where they discovered that the Hurricanes had moved to Monywa, but the detachment stayed at Ywadon to service Spitfires for 17 Squadron.

On 13 February B Flight moved by road to assist 221 Group HQ at Monywa in establishing a working site and they were joined there on 5 March by A Section who were to be airlifted to Meiktila at first light next day. At Meiktila they would be very much involved at the sharp end of *Extended Capital*, for although the town had fallen to a swift assault by Major-General Cowan's 17th Division and its tank brigade on 3 March, the Japanese were in the country all around and counter-attacking fiercely.

Ken Hurst was with A Section at Ywadon:

> We were told to take down all badges and remove all unit markings. We left late one night for Monywa and spent three days living in the open. We then embarked in American C46 Commandos for an unnamed airstrip.
>
> Here we joined the army in a push down to Meiktila, letting the enemy close in behind us as we went. We spent our first night in the town which was almost destroyed and we spent our spare time practising our section drills and procedures.
>
> We occupied an airstrip astride the junction and close to the lake. There was a Brigade Box, an Artillery Box

Burma – receiving medical attention. Servicing Commandos being treated by LAC Patrick O'Shea, medic–LAC Harold Craddock and LAC Paddy Bugby.

> and an Airstrip Box. We were joined by the RAF Regiment who operated forward listening posts and took most of the defence off our hands, leaving us free to deal with aircraft. These were mainly fighters: Spits, Hurricanes and Thunderbolts, and Dakota and Commando transport aircraft. Some of these dropped in *en route* to China where, by flying 'The Hump', they were able to support Chenault's Tigers with their Tomahawks. We had with us an American anti-aircraft unit with a large tripod-mounted machine gun, something like a large Vickers. Needless to say we swapped rations, Spam for bully beef. When things got a little hectic later on, we took the Yanks in to stand guard with us on a one-to-one basis.

On 9 March the CO was evacuated from Meiktila suffering from dysentery. Soon after his departure enemy activity increased: aircraft taking off and landing came under mortar fire and several aircraft were damaged or destroyed at the dispersals. On 16 March all unit personnel were ordered to the RAF Regiment's lines to help defend the airfield, and four battle sections were despatched to man the foxholes on the perimeter where a Gurkha unit was under constant small arms, shell and mortar fire. They remained at the perimeter until the RAF Regiment had driven off the Japanese attack, whereupon the MO and an orderly went out with the tanks and infantry to pick up the regiment's dead and wounded.

Heavy shelling of the airstrip continued for the next two weeks. The CO returned from hospital on 22 March, while the Armament Officer flew out for a rest and was shelled while taking off, after which the strip was closed all day due to heavy shelling. The next day a Beechcraft landed, bringing USAAF and RAF officers to Meiktila for a conference and took off again immediately with battle casualties. At 14.00 hours two Dakotas landed to evacuate more casualties. One aircraft got away, but the port engine of the second aircraft refused to start. Ken Hurst describes the incident:

> The transports came in and off-loaded ammo, spares, stores and food, the priority being roughly in that order. They then took out any wounded, or captured equipment if it was needed. It was during one of these sorties that a Dakota full of wounded was hit and caught fire. Sgt 'Buster' Brown rounded some of us up and we off-loaded the wounded first and then the dead and only just in time. It was a mortar shell that started it. This was a favourite pastime for the Japanese, and mortar shells also landed in the RAF Regiment's lines and caused casualties. A sortie by the regiment to find the mortars resulted in the death of Wg Cdr Landon their CO. We had two casualties, Dixon and Dagnell, who were eventually flown out. The dead we wrapped in blankets and buried. We had the job of burying a Major who had been in command of an Indian unit and was directing fire from a tank when he was hit. When we arrived at the grave with his body the Padre refused to bury him until we had made the grave longer, wider and deeper, so it was shirts off and get digging whilst he lay in the back of the vehicle. There were so many dead around, mainly unburied Japanese, that you became immune to death in its many ghastly forms and we were only too glad to assist in burying our own dead, when asked. Death has its own sickly smell, and everywhere you went you could not avoid it.

While this was going on another Beechcraft tried to land and was hit by shell or mortar fire, crashed and was burnt out. Sgt Brown, seeing yet another aircraft in the circuit, went out onto the strip and warned the aircraft off. Later in the afternoon, the CO and Sgt Brown returned to the Dakota to remove as much equipment as they could, in case the enemy should totally destroy the aircraft.

> The idea of us being in Meiktila was to hold the crossing until Slim took the town of Mandalay. We hung on, and on and after the Japs, in a desperate effort to dislodge us, denied us the use of the airstrip by attacking every movement on it we were on to quarter rations and one bottle of water each day. Some days we got the strip open and as soon as the first aircraft tried to land the fun started. It was during one of these periods that a Wing Commander flew in, and remonstrated with our CO about us being unshaven. Even on one bottle of water a day he thought we should have given up a part of it for shaving, but we were not impressed as he spent most of his time safely behind the lines with all the water that he wanted. Just then the Japs opened up and a mortar shell landed near his aircraft. Needless to say we did not see him for dust, nor for a long time after that. As soon as he had gone the CO rescinded the shaving order and we could quench our thirst in peace.
>
> We drew our water from the lake and each time we followed a routine. Both us and the Japs would arrive to fill the bowsers. Each kept an eye on the other. When we saw their vehicle

Burma – Servicing Commandos Sgt A 'Buster' Brown (with shaven head), Sgt Eddie Block and WO S G Green.

was on the move it was get to hell out of it, whether we were full or not, before the mortars arrived. We played this game nearly every day.

We lived in foxholes and slept where and when we could. We repaired holes in the airstrip with biscuit tins and doped the patches. We had one Hurricane land and go U/S in spite of all our efforts. It had a nice cartoon of a six-shooting bumble-bee on one engine cowling. As soon as it got dark we moved the aircraft to fool the Japanese and took the cowling back into the box with us. Good job we did, as they found the Hurricane and blew it up. Next day, when the pilot came to collect it we gave him his cowling as all that was left.

A and B Sections of 3207 were kept busy on 24 March. They were responsible for fifty yards of the perimeter and all night the Japanese could be heard digging in and talking. From dawn onwards there was steady shelling of the airstrip and it was not possible to recover more equipment from the Dakota. At around 08.00 hours intense small arms fire broke out in the north-west corner of the defensive box and the two sections moved up to give assistance. It was later pointed out by the CO that this action had been voluntary and he was exceptionally proud of them. The CO himself was in the sector to determine what was happening and discovered that a party made up of Ghurkas and RAF Regiment personnel were doing their best to eliminate a group in Japanese in a Pagoda several hundred yards away. One infantryman, obviously wounded, attempted to return to the perimeter but collapsed before he reached it. The CO went out to help and, finding that the soldier had a bad wrist wound, he dressed the wound and got the man under cover inside the perimeter. As there were a number of wounded out beyond the wire the CO and a few men from the unit took stretchers and evacuated the wounded men from the battle area.

Ken Hurst admired the Ghurkas:

They frequently took off on forays and harassed the Japs when and wherever they could. It was amazing how quietly they could move, even when loaded with packs and weapons. 'Nobby' Coxhall went out on patrol with them and they were ambushed on a railway line, which was most unusual for the Ghurkas. He tried to carry a wounded Ghurka back to our positions, but he died in spite of Nobby's efforts. He, like 'Buster' Brown, got the Military Medal for his exploit. The dead Ghurka had a brother in the same regiment and he persuaded his father that instead of accepting the dead boy's Kukri, which was the custom, he should present it to Nobby, who was very proud.

On 25 March intermittent shelling went on throughout the day. There were 250 RAF men in D box and casualties from wounds, sickness and cases of neurosis had reached thirty per cent and were mounting steadily. The CO therefore decided to move all RAF personnel from D box to a safer area, unless Brigade could guarantee to clear the strip within two days. He visited Col Young at Brigade Headquarters to tell him of his intention, but Col Young objected and said that it would weaken the defence. The CO then pointed out that the majority of the RAF men were technicians and would be essential for the servicing of aircraft when the strip reopened and that the way that casualties were mounting there would soon be insufficient men to carry out the task. Col Young agreed at last, but would not release the RAF Regiment or the men of 3207 SCU because they were actively

Burma – Servicing Commandos Cpl Walter Robinson and LAC Jeffrey Russell.

engaged in defending the perimeter of D Box. The CO then reiterated that his men were primarily technicians who would soon be needed for the servicing of aircraft but Col Young was adamant that they should stay. The CO decided that he would fly to Headquarters 221 Group to inform the AOC of the position, but on the airstrip he met Wg Cdr Gladding who returned with him to Col Young to press the case. Col Young refused to change his mind. The two officers then flew off in an L5 to see the AOC, who gave his sanction for the move. The unit Adjutant, Flt Lt Hopkins, was also at Headquarters and he and the CO decided that C and D Flights should be brought in from detachment to reinforce A Section as soon as the airstrip was cleared of Japanese.

On 28 March A and B Flights moved to a safer place on the west side of Meiktila Lake, and by the evening everyone was feeling, and looking, a lot better, having washed their clothing and themselves in the waters of the lake.

The next day the CO discovered that an aircraft of 656 Squadron was in trouble with two of its L5s, and Sgt Brown, six riggers and two fitters were detailed to repair the badly damaged aircraft. Repairs were carried out using a brazier borrowed from a tank brigade and patches were brazed onto aircraft that had been thought to be irreparable, although the use of a welding flame on the damaged parts was hardly in accordance with the practices laid down by the engineering manual for the RAF.

By 3 April C and D Flights had arrived at Meiktila, where things had quietened down. The battle for the town had caused heavy losses to the Japanese and the fall of Mandalay on 20 March had seen the 15th Army virtually destroyed by Allied air attacks from heavy bombers. On 5 April Air Commodore Mills, the AOA of 221

Group, gave an informal talk and thanked the men of 3207 for their magnificent work carried out under very trying conditions.

By the middle of the month the CO was back in hospital with dysentery, and the servicing of 17 and 285 Squadrons, plus all visiting aircraft, was handed over to the squadron personnel. On 23 April A section moved by road to Lewe to service Spitfires of 607 Squadron. On 25 April HQ and B Sections moved to Tennent airstrip and A Section moved from Lewe to Malewa, about two miles from Tennent. B Section serviced Spitfires for 17 Squadron, while A Section serviced Hurricanes and Spitfires for 28, 60 and 607 Squadrons.

Early in May A Section left Malewa for Mingaladon airfield at Rangoon. The Japanese had abandoned Rangoon on 29 April but the advancing troops had no idea that they had left until Wg Cdr Saunders, the CO of 110 Squadron, flew over the town in his Mosquito and saw the words 'Japs gone. Extract digit' painted on the roof of Rangoon Jail. He immediately landed at Mingaladon, checked out the accuracy of the message with the inmates of the jail and, having damaged the undercarriage of his aircraft on craters in the airfield runway, borrowed a motor launch and set off up the Rangoon River to tell the army the good news.

Ken Hurst was with A Section as they progressed from Meiktila to Mingaladon:

> Eventually Slim took Mandalay and we were able to drive the Japs off and open up the strip again. We then moved on and began servicing Hurricanes and Spitfires at a series of advanced strips, until the push on Rangoon when we dashed down there. Our Jap friends had blown all the bridges and downed trees, so we had to work pretty hard getting round, over or through the obstacles.

Burma – Servicing Commandos and twin brothers LACs Robert and Wallace Clark.

One night, when proceeding to a forward airstrip, the convoy was actually bombed by the Japanese — they must have been getting a bit desperate.

Unfortunately, when we reached Mingaladon the seaborne landing had beaten us to it and we took on a turnround servicing role for anyone who needed it. I remember 28 Squadron's Hurricanes and a Group Communications unit with L5s, also bags of Dakotas and C46 Commandos. One of the latter ran off the strip during the rains and bogged up to his mainplane. We had to progressively jack up and shore up till we were able to drag him free, none the worse for wear. I even found time to learn to fly a Sentinel L5 we had acquired.

It was decided to attempt a seaborne landing (on Singapore) from Rangoon and we were pulled back to billets at Insein Barracks to sort out our equipment and to service our vehicles. We also took part in the Victory Parade through Rangoon, dressed in starched jungle green bush hats with white blancoed webbing belts, gaiters and rifle slings. It bucketed down with rain! Mountbatten, Slim, Keith Park and the senior naval boss were all on the saluting base and they too were soaked. We didn't care. We came swinging down the avenue, all sporting a single ribbon of the newly-awarded Burma Star. 'One inch per man, return it after the parade'. The blanco ran down all over us, but we couldn't have cared less. We were a very proud bunch.

We finally shipped out (for Singapore) after helping load our own vessel, the 10,000 ton British India ship *Risaldar*, skippered by an Anglo-Indian who paced his bridge without his shoes and socks on. We acted as transport to the Defence of Merchant Shipping unit who managed the anti-aircraft guns aboard the ship. The DEMs were only too glad to show us how to operate their guns and have us share watches with them. It was during one of these watches that the cruiser *Sheffield* came down the convoy to advise us that three Japanese aircraft would fly over the convoy, painted white with green crosses on them, on their way to Rangoon to negotiate a surrender. We were not, repeat not, to fire on them. We didn't believe it, so we kept one up the spout and the safety catch off whilst they flew over us. Some time later the *Sheffield* came back to say that terms had been agreed and we might get a peaceful landing yet.

We finally reached Singapore on 5 September 1945. We off-loaded at the docks and were driven in convoy through the town in captured Japanese vehicles to occupy Kallang, the civil airport. Japanese with rifles and bayonets lined the route, as did the cheering Chinese, with some PoWs amongst them. Again we were suspicious and had one up the spout. The first firecracker that was thrown nearly caused a nasty incident.

On arrival at the airport there was a Dakota in the circuit. It was *Hapgift* or *Mercury*, one of Mountbatten's aircraft, bringing in either General Rees or General Lees. Suffice to say we chased away the Japanese Air Force and saw it in, much to the surprise of the occupants. We slept the night in the terminal building at Kallang and it was in the main hall that we heard for the first time of the decorations that had been awarded to the unit.

The decorations to which Ken Hurst refers were the Military Medals awarded

Burma invasion – RAF ground staff unloading a light aircraft from a landing craft.

to Sgt Brown and Cpl Coxhall for their courage and devotion to duty at Meiktila, but notification was not officially received until the middle of October.

Our main task at Kallang was to act as a staging post for all kinds of aircraft. These included Lancastrians or Quantas flying boats which were operating from Singapore Roads, but using the small inner harbour alongside the airport. We also had Dakotas of 31, 32 and 34 Squadrons of the RAAF, and 31, 48, 215 and 267 Squadrons of the RAF, all engaged on ferrying prisoners of war. The turnround was roughly 100 aircraft every day. 48 Squadron were ferrying the PoWs released from Java and Sumatra back to Singapore, including women and children. These were the most distressing sights — of women so thin, and kids with distended tummies, but oh, how cheerful they were, and so grateful to be free. We had to keep the Jap prisoners off the 'drome the day the first batch came in or we would have cheerfully killed them. A nurse, a hardened veteran of World War I, broke down and wept when we opened the doors of the first aircraft. Of course we made the mistake of giving the kiddies our sweets, which were too rich for the poor little things and they were instantly sick. After that we gave them to the mums to ration out. There was a steady stream of PoWs and we turned the aircraft round as fast as we could. The aircrews worked miracles, flying long hours and many trips. We also brought back PoWs of other nationalities, including the Dutch.

During this time we vacated the terminal building and set up in two houses and a block of flats on the seafront, known as Meyer's Flats. We also liberated transport, including a Ford open touring car, from the Japanse officers who were riding in it at the time, and an old ex-service BSA 500cc motorbike which I learned to ride. We used lorries and vans liberated by civilians to ferry our equipment from the docks — unescorted until we started losing stores. Then we sent out escorts, some of whom lived the life of Reilly till they too were rumbled. We refuelled the civilian vehicles from the low-octane fuel dumps left behind by the Japanese. We gave away thousands of gallons of the stuff to make way in the bulk installations for our own high-octane fuel.

The Singapore Swimming Club began operating and the Worlds amusement park, started up again, as did the brothels in Lavender Street. The Worlds were The New, The Old and The Happy World. They started wrestling at The Happy World and service contenders, supported very vocally by their respective colleagues, were a great attraction. The taxi drivers did a roaring trade, as did the trishaw parade around the Padang in the town. At about this time, whilst the Singapore brewery was getting under way, some Singapore saki was released. It was very crude and blindness and some deaths occurred from drinking this rot-gut. The beer company used the image of a baby tiger to advertise their Tiger beer. Scratching at the trees to sharpen his claws this creature gradually grew bigger, with the caption 'Tiger beer getting stronger'.

The single-decker trolley buses had not been used during the occupation and had been standing still so long their solid tyres had developed flats. When they did start again it was a very bumpy ride. The old buses

Burma — RAF ground crews struggling to erect their mobile workshop with a high wind blowing.

> started too, I think they were Albions. The colour scheme, I remember, was green, with white tops. Whilst we were at Kallang we found a Hucks Starter vehicle and evidently some Jap aircraft were still started by this method, which goes back to the First World War. We stripped the gear off and used the vehicle as a pickup truck. If only we had known what a valuable find it would have been today.

Christmas at Kallang was thoroughly enjoyable. A comic football match was staged between officers, NCOs and airmen, with everybody dressing up for the event and some highly original costumes were designed. Christmas dinner was a credit to the cookhouse staff. Souvenir menus were printed and the CO had a busy time signing them. After dinner the CO made a speech, during which he told the men that the unit was to be split up as there was no further need for Servicing Commandos.

Work continued at Kallang throughout January 1946. The CO was told that unit personnel would be absorbed by 67 Staging Post and postings and attachments soon began, with the Electrical Section being very much depleted. In February 116 men were posted to the staging post and by the end of the month there were only sixty-one airmen still on the strength.

During March the flow of transport aircraft handled by the unit was running at approximately fifteen aircraft every day receiving between flight inspections and daily inspections. The percentage of unserviceability was high and could be roughly divided into faults that took an hour or so to rectify, and engine changes. The engine changes were all on American aircraft. As the American aircraft had completed many flying hours and were often three or four years old, airframe unserviceability was understandable but the average life of an American built aircraft engine seemed to be around 350 hours.

The release rate of airmen at Kallang was beginning to outstrip the training of the higher demobilisation groups who were to take over the servicing of aircraft. On 14 March the remaining personnel of 3207 SCU were posted to SHQ, RAF Kallang, and the unit was officially disbanded on 31 March 1946.

3209 SCU

3209 SCU landed at Bombay in mid-January 1945 and, after a period of PT and drills at Worli Transit Camp, went by special train to Singarbil where, as had so often happened throughout the history of the SCUs, they were to assist on R&SU instead of taking part in operations at a forward landing ground.

At RAF Singarbil the unit was temporarily accommodated in bashas and messed with 142 R&SU until their tents and cooking equipment could be sent up from the coast. After two days of intensive training in the requirements of the R&SU, the unit started work on Monday 5 February, while the CO, Flt Lt Wood, flew to 230 Group's HQ to discuss the future of the unit with the AOC in the hope of seeing some action. He returned from seeing the AOC with instructions to send men on detachment to other R&SUs and by the middle of the month thirty-six men and four NCOs were assisting other units.

The majority were at Imphal with 124 R&SU and it was here that Flg Sgt Evans and his party were involved in an explosion in the bomb dump, distinguishing themselves in taxying aircraft and driving MT vehicles out of the danger zone. By the end of February men of 3207 Servicing Commando were working with 82, 101, 124, 126 and 142 R&SUs.

Work with these units went on in conjunction with the training of all tradesmen on all types of aircraft currently in service with South East Asia Air Command, with particular reference to training airframe fitters on propellers, as past experience had shown that all too often there had been a surplus of airframe fitters and insufficient engine fitters for this type of work.

While acknowledging the usefulness of the unit's work with the various R&SUs, the CO was still fretting that 3209 were not actively involved in operations and more suitably employed on work for which they were intended. He wrote:

> Efforts to maintain the fitness and morale of the unit at the very high standard desirable, by parades, strict attention to dress, cleanliness and smartness of deportment, by sports and welfare activities have so far been successful, but it has been adequately proved by past experience that the unit enjoys its greatest efficiency when fully employed in an operational or operational training role. Long periods of comparative inactivity such as working with the R&SUs, MUs, etc, are not conducive to the best results in personnel with a highly developed sense of unit pride and with a mentality moulded around the word 'Commando'.
>
> When operational in the UK and France, this unit handled on some days as many as 600 to 700 sorties. It is only this type of training which will tune the unit up to the maximum efficiency required for the part it is required to play in an assault landing.

Ironically, the CO was in hospital suffering from typhoid when on 24 March an 'immediate' signal was received from HQ Bengal/Burma instructing the Officers Commanding 3209 and 3210 SCUs to report to a Wg Cdr Thomas at Admin Plans X group in Delhi. As Flg Off Blake was already in Calcutta with the CO of 3210 it was decided that he should proceed to Delhi. While he was away, Air Commodore Blockley, the AOC of 230 Group, called on Flg Off Powell, who was acting deputy CO, with the information that 3209 and 3210 had been selected for a forthcoming operation and would probably be moved to the Bombay area within the next few days. Action was immediately taken to recall all the detachments and when Flg Off Blake returned from Delhi he was able to give more details of the operation, code-named *Roger,* which was to provide air cover for *Operation Dracula,* the name chosen for a seaborne assault upon Rangoon. It had originally been planned that 3209 were to land on D-Day, with 3210 landing nine days later, but the order was reversed due to the indisposition of Flt Lt Wood.

After the withdrawal of the detachment and the working parties with 101 and 142 R&SUs, a concentrated programme of-technical and non-technical training was drawn up on a day-to-day basis as the time available before movement to the Concentration Area was not expected to exceed a week. This programme included the training of all fitters and riggers on Mosquitos and Thunderbolts, on aircraft borrowed for this purpose. Bayonet fighting and grenade throwing were also included and during the heat of the afternoon lectures were given on technical subjects, organisation of a forward landing strip, first-aid and amphibious assaults in general.

On 6 April the AOC informed Flg Off Powell that the operation had been postponed indefinitely and the training programme was extended to include range firing and unit scale defence exercises, by day and night. Conferences were held after each exercise, and the umpires pointed out mistakes and gave instructions for their remedy. Later in the month Sqn Ldr Abbott arrived at Singarbil to become

CO of the unit and some of the tradesmen returned to work with 142 R&SU engaged upon dismantling irrepairable aircraft.

Throughout their time at Singarbil 3209 had no transport of their own and had been unable to collect their technical equipment from Calcutta. They had also failed in various attempts to have it taken up to Chittagong, but on 1 May a detachment of two warrant officers, four NCOs and thirty-four other ranks was sent to RAF Red Road, Calcutta, to sort out their equipment for the operation. The entire unit was looking forward to taking part in the invasion of Rangoon, but the Japanese retreated from the town before *Operation Dracula* had a chance to use its fangs, and in the absence of the opposition there was no need for *Operation Roger*.

May was not a merry month for 3209 at Singarbil, as everybody had been 'keyed-up' at the prospect of some action and there was general disappointment at the cancellation of the operation. The dismantling of damaged aircraft went on throughout the month, but in June the fitters, riggers and ancillary trades were taken off that job and transferred to productive work, five aircraft being allocated to them for major operations.

On 10 June a signal came from HQ BAFSEA warning that the unit should stand by for an immediate move to 374 MU at RAF Korangi Creek, outside Karachi. 3209 handed over all their work to 142 R&SU and kicked their heels at Singarbil until 28 June when A Squadron, under the command of Sqn Ldr Abbott, left by train for the journey to Calcutta, after some confusion with RAFMOVE Calcutta as to their destination. They were followed the next day by the majority of B Squadron, a small party being left at Akhaura railway station to escort the unit's heavy kit, their equipment and a jeep and a three-tonner which were to go by goods train.

At Calcutta the unit were alloted eight three-ton trucks, one van and a water tender, which brought the unit's vehicle strength up to nine three-tonners, one jeep, one van, one water tender and two motorcycles, although the jeep and one three-tonner were still at Singarbil. On 29 and 30 June, 3209 left Calcutta in two parties on military trains. Two escort parties, one with the equipment from Singarbil the other with equipment collected at Calcutta, were somewhere in India on goods trians heading for Karachi, and on 2 July a further party, under Flg Off Anstees, set out from Calcutta with the unit's vehicles on the long drive to Karachi, via Benares, Delhi and Lahore.

A Squadron arrived at Lahore on 2 July and proceeded to Karachi in two parties, one staying overnight. Flt Lt Powell arrived with B Squadron at 10.30 on 3 July and they too were split in half, one half leaving for Karachi at 18.15 hours next day while the other half was forced to hang around Lahore until the morning of 7 July. No official arrangements had been made for feeding any of the parties at Lahore, but the Toc H Club were very helpful and provided food, although all personnel who wished to eat had to pay for their own meals.

By 14 July, 3209 SCU was established at Korangi Creek, complete with all equipment and all vehicles except the jeep and one three-tonner still *en route* from Singarbil. Although small parties of airframe and engine fitters were sometimes required to help dismantle damaged Catalina flying boats, the unit, for the most part, were unemployed at Korangi Creek. The amenities, together with the drier and more temperate climate, should have made their stay something of a holiday, but there was considerable discontent amongst all ranks at the unskilled and unproductive work on which they were employed — when they had any work at all. The general health of the unit showed an astonishing decline. Dysentry was rife and many of the men were suffering from skin complaints, probably contracted on the journey across India.

On 7 August another signal came from RAFSEA, stating that 3209 was to move to Bobbili, with full technical and domestic equipment and to be installed there not later than 22 August. On 15, 16, 17 and 18 August the unit left Karachi in four parties in ordinary trains to travel via Lahore, Delhi, Jagpur and Raipur, to detrain at Denkinsa for Bobbili, where they arrived on 20, 22 and 24 August to find that, once again, there was no work.

Flg Off Anstess took a party of drivers to Madras to collect new vehicles that had been allotted to 3209, returning early in September, by which time the unit had begun to service aircraft of 131 and 258 Squadrons, but on 3 September the unit was alerted to stand by for movement to Madras, for embarkation to take part in operations *Zipper* and *Masterdon*. *Zipper* was intended to retake Malaya and Singapore from the Japanese, while *Masterdon* was the code-name for the invasion of Thailand and French Indo-China. A Squadron was earmarked for *Zipper* and B Squadron for *Masterdon*.

By this time, of course, the war was over, but news of the Japanese surrender did not reach them until 5 September and in the meantime the members of 3209 were delighted at the prospect of seeing some action at last.

On 4 September the unit was withdrawn from aircraft servicing and preparations for the move began. As the equipment was still crated it took up a lot of space and once it had been loaded on the trucks there was no room for unit personnel. A truck, with a party of ten drivers, was despatched to Vizagapatam some seventy-five miles away, to borrow trucks, and when they returned early in the morning on 7 September the convoy was soon under way.

They were now running behind schedule

Thailand — RAF officers at Bangkok aerodrome raising the Ensign.

and the CO decided that they should press on through the night in order to catch up. The roads were very dusty and at 22.00 hours LAC Harkness, driving a three-ton truck full of equipment, hit the parapet of a small bridge. The lorry somersaulted and landed on its back in the bed of a small stream. Happily, neither the driver or his mate was hurt, but the truck was written off and transferring the equipment to another vehicle delayed them even more, so the convoy did not arrive at Avadi until 13.30 on 12 September.

In the event only *Zipper* went ahead, as a policing operation, and without A Squadron. Instead of facing a protracted struggle with the Japanese, the 100,000 men who landed in Malaya found themselves rounding up their erstwhile enemies and disarming them.

On 24 September A Squadron sailed from Madras aboard an LST bound for Rangoon to be followed two days later by B Squadron aboard another LST. A Squadron arrived at Rangoon on 28 September and sailed for Thailand at the beginning of October, disembarking at Bangkok a fortnight later and proceeding to RAF Don Muang twenty miles outside the town. B Squadron disembarked at Rangoon from their LST and on 2 October they embarked again, this time on board the troopship *Circassia* on which they sailed for Saigon in French Indo-China, arriving on 10 October to proceed next day to Saigon airfield. The MT *Fort Turtle* carrying the unit's transport arrived off Saigon on 13 October and was fired upon from both sides of the river by Annamite Nationalists, causing some minor damage.

3209 was permanently split, never to be reunited. Of A Squadron's activities at RAF Don Muang there is little to report. Their function was the servicing of all British transport aircraft and all other aircraft visiting Bangkok. They loaded and unloaded freight and provided a twenty-four-hour guard on the armoury and freight sections. The Official History for the period states, 'The morale and discipline of the Squadron at Bangkok is reported by the Commanding Officer to be of an exceedingly high standard. Airmen have plenty of time to themselves, and the various amenities available for their amusement and relaxation have kept them occupied and happy'.

At Saigon, B Squadron had a rather more exciting time at first, taking part in operations in the surrounding country, searching villages for terrorists, arms and ammuntion. They also formed part of the Defence Wing on the airfield, as skirmishes with the terrorists on the perimeter took place almost every night. The remainder of their time during the first few weeks was spent in uncrating their equipment and maintaining it in good condition. Things settled down however and by November B Squadron, like A Squadron at Bangkok, was engaged upon the servicing of British and visiting aircraft. According to the Official History, 'There has been a very happy atmosphere in B Squadron, which first became apparent when we left Madras. The officers and men have all worked in the closest harmony, reminiscent of the more flourishing days of the unit when operational in England and in France. The morale and discipline of the unit as a whole have greatly increased throughout November. After such a long period without having any really productive work, the airmen now feel that they are doing a useful job'.

3209 Servicing Commando was officially disbanded on 22 November 1945.

3210 SCU

3210 disembarked at Bombay on 14 January 1945 and, like the other SCUs before them, proceeded to the transit camp at Worli, where a rigorous course of route marches, swimming and PT quickly overcame the inevitable deterioration in the physical condition of all personnel brought on by the long sea voyage.

At this time unit strength stood at three officers, sixteen SNCOs and 152 other ranks. There was some disenchantment with the KD clothing that had been issued to the airmen. Practically all of it was three or even four sizes too large except the trousers, which were too narrow and too tight. In addition long-obsolete pith helmets had been issued which, it was felt, heaped ridicule upon discomfort. The only remedy available was for the men to buy new 'Khaki Drill' and more up-to-date headgear out of their own pockets, which could not be regarded as a popular solution.

3210, together with personnel from other units, entrained at Bombay on 3 February for the journey to Calcutta. A kitchen car was not included in the train but very good dry rations had been issued and the men found the long train ride across India both instructive and enjoyable, in spite of inadequate facilities for brewing tea.

The unit arrived safely at Calcutta on 7 February, where transport to RAF Red Road was provided by 134 R&SU who made the unit very welcome. On 9 February, after two months of enforced idleness, repair and servicing work began on Hurricanes and Spitfires and such was the demand for fighter aircraft that a night shift was instituted later in the month.

As 3210 was somewhat under strength, Flt Lt O'Malley, the CO, visited HQ 230 Group to explain the unusual nature of a Servicing Commando and ask if Group would screen all personnel scheduled to be posted to the unit. This was readily agreed and by early March the establishment stood at three officers and 175 other ranks, Group having been most helpful in sending suitable technicians.

The R&SU work was a useful 'shakedown' period for the new members of the unit, enabling the tradesmen to acquaint themselves with the types of aircraft that they could be called upon to service under operational conditions, although the unit was still without transport and short of fifty cases of equipment and could hardly be considered to be ready for an operation.

Nevertheless, on 19 March the AOC 230 Group called the CO to Group HQ to tell him that the unit would take part in a forthcoming operation, and a week later the CO, together with Flg Off Blake of 3209, went for a briefing at the Admin Plans office in Delhi, returning on 30 March with the details of *Operation Roger*. This information was not transmitted to the other ranks, but when the unit was sent to Alipore two flights at a time for battle training with the RAF Regiment, there was a general feeling of anticipation. There were some minor injuries at Alipore, where the instructors quite expected that ten per cent of trainees would be casualties, but throughout April the anticipation heightened with intensive training and the preparation and the waterproofing of the technical equipment.

On 27 April the CO flew to HQ 227 Group at Bombay for instructions and the movement order finally came through. On 29 April members of the unit were loading their equipment on to railway trucks at Howrah station and arrangements had been made for all personnel to entrain at 18.30 hours that day when the move was cancelled without any explanation.

3210 was in a difficult position. Apart from general disappointment and confusion and the depressing knowledge that the kitchen equipment was packed away on board the train, the unit had no home, as Red Road airfield was to be closed down in a few days' time. The CO called BAFSEA on the telephone and they confirmed that the movement order had been cancelled and gave instructions that all equipment should be unloaded from the train.

The cancellation of *Operation Roger*, the shortage of accommodation in the Red Road area and the difficulty of finding

Java – men of 3210 SCU fitting rocket projectiles to Mosquitos.

work for the unit as a whole meant that a dispersal policy had to be adopted and as soon as possible.

D Flight was sent to help 1 CMU carry out modifications to Thunderbolts and Mosquitos at Kanchrapara, while C Flight went by air to help 5 CMU at Aharda Road. B Flight was sent to Dum Dum for repair and salvage work on Liberators and Dakotas with 134 R&SU, and A Flight went by rail to Ranchi to assist the squadrons. At the end of May D Flight was withdrawn from Kanchrapara and sent to help repair storm damaged Thunderbolts and Spitfires at Chakulia. Meanwhile Headquarters Flight, with the equipment, stayed at RAF Red Road. Owing to transport difficulties and other factors, employment in the forward areas of Burma was impractical or so 3210 were told. Nevertheless, all flights were within easy access of Calcutta and could be recalled at a moment's notice at the prospect of an operation.

This was the pattern of employment for the unit until the middle of July, when the CO received instructions to prepare the unit to take part in *Operation Zipper*. HQ Flight moved to RAF Dalbumgarh on 14 July and all detachments were recalled. The remainder of the month was spent in gathering equipment for the operation, including spares for Thunderbolts, but, as few men from the unit had tackled Thunderbolts before, training was arranged with the officer commanding the USAAF airbase at Dum Elmundi. The unit had at last received its full complement of MT vehicles, but difficulties were experienced with issues of green battle-dress, although orders for it had been placed in early June. A bomb disposal squad was formed and sent on a special training course, but this was rendered non-effective by a disruptive outbreak of prickly heat and other minor skin complaints that were common in Bengal at that time of year.

On 5 August the unit was still waiting at Dalbumgarh, where personnel were disappointed at the news that, under the terms of an Air Ministry order, they were not to be awarded the 1939/45 France and Germany Stars because they had not served for the prescribed six-month period in that theatre of war. The men felt very strongly that their service in the assault phase of *Operation Overlord* had not been recognised, but in this respect they were in a similar position to the Army and Marine Commando Units.

On 9, 10 and 11 August, 3210 returned in three separate convoys to Red Road. On 15 August news came of the Japanese surrender, but preparations for *Operation Zipper* went ahead, with vehicles being waterproofed at 329 MU by the unit's MT drivers, in accordance with a signal from the AOC of 224 Group sent on 17 August. On 20, 21 and 22 August the unit moved in three rail parties to 35 Personnel Training Centre in Calcutta.

By 10 September, 3210 was on board the SS *Dunera,* bound for Malaya, while the unit's vehicles were following on board ship M 78. The SS *Dunera* dropped anchor off Morib beach on 17 September, all personnel transferring first into LCIs and then to LCAs some distance from the shore. The men waded the last quarter of a mile, with full kit, through four feet of water and then marched nine miles through pouring rain to the Assembly Area, where contact was made with Sqn Ldr Hadfield. The majority of the unit

Burma — bombing up fighter-bombers.

bivouacked beneath the trees, but the remainder were collected in two trucks and driven to Kellanang airfield where they were given a hot meal.

The rest of the unit hitch-hiked to Kuala Lumpur the next day to find that the Japanese were still occupying the billets, but they were soon cleared out and the airmen occupied three huts. Due to the enormous number of vehicles landed at Morib, the MT ship had moved up to Port Swettenham and all the MT drivers were sent to the airfield to await the vehicles. C and D Flights were also sent to Port Swettenham airfield to service Thunderbolts of 131 and 258 Squadron, while A and B Flight serviced other fighter aircraft at Kuala Lumpur and Kellanang airfields, most of these aircraft having flown from India and Burma.

Alan Smedley, who served with 3210 at Kellanang, wrote the following account of his experiences:

> From Kellanang I had two very interesting trips in a small two-seater aircraft, which was probably an Auster.
>
> The first occasion was with Air Vice Marshal The Earl of Bandon, who wished to take a passenger on a short trip to another airstrip a few miles inland. I was asked to be suitably armed and when we landed at this other airstrip the aircraft was parked at the edge of the field and was immediately surrounded by dozens of the local inhabitants. I was required to guard the aircraft from their curiosity.
>
> Nobody was aware that we had arrived and the Air Vice Marshal wanted to contact the Group Captain in charge. The only way that he could do that was to reach the huts that we could see in the distance. He decided that the best way to get to them would be to hitch a lift along the road that ran nearby. In his rather voluminous shorts and his Australian type hat with RAF headband, the only evidence of his rank were his shoulder epaulettes. As he stood at the roadside thumbing army lorries he was greeted with shouts of 'F---ing RAF'. He did finally get there, however, and when we left we were escorted out in grand style, with aircraft in V formation flying on either side of us.
>
> The other flight was with a Flight Lieutenant who sought a passenger to go with him to Kuala Lumpur Airport. Kuala Lumpur and the airport were still administered by the Japanese, all fully armed and complete with their Samurai swords. Altogether there were some 3,000 on the airport which, being fairly well inland, had not been reached by British troops.
>
> We flew into this place and a party of Japs came out to the aircraft, led by their Commanding Officer. When we climbed out he asked, in quite good English, where did we want our billet. The Flight Lieutenant very quickly asked him, 'Which is yours?' and when a splendid residence was pointed out to us, he said 'That will do'. We were escorted to the house, and had Jap servants literally crawling around us. They would knock on the door and crawl in on their hands and knees.
>
> From the moment of landing we were both naturally terrified, but tried not to show it. We decided that we would walk round the camp and 'show the flag'. On the first excursion we had only gone a few yards when we heard the most bloodcurdling yells and screams, and we both said 'This is it'. However, we soon found that the Japs had seen us coming and were calling out the guard in our honour. We received this sort of

treatment for about three days, with troops breaking into goose steps when they passed us, until the army eventually arrived and the surrender of the Samurai took place. I have a photograph of this.

Another interesting recollection of these three days was the dressing down which took place through the ranks of the Japanese. The Commanding Officer would call his senior officers around him in a circle, harangue them for about five minutes and then walk round and slap each one across the face. They, in turn, would do the same thing to their immediate subordinates, and so it carried on through the various levels of rank so that the punishment at the end of the line far exceeded the crime.

We also found a hangar piled high with crates of American-made precision instruments, micrometers, etc. I filled a kitbag with these and made quite a bit of money when I eventually got to Singapore.

I still feel quite proud to be the first person, together with the Flight Lieutenant, to set foot in Kuala Lumpur after the invasion.

On 21 September a signal came from 224 Group warning that the unit was to move on to Batavia, via Singapore. The CO and the Adjutant flew down to Singapore to contact 224 Group and collect accumulated mail. In the event the unit sailed from Port Dickson, not from Singapore, all personnel and vehicles aboard four LCTs. The voyage was very much enjoyed by all. The men slept in or underneath the lorries and the clean sea air soon cleared up any vestiges of skin complaints.

Monsoon conditions in Burma, 1945. A group of RAF Spitfire pilots are seen here on a forward airstrip. The flooded airfield and lowering clouds give an idea of the terrible weather conditions encountered by both pilots and Servicing Commandos.

They went ashore at the port of Batavia, Java, on 12 October at 10.00 and soon moved off in convoy to the airfield at Kemajoran. The officers and men of the staging post advance party had prepared the billets and the unit took over the camp cookhouse and set up their HQ. A curfew was in force at 18.00 throughout the island and all personnel were told to carry arms and ammunition.

A small detachment from the army had been guarding the airfield, but they pulled out when 3210 arrived and the SCU took over the airfield defence duties. For a week or so the unit had the only RAF MT in the island. They brought up petrol from the docks, serviced all aircraft visiting the staging post, refuelled the Dutch RAPWI aircraft that was flying out Dutch internees and serviced two squadrons of Thunderbolts. Due to a serious situation that had developed at Soerabaja, two squadrons of Mosquitos arrived at Kemajoran, together with sixteen Dakotas which were to be used to drop supplies and all these aircraft added to the unit's workload.

The situation in the Dutch East Indies was extremely tense, yet no aircraft ammunition was available for the first few days. Supplies of 100 octane petrol were very short and had to be flown in. Hand-to-mouth refuelling was the order of the day. All in all, October had been an interesting month. All personnel were happy and the unit was, at last, performing its proper function when it was suddenly disbanded on 31 October 1945.

CHAPTER 9
Uses and Misuses

Over the years there has been a tendency for the RAF to glorify the exploits of the Squadrons during World War II and to ignore the activities of the SCUs. They were never talked about, were rarely mentioned in the records and their contribution to the Allied victory, both in Europe and in South East Asia, has been generally played down. As a result the majority of people, including many who served with the armed forces between 1939 and 1945, have no knowledge of the brief existence of the RAF Servicing Commandos and this official reticence is hard to understand.

During his time as 'Supremo' of the Combined Operations programme, the late Earl Mountbatten was an enthusiastic advocate of the SCUs. His faith in them was more than justified by the successful deployment of the first three units in *Operation Torch*, where their efforts with the front-line squadrons earned warm applause from the Air Officer-in-Charge of Administration at HQ, Eastern Air Command, and led to the formation of a further dozen units. Yet in April 1944 the Air Commander-in-Chief, *Operation Thursday*, made the following comment in a letter to the Chief of the Air Staff:

> The idea of a separate Air Unit to support specific land formations was strongly opposed by the RAF as being unnecessary and fundamentally unsound. Hence the desire to disband the Air Commando Force on completion of its operations in May 1944.
>
> While the record of the small force of selected personnel with first-class equipment which constituted the Air Commando was naturally good, this record could not be advanced in support of extending the principle of Air Commando Units.

On 12 April 1944 the CAS replied:

> This view is upheld by the Air Ministry, it being agreed that the principle of the Air Commando Units gave rise to the danger of tying down air forces permanently and exclusively to one particular army formation, with the consequent risk of duplication and lack of flexibility.

As flexibility was what Combined Operations, and the Servicing Commandos, was all about, these extraordinary statements, although specifically referring to the Servicing Parties that had been formed in India, make it quite clear that the Servicing Commandos suffered at the time, and indeed have suffered ever since, from a certain lack of friends amongst the higher echelons of the RAF.

Looked at in the light of these remarks, so dismissive of No 1 Servicing Party's achievements in the danger and discomfort prevalent at Broadway, an analysis of the history of the Servicing Commandos does lead one to wonder if they might not so frequently have been misemployed, or unemployed, due to a feeling of resentment in high places at having such unorthodox, dual-purpose units foisted on them.

Certainly the Commanding Officers of the SCUs were often irritated and perplexed by the lack of orders and co-operation from Group and Wing Commanders who did not deploy or utilise the SCUs to the best advantage or allow them to fulfil their proper front-line rôle. As the histories show, the SCUs were often sent on hazardous and lengthy journeys to destinations where there was no work and the members of the units sometimes felt that these moves, which wasted so much petrol, time and manpower, served no useful purpose other than to keep them occupied.

Considerable frustration was also felt throughout the units at the failure of the RAF to accept responsibility for finding suitable employment for the SCUs in other theatres when an operation had been successfully completed, instead of wasting well-trained and enthusiastic tradesmen, capable of handling four operational squadrons at a time, on transporting petrol, oil and ammunition boxes from one place to another, as so often happened.

In some cases too many units were allocated to an operation. For example, eight units went to Sicily for *Operation Bigot Husky,* and some of them accomplished very little, due partly to the practice of separating the SCUs from their vehicles and equipment for transportation to the island and the subsequent and unforeseen delays in reuniting them. With the benefit of hindsight, five units would have been enough and could have been fully utilised at forward airfields on the tasks for which they had been trained. Then there would have been sufficient servicing and salvage work to keep five units usefully employed once the island was in Allied hands.

The same eight Servicing Commando Units were sent to Italy for *Operation Avalanche.* This was the ideal number to employ, bearing in mind the size of the country and the location of the Italian and German airfields. During the first phase of the operation all eight units were kept busy, but there appeared to be no forward planning by either Combined Operations or the RAF for deploying the eight units in other areas once the fighting had died down, and much to everyone's surprise seven of the eight were suddenly pronounced redundant, and either disbanded in Italy or shipped back to the United Kingdom to be disbanded. At this stage of the war, men and equipment were urgently required in India to oppose the threat of Japanese invasion and Wingate's Chindits, operating inside Burma, were desperately in need of vital air support. The High Command missed an opportunity to boost the RAF in South East Asia by not sending these seven units out to India where their commando training and equipment would have proved most useful. Instead, they were summarily disbanded and, at a later date, High Command was obliged to withdraw four SCUs from Northern France only two months after D-Day for service in the Japanese Campaign. Then, as the records show, all four units that were sent to India arrived at Bombay without their transport or equipment.

Although a great deal of time and effort was expended on the training of the fifteen SCUs and the three smaller units known as Servicing Parties, they rarely had the opportunity to demonstrate their full potential. 3225 SCU spent most of its time in Palestine and Egypt and had no opportunity at all to show what it could do, although it may have been intended for an operation in the Dodecanese Islands, or possibly in Crete or Greece. No 2 Servicing Party played no part at all in the very campaign in Burma for which it had been formed.

When given the opportunity during peak periods of active service in the initial stages of an operation, the men of the SCUs worked night and day, in great danger and discomfort, and often had to find the time between refuelling and re-arming a constant stream of combat aircraft, to change propellers or an engine, or to cannibalise a damaged aircraft for unobtainable spare parts.

As the frequent misuse of such efficient units can hardly be regarded as a conspiracy or plot, one must look elsewhere for a reason, other than the good old-fashioned service prejudice, which must have played its part, especially as the Servicing Commandos wore a mixture of RAF and Army uniform with Combined Operation flashes. The very fact that, in the later stages of the war, squadron personnel and not the SCUs were so often sent to operate at forward airstrips suggests that the RAF had grasped the obvious advantages of having well-equipped and mobile ground crews who could be rapidly deployed to provide the back-up services for front-line air support. It was the Servicing Commandos who had shown the way.

It seems a pity that they were never given credit for it.

CHAPTER 10
Military Awards and Roll of Honour

According to the qualifying period, all officers and other ranks would be entitled to various medals, depending upon the theatre of war they served.

Eight British Campaign Medals were approved by HM King George VI, also the War Medal 1939-1945 and the Defence Medal, covering the whole period of World War II, with the following description:

Campaign Stars, Clasps and Medals

instituted in recognition of service

in the war of 1939-45

THE AWARDS ISSUED ARE MARKED X
ON THE ACCOMPANYING SLIP

Order of Wearing	*Description of Ribbon*	*Clasp or Emblem (if awarded)*
1 **1939-45 Star**	Dark blue, red and light blue in three equal vertical stripes. This ribbon is worn with the dark blue stripe furthest from the left shoulder.	Battle of Britain
2 **Atlantic Star**	Blue, white and sea green shaded and watered. This ribbon is worn with the blue edge furthest from the left shoulder.	Air Crew Europe or France and Germany
3 **Air Crew Europe Star**	Light blue with black edges and in addition a narrow yellow stripe on either side.	Atlantic or France and Germany
4 **Africa Star**	Pale buff, with a central vertical red stripe and two narrow stripes, one dark blue, and the other light blue. This ribbon is worn with the dark blue stripe furthest from the left shoulder.	8th Army or 1st Army or North Africa 1942-43
5 **Pacific Star**	Dark green with red edges, a central yellow stripe, and two narrow stripes, one dark blue and the other light blue. This ribbon is worn with the dark blue stripe furthest from the left shoulder.	Burma
6 **Burma Star**	Dark blue with a central red stripe and in addition two orange stripes.	Pacific
7 **Italy Star**	Five vertical stripes of equal width, one in red at either edge and one in green at the centre, the two intervening stripes being in white.	
8 **France and Germany Star**	Five vertical stripes of equal width, one in blue at either edge and one in red at the centre, the two intervening stripes being in white.	Atlantic
9 **Defence Medal**	Flame coloured with green edges, upon each of which is a narrow black stripe.	Silver laurel leaves (King's Commendation for brave conduct. Civil)
10 **War Medal 1939-49**	A narrow central red stripe with a narrow white stripe on either side. A broad red stripe at either edge, and two intervening stripes in blue.	Oak leaf

A slip was sent with the medals indicating the awards made to each serviceman.

MILITARY AWARDS

LIST OF AWARDS TO SERVICING COMMANDO PERSONNEL IN UNIT ORDER

Unit	Number	Rank	Name	Award
3201 SCU	810118	A/F/Sgt	Bannon	BEM
	551351	Cpl	Frazer H	BEM
	962736	L/A/C	Strange W R	BEM
	1428680	Cpl	Dann E	MID
	623099	Cpl	Cooper V A	MID
	1580175	A/C2	Fear C A	MID
	1012113	L/A/C	Garlick A C	MID
	977875	Cpl	Holton J	MID
	1267277	Sgt	Tee E M	MID
	1178541	L/A/C	Williams D I	MID
3201 SCU & 3202 SCU	Units Devotion to Duty in command DROs by AOC Eastern Air Command.			
3202 SCU		Flt/Lt	Wheadon B E	MBE
	566248	W/O	Draycott W E	MBE
		F/O	Hatton M F	MID
	1136053	L/A/C	Valance R W	MID
3203 SCU	520716	F/Sgt	Flanders L J	MID
	930768	L/A/C	Emms E J	MID
3204 SCU	None on records.			
3205 SCU	Unit Commendation — ACSEA.			
3206 SCU	None on records.			
3207 SCU	803379	Sgt	Brown F	MM
	1433683	Cpl	Coxhall	MM
	47948	Flt/Lt	Smith C F	MID
3208 SCU	None on records.			
3209 SCU	None on records.			
3210 SCU	Unit Commendation — AOC 85 Grp			
	1404004	L/A/C	Warren	MID Commendation for Bravery

3225 SCU	Unit Commendation — CO's 13 and 614 Sqns			AM
	626130	Cpl	Greenstreet J G E	MID
	615453	Sgt	Tamblin	MID
	1072522	L/A/C	Moffett	MID
	137718	L/A/C	Barge	MID

3226 SCU None on records.

3230 SCU None on records.

3231 SCU None on records.

3232 SCU None on records.

THOSE WHO DIED — ROLL OF HONOUR

On a careful study of the Official Permanent Historical Records for each of the SCUs, together with other information supplied by ex-members of the units where sections of the Official History is missing, the recorded total number of deaths was fortunately very low.

When bearing in mind the kind of Army-type Commando training that was undertaken, the invasion landings, air raids, artillery shelling of airfields, bombing and strafing that were encountered, only seventeen names are listed out of approximately 2,400 officers and men who volunteered or were posted to the units.

Their known graves are now given in accordance with the records held at the Commonwealth War Graves Commission, Head Office at Maidenhead, Berks, together with those lost at sea.

All units had casualties caused through motor vehicles, accidents, mishaps or other causes. The total loss of life, together with the vital loss of unit technical equipment for the whole period of the various SCUs was a very low percentage.

Even though the landings on the Normandy beaches had their problems for the units involved, with a landing craft being blown up by an E-boat and two trucks failing to make the shore, the loss of life was nominal, bearing in mind the circumstances that prevailed at the time.

The names of those who died are recorded in style at the RAF Memorial at Runnymede in the atmosphere of a quiet intimate garden, with a cloister and shrine on a hilltop overlooking the River Thames, with Windsor Castle in the distance, but without reference to the RAF or Commonwealth War Graves Commission records, this Memorial does not tell us where servicemen have died, or where they have been buried. Many ex-Commandos never know where their dead colleagues are buried or even attended the burial service.

So now, after many years, we the ex-members of 15 SCU's, now honour our dead, with a list of their names in unit order, together with other details as officially recorded:

SCU

3201 612453. SGT BENJAMIN PICKERING
RAF 17 November 1942. Age 22
DELY IBRAHIM WAR CEMETERY, ALGERIA
3H10

3201 1240138. AC1 GEORGE CLARKE
RAF (VR) 22 November 1942. Age 31
MEDJEZ-EL-BAB WAR CEMETERY, TUNISIA
6C1

3201 1035703. LAC STANLEY ARTHUR GALLAGHER
RAF (VR) 22 November 1942. Age 22
MEDJEZ-EL-BAB WAR CEMETERY, TUNISIA
GC2

3202 618375. SGT LEONARD VICTOR SNAPE
RAF 18 January 1944. Age 23
BARI WAR CEMETERY, ITALY
15D14

3205 1312615. LAC OWEN WILLIAM SWALLOW
RAF (VR) 30 January 1945. Age 31
TAUKKYAN WAR CEMETERY, RANGOON, BURMA
5C8

3206 1384610. LAC LEONARD CHARLES LANSDOWNE
RAF (VR) 12 September 1944. Age 32
MARISSEL FRENCH NATIONAL CEMETERY, FRANCE
Grave 324

3207 1678283. LAC JACK HENSON CROFTS
RAF (VR) 7 June 1944. Age 20
RUNNYMEDE MEMORIAL, EGHAM, SURREY
Panel 241 (LOST AT SEA – NORMANDY LANDINGS)

3209 1460523. AC1 EDWARD JOHN SKEGGS
RAF (VR) 8 June 1944. Age 23
RUNNYMEDE MEMORIAL, EGHAM, SURREY
Panel 243 (LOST AT SEA – NORMANDY LANDINGS)

3209 648591. CPL CHARLES MERVYN WALKER
RAF 10 October 1945. Age 23
MADRAS WAR CEMETERY, INDIA
9E3 (WHILE REJOINING UNIT IN BURMA – SIAM AREA)

3225 612613. SGT JOHN EDWIN SAVAGE
RAF 22 October 1943. Age 26
KHAYAT BEACH WAR CEMETERY, ISRAEL
DB6

3226 1107082. CPL HUGH McCULLOCH MONTGOMERIE
RAF (VR) 11 August 1943. Age 26
CATANIA WAR CEMETERY, SICILY
IF 46

3231 1305857. LAC ERNEST NUTTALL
RAF (VR) 30 June 1943. Age 22
PEMBROKE MILITARY CEMETERY, MALTA
Plot 5. Row 4. Grave 9

3231 1342823. LAC JAMES RENTON TAYLOR
RAF (VR) 30 June 1943. Age 22
PEMBROKE MILITARY CEMETERY, MALTA
1117

3232 649555. CPL HAROLD MOORE
RAF 11 May 1943. Age 27
THE ALAMEIN MEMORIAL, EGYPT (Column 272)
(LOST AT SEA – GIVATE OLGA BEACH, ISRAEL)

3232 1024016. LAC HORACE HUGHES
RAF (VR) 11 May 1943. Age 23
KHAYAT BEACH WAR CEMETERY, ISRAEL
CB16 (LOST AT SEA – GIVATE OLGA BEACH, ISRAEL)

3232 1233431. AC1 JOHN WILLIAM CANNON
RAF (VR) 21 June 1943. Age 22
MALTA (CAPUCCHINI) NAVAL CEMETERY, MALTA
Prot Sec (Men's) Plot F Coll. Grave 36

3232 1172764. LAC REGINALD JAMES ALGRED GOODMAN
RAF (VR) 21 June 1943. Age 24
MALTA (CAPUCCINI) NAVAL CEMETERY, MALTA
Prot Sec (Men's) Plot F Coll. Grave 36

THE FALLEN

Silent troops lined row on row,
No trumpet call, no nearby foe.
Battles faded into dreams,
Blood run cold like icy streams.
Memories faded like the years,
Only stories, bravery blurs.
Souls risen, matters not the low,
Rank means nothing where we go.
We'll just wait here, we are the blessed,
There is no war where we must rest.

Gwyneth Pritchard

POSTSCRIPT

On behalf of the Erks — Airmen, NCOs, W/Os and Officers who were members of the various Commando Units, coupled with those from the three Servicing Parties, our history set new traditions within the RAF for the deployment of aircraft tradesmen, which can now be told.

Although the world at large may not have heard about us, or the existence of such units, our history can now be added to the annals of World War II Royal Air Force records, where it justly belongs, even though these events took place more than forty years ago.

Through the joint efforts of the ex-Commandos who have survived and now attend the reunions held by the Association at the RAF Museum at Hendon, the same high morale, coupled with *esprit de corps* still exists between the ex-units today, the same as we had in those bygone days.

Although the Air Historical Branch (RAF) at the Ministry of Defence, the Imperial War Museum, RAF Museum and the Public Records Office may hold in their archives various items of information, no attempt appears to have been made until now to present the complete history of the Royal Air Force Servicing Commandos.

The authors have spent over four years seeking the various facts and other general information about the units, which we condensed into this book so that at last our story can be told, showing how we fitted into the Combined Operations invasion planning, etc.

There is no doubt that the brutal experience gained from the rapid advance of the German armies across Europe during the spring and early summer of 1940, showing how close support of the Luftwaffe gave to *Blitzkrieg* method of attack, by providing fighter and fighter-bomber aircraft to support their armies, destroying hundreds of Allied aircraft on the ground before they had the chance to fight back, also hitting hard any strong points of resistance, or lines of communications, soon caused a rapid collapse of any formidable fighting force that stood in the way of the German might.

The Allied Chiefs of Staff were faced with a tremendous task after the fall of Western Europe, to modernise all the armed Allied forces that were in the United Kingdom, although the little ships of the summer of 1940 saved the best part of a stranded army, plus those airmen that had to fend for themselves to get back to England after airfields and aircraft were destroyed by the superior fighting tactics of the German dive-bombers.

Further major problems occurred when the Italians declared war, starting the Middle East War, attacking the British forces in Egypt from Libya and those at Aden by sending bomber aircraft from the airfields in the Eritrea Somalil area.

Slowly, all the demands for men, tanks and aircraft, together with a build-up of shipping, in spite of losses sustained by U-boats, to move the new build-up of armies and their supporting units to all parts of the world as quickly as possible. This was no easy task for the planners when studying all the facts and problems that faced them at that time.

The next fatal blow to hit the British

forces was the rapid advance once Japan started war in the Far East against Singapore and with many other important places and islands. Again many lessons were to be learned on how Japan used her superior naval and army air forces to pave the way for their armies to invade the Far Eastern Continent or island ports and bases.

It was not until the might of the German Luftwaffe, the Italian Regia Aeronautica and the Japanese Army and Naval Air Forces lost their air supremacy that the Allies, including the Russians on their fronts, were able to hit back and slowly to press home the advantage of attacking the enemy, thus gaining control of the battlefields, hitting the enemy wherever he could be found, destroying his lines of communications, the factories that were making his tanks, aircraft and other military equipment to bring the enemy to his knees and to make him surrender.

In all walks of life innovations are necessary, even today the present military forces have to adapt to meet continual changing circumstances. The Falklands Campaign gave an updated version of how Combined Operations form a vital part of how the British Army, Navy and Air Force had to meet a new situation to fight invading forces on islands, thousands of miles away from their home bases.

Even though the RAF Servicing Commandos were formed by Lord Mountbatten and Lord Portal, there were many high-ranking officers during the 1942-46 period who were against the formation of these units, with the result that once they were formed the units were often misused by the failure of those senior officers to take full advantage of the special tradesmen units that were able to carry out many duties at a few moments notice.

Mobility is still the essential factor for any modern military force. Even today the lessons we were taught over forty years ago are still being applied in different ways. Tradesmen must be readily available to refuel, re-arm and service all types of modern aircraft at short notice.

The authors have tried to give an insight of our part in RAF history, gathering the facts from official records, stories from ex-Commandos, together with other general information has now been given, with suitable photographs, thus giving a complete picture and spectrum of events during the 1942-46 period. At last we can say we have honoured our dead, when our Roll of Honour was called at a church service held on Sunday, 7 June, 1987 at the RAF Central Church, St Clement Danes, The Strand, London, in the presence of a full congregation.

Although many of us never received a word of thanks for the duties that we carried out, at least we can now say, 'Justice has been done'. Today the ex-Servicing Commandos enjoy attending their reunions, meeting old friends and colleagues, representing the units they once took an active part in. The tasks that we carried out then were in the best traditions of the RAF. We were all proud to have been the forerunners of today's mobility — The Royal Air Force Servicing Commandos.

J P Kellett J Davies

Index